Best 1

in Southwestern Colorado
around Ouray, Telluride, Silverton
and Lake City

Diane Greer

Boot Jockey Press

Best Hiking in Southwestern Colorado around Ouray, Telluride, Silverton and Lake City

1st Edition, February 2017
2nd Edition, March 2019
Revised & Updated December 2021
ISBN: 978-0-9974780-4-4

All photos and original maps by the author
Cover photo: Blue Lakes and Blue Lakes Pass (Hike 1)

Your Safety is Your Responsibility

The author assumes no responsibility for the safety of users of this guide. Outdoor recreational activities involve a certain degree of risk and are by their very nature potentially hazardous. It is not within the scope of this guide to allow for disclosure of all potential hazards and risks involved in outdoor activities. All participants in such activities must assume the responsibility of their own actions and safety.

Furthermore, the author has done her best to make sure the information in this guide is as accurate and useful as possible. However, things can change, trails get rerouted, road conditions change, regulations are modified, etc. Hikers using the information in this guide should make allowances for the possibility that it may not be correct.

Even the best guide and maps can't replace good judgment and common sense. Be prepared and cautious. You will have a safer and more enjoyable trip.

Table of Contents

Introduction

Best Day Hikes in Southwest Colorado around the towns of Ouray, Telluride, Silverton and Lake City   1

The Basecamps

Ouray, Colorado   3
Silverton, Colorado   5
Telluride, Colorado   8
Lake City, Colorado   10

Locator Map

List of Hikes and Locator Maps   13

Ouray Hikes

1. Blue Lakes Pass   16
2. Bridge of Heaven   20
3. Bear Creek National Recreation Trail   24
4. Wetterhorn Basin   27
5. Blaine Basin   30
6. Upper Cascade Falls   34
7. Portland Trail   37
8. Alpine Mine Overlook   39
9. Richmond Pass   42
10. Governor Basin   46
11. Hayden Trail   51
12. Ouray Perimeter Trail   56
13. Baldy Trail   59
14. Oak Creek   62

Silverton Hikes

15. Ice Lake Trail   66
16. Columbine Lake and Pass   71
17. Porphyry Basin   75
18. Highland Mary Lakes   82
19. Crater Lake   88
20. Colorado Trail: Little Molas Lake to Lime Creek   91
21. Spencer Basin   94
22. Pass Creek–Engineer Mountain   99
23. Rico-Silverton   104

Telluride Hikes

24. Sneffels Highline 107
25. Lewis Lake and Mine 111
26. Blue Lake (in Telluride) 115
27. Bridal Veil Falls 118
28. See Forever / Bear Creek Loop 121
29. Wasatch Trail 125
30. Bear Creek Falls 129
31. Lake Hope 131
32. Lizard Head 134
33. Cross Mountain 138
34. Old Railroad Grade 141
35. Navajo Lake Trail 143
36. Kilpacker Trail to Navajo Lake 146
38. Liberty Bell/Marshall Basin 148
38. Swamp Canyon 154
39. Ajax Peak 159
40. Hawn Mountain 162
41. Iron Mountain 165

Lake City Hikes

42. Handies Peak 169
43. Uncompahgre Peak 172
44. Cataract Lake (aka Cataract Gulch) 175
45. Grizzly Gulch 178
46. Redcloud and Sunshine Peaks 180
47. Devil's Lake (aka Devil's Creek) 182
48. Powderhorn Lakes 184
49. Cooper Lake 187
50. Crystal Lake 189
51. Waterdog Lake 192
52. Spring Creek Pass East to Snow Mesa 194
53. Spring Creek Pass West to Jarosa Mesa 197
54. Cannibal Plateau 200

Appendices

Appendix A: Hiking Tips 204
Appendix B: Ouray – Food, Services, Resources and Links 207
Appendix C: Silverton Food, Services, Resources and Links 209
Appendix D: Telluride Resources and Links 211
Appendix E: Lake City Resources and Links 212

Best Day Hikes in Southwest Colorado around the towns of Ouray, Telluride, Silverton and Lake City

An opinionated guide to the best day hikes in one of Colorado's best hiking areas, the western San Juan Mountains

If you're like me you love to hike and want to spend as much of your vacation and time off as possible on the trail. The challenge is weeding through all the online and hardcopy information to find the best hikes -- the trails that take you above timberline to beautiful mountain lakes nestled in dramatic cirques, to passes with see forever views and to glorious alpine meadows filled with wildflowers.

This opinionated guide does the work for you, choosing the best day hikes in one of Colorado's best hiking areas, the western San Juan Mountains around the towns of Ouray, Telluride, Silverton and Lake City. The San Juan Mountains, the largest range in Colorado, encompasses more than 10,000 square-miles of some of the most spectacular peaks, ridges and glacial valleys in the state with sixteen peaks towering above 14,000-ft. and hundreds topping 13,000-ft. Three national forests and seven wilderness areas protect huge swathes of this amazing landscape.

The trails in this guide, best hiked between mid-July and mid-September, appeal to day hikers who like to go high and walk 6.0 to 12.5 miles/day. Elevation gains range from 1,000 to 3,500-ft. Many of the trails offer great intermediate turnaround points for those seeking shorter hikes. All are reached in less than an hour drive from four great base camps; Ouray, Telluride, Silverton and Lake City.

Ouray, Telluride and Silverton are beautifully preserved Victorian era mining towns, each with its own distinct personality. The towns are linked by the stunning San Juan Skyway scenic drive, a 233-mile loop traversing the heart of the San Juan Mountains. Along the way the drive also passes through Durango, Cortez and numerous historic sites.

A little further afield is Lake City, a small, remote Victorian town linked with Ouray and Silverton by the Alpine Loop National Backcountry Byway, a network of jeep roads traversing stunning scenery, visiting interesting ghost towns and crossing passes up to 12,800-ft. in elevation. Visitors driving passenger cars reach the idyllic little hamlet along Highway 149, aka the Silver Thread Scenic Byway, a road with some really beautiful scenery and a good dose of history.

Each town offers accommodations, campgrounds, restaurants and bars catering to all budget levels. Groceries, outdoor stores and laundromats along with bakeries and internet cafes provide the essential services needed by outdoor travelers.

The first section of this guide describes the towns, identifying local services, highlighting nearby attractions and suggesting activities for non-hiking/rainy days. The second section offers detailed trail descriptions with photos, maps, elevation profiles and driving directions for the recommended hikes. The final section includes an appendix for each town with links to lodging, food, retail stores and other websites to help plan your trip.

Extensive photo galleries and interactive maps with GPS tracks of the hikes are available on a companion website – www.hikingwalking.com.

I love feedback and would like to hear your opinion on how to improve the guide and the website. Obviously the selection of the best hikes is subjective, based on my personal opinion. Send an email (bootjockey@hikingwalking.com) or post a comment on the website about the pros and cons of a particular hike or if you believe other hikes should be included in the "best of" list.

Trail and Road Conditions

Avalanches, rockslides, heavy rains, snow/ice storms, blowdowns and other events can quickly change the condition of a trail and/or backcountry road. Access to some trails is vehicle dependent. Clearance and traction are importation on rutted, rocky and steep roads, when crossing creeks and driving on muddy roads. Always check on current road and trail conditions at the local visitor center, forest service office and/or outdoor store. Don't hesitate to turn around if you encounter unsafe conditions. Walking an extra mile or so to the trailhead is always a much better option than ruining your car.

About the Ratings

All the hikes in this guide are recommended. That being said I want to make it easier for hikers to differentiate between trails. As such, hikes within a region are rated in relation to other hikes in the area. That does not mean that a hike rated as three stars is not worth doing. It just means if you only have a few days in a given area you might want to consider tackling the higher rated hikes first.

Abbreviations

RT – Round-Trip, NF – National Forest

Ouray, Colorado

Location: On Highway 550, 35 miles south of Montrose, CO and 70 miles north of Durango, CO.

Ouray (7,746-ft.) is a pretty little Victorian mountain town nestled beneath a dramatic granite amphitheater and surrounded by 12,000-ft. peaks. A variety of accommodations and services along with its close proximity to some of the region's best hikes makes the town a perfect base camp for outdoor enthusiasts.

The town is located in the heart of the Uncompahgre National Forest in southwest Colorado, 35 miles south of Montrose and 70 miles north of Durango, CO on Highway 550. Distinctive Mt. Sneffels (14,150-ft.), rising to the west of town, is the center piece of the 16,500-acre Mt. Sneffels Wilderness. Northeast of Ouray is the 99,000-acre Uncompahgre Wilderness, home to two fourteeners, Wetterhorn Peak (14,015-ft.) and Uncompahgre Peak (14,309-ft.), along with numerous peaks over 13,000-ft.

Around Town

During the day Ouray (pronounced "you-ray" by the locals) is a popular stop for sightseers driving the San Juan Skyway, a stunning 233-mile loop that crosses four high passes and connects Ouray to Silverton, Durango, Cortez, and Telluride (going clockwise around the loop). The Skyway's steady stream of tourists helps support a good selection of restaurants, bars and breweries along with a range of accommodations that includes condos, cabins and vacations rentals, B&B's, hotels/motels and campground/RV parks.

By 4pm the day trippers plying the scenic byways disappear and the town takes on a more laid back, family atmosphere. Be sure to spend at least one of your evenings strolling Ouray's back streets admiring the beautifully restored Victorian architecture. The entire town is listed on the National Register of Historic Districts and most of its structures, built between 1880 and 1900 during the area's mining boom, are still standing.

My favorite place in town is Ouray's Hot Springs. After a hard day of hiking nothing is better than soaking in the pools fed by natural hot springs while admiring the red sandstone and granite cliffs towering above town. The facility is configured into different pools ranging in temperature from 96-105 degrees and includes a cooler lap swimming section, diving area and kiddie wading pool. The adjacent park is a nice place for a picnic. The Ouray Visitor Center (visitouray.com) is located next to the facility.

A short walk in town to the end of east 8th Avenue will take you to the base of Cascade Falls, the lowest segment of a series of seven waterfalls draining snowmelt from the peaks above town. Box Canyon Waterfalls and Park, located on CR 361 off Highway 550 just south of Ouray, is an interesting geological formation featuring a 285-ft. waterfall plummeting through a narrow box canyon. It is worth the entrance fee and the hour or so spent viewing the formation and walking the three interpretive trails. Another nice walk is the Uncompahgre River trail, which starts on the west side of town just north of the Hot Springs and meanders along the river to Ouray's northern border.

The Ouray Perimeter trail is a good option for visitors looking for a longer walk. (See the trail description in this book for more information.) The 5.9 mile trail, which can be accessed from several spots around town, visits Cascade Falls, the Baby Bathtubs and crosses over Canyon Creek's spectacular gorge. Along the way enjoy great views of Mt. Abrams, Hayden Mountain, Whitehouse Mountain, Twin Peaks and the Amphitheater. An optional detour includes a visit to Box Canyon Park. A map and additional information about the Perimeter Trail is available at the Ouray Visitor Center.

Nearby Attractions

There is plenty to do around Ouray if you decide to take a day off from hiking. Most people drive the Million Dollar Highway, the 24 mile section of the San Juan Skyway between Ouray and Silverton. The route travels by jaw dropping scenery littered with mining relics and climbs over 11,018-ft. Red Mountain Pass. A full day needs to be allocated to drive the entire San Juan Skyway. This trip is better done as part of an extended trip with overnight stops in Silverton and Telluride.

Another interesting diversion is a trip to one of the area's ghost towns. A few are accessible with a passenger vehicle but most require a 4WD (tours are available). The Ouray Visitor Center located by the Hot Springs has a complete list of the options along with directions and recommendations.

Those with a 4WD and taste for adventure may want to drive the area's famous backcountry roads. Yankee Boy Basin, to the southwest of town, provides opportunities to visit several ghost towns, view beautiful Twin Falls and, during late July/early August, see spectacular displays of wildflowers. The Alpine Loop is another popular route leading over 12,000-ft passes to the Lake City and back. Be sure to check with the local tourism office about road conditions and the skill level required to drive each of the routes.

A tour of the Bachelors Syracuse Mine is a good option for a rainy day. (See also Old Hundred Gold Mine Tour outside of Silverton.) A guide with experience working the mine takes visitors 1,800 feet horizontally into Gold Hill to a work area used to extract the silver and other minerals. The tour includes a complete presentation of the equipment and techniques used to extract the ore.

Food, Lodging and Services

Just about all the basic services you need are found along Main Street, a six block section of Highway 550 running through the center of town. The

Ouray Visitor Center, open 7 days a week during the summer, is located at 1230 Main Street, next to the Hot Springs Pool.

The Ouray Grocery, a small grocery at 621 Main Street, offers the basics for making a meal. Those looking for the wider selection should travel 11 miles north to the Ridgway Mountain Market (490 Sherman St, Ridgway) or purchase groceries in Montrose or Durango. Coffee along with a great selection of chocolates is available at Mouse's Chocolates and Coffee (520 Main Street). Ouray Mountain Sports (732 Main St.) stocks clothing and gear for climbers and hikers. A surprisingly good selection of maps, guides and leisure reading material can be found at Buckskin Booksellers at 505 Main St.

Silverton, Colorado

Location: On Highway 550, 23 miles south of Ouray and 50 miles north of Durango.

Silverton (9,318-ft.) is a wonderfully preserved mining town set in a high mountain valley surrounded by 13,000-ft. peaks. Primarily constructed between 1882 and 1910, the entire town is a national historic landmark and considered one of the most intact sites of its kind in the country.

Silverton is a little grittier and rougher around the edges then nearby Ouray. What the town lacks in polish it makes up for with location, surrounded by BLM land and three national forests featuring stunning alpine valleys, emerald green meadows and towering peaks. The Weminuche Wilderness, the State's largest, is located southeast of town. The Continental Divide and the Colorado Trails traverse the high country to the south and east.

Getting to Silverton is its own adventure. The town lies sandwiched between two high passes on Highway 550, aka the Million Dollar Highway, 23 miles south of Ouray and 50 miles north of Durango. Driving south from Ouray on 550, the narrow, winding highway ascends through fabulous scenery littered with mining ruins to cross Red Mountain Pass (11,018-ft.) before dropping to Silverton. The route north from Durango is just as spectacular, crossing Coal Bank (10,640-ft.) and Molas (10,970-ft.) Passes along the way.

Around Town

During Silverton's heyday in the 1880's, millions of dollars in gold and silver extracted from nearby mines fueled construction of lavish hotels and ornate homes, occupied by the town's law-abiding and respectable citizens, along with dance halls, brothels and saloons frequented by a rougher crowd. Because Silverton never experienced a major fire a good number of these buildings are still standing.

Today the town boasts of its dual personalities, the respectable half west of Greene Street (the town's main drag) and the "red light district" east of Greene around notorious Blair Street, once home to over 40 saloons and brothels. Many of the restored structures on Greene, Blair and the adjacent side streets are now eclectic gift shops and restaurants catering to tourist.

Tourism is the mainstay of Silverton's economy. During the summer and early fall the Durango and Silverton Narrow Gauge Railroad (D&SNG) makes the 45-mile run between Durango and Silverton several times a day, bringing an influx of tourists who spend a few hours sightseeing, shopping and eating before returning to Durango.

The town is also is a popular stop for sightseers driving the San Juan Skyway, a 233-mile loop with stunning scenery that crosses four high passes and connects Silverton to Ouray, Telluride, Cortez, and Durango (going clockwise around the loop).

By late afternoon most of the train tourists are gone and the town takes on a more relaxed and authentic atmosphere. The evenings are a good time to stroll the streets and appreciate the historic buildings. Take time to tour the backstreets west of Greene to see beautifully restored Victorian homes along with buildings undergoing restoration.

For a bird's eye view of Silverton and the surrounding area take an evening stroll to the Christ of the Mine Shrine, a huge statue of Jesus in a stone alcove located 500 feet up the slope of Anvil Mountain north of Silverton. Reach the shrine by walking northwest on 10th Street to its end at Keystone Street where an obvious trail ascends the hillside to the statue.

Visit the tourist office for more information on other nearby short hikes. Good options include visiting the local Cemetery (2 miles), ascending to the Idaho Mine (3.1 miles) or walking along the Animas River south of town (1.6 miles)

The San Juan County Museum, located in the old San Juan County Jail at the northeast end of Green Street, is worth a visit and a good rainy day diversion. The museum features artifacts and displays explaining the history of the town, the area's mining legacy and the D&SNG railroad.

Nearby Attractions

When you need a break from hiking visiting Animas Forks, a ghost town located 15 miles northeast of Silverton on County Road 2, is an interesting option. A surprising number of buildings and mining structure still stand at the site, inhabited from the 1870's to the 1920's. BLM plaques describe the structures and the history of the town. The dirt road leading to the site is typically accessible to passenger vehicles. High clearance is better. Check at the Visitor Center for current road conditions.

Another good diversion is the drive to Ouray along the 24-mile stretch of Highway 550 dubbed the Million Dollar Highway. The drive features incredible mountain scenery, deep canyons, sheer cliffs and numerous mining ruins. Ouray (7,746-ft.) is a pretty little Victorian town nestled beneath a dramatic granite amphitheater and surrounded by 12,000-ft. plus peaks. See the Ouray section of the guide for more information.

A tour of the Old Hundred Mine is a great option for a rainy day. To reach the mine travel 4 miles northeast from Silverton on County Road 2. Turn right onto Country Road 4A and follow the signs for 0.75 miles to the mine. The tour takes visitors 1,500-ft. into a gold mine for demonstrations of mining equipment and operations.

Self-guided tours are available at the Mayflower Gold Mill, a National Historic Landmark located 2 miles northeast of Silverton on County Road 2. The tour explains the operation of the largely intact Mill that processed gold and silver for almost a half century.

Hikers with a 4WD vehicle or a mountain bike might want to investigate the old mining roads crisscrossing the backcountry around Silverton. Many lead to ghost towns, mining ruins and spectacular vistas. Be sure to check at the Silverton Visitor Center (414 Greene Street) regarding road conditions and the skill level required to navigate the roads. Jeep rentals and 4WD tours of the backcountry are offered by various businesses in town.

The Alpine Loop, a National Backcountry Byway, is the area's most popular backcountry adventure. From Silverton the 65-mile 4WD route starts at the ghost town at Animas Forks, climbs over Cinnamon Pass (12,620-ft.) and drops down to Lake City on Highway 149. From the south end of Lake City the return route follows the Henson Creek drainage to Engineer Pass (12,800-ft.) and then drops back down to Animas Forks. Along the way the route traverses beautiful mountain landscapes with panoramic vistas and passes historic ghost towns and mining sites.

Food, Lodging and Services

Greene Street (the town's main drag), Blair Street and the adjacent side streets are lined with restaurants, cafes and quaint shops catering to tourist and outdoor enthusiast.

Accommodations range from B&B's and small hotels, situated in historic buildings with period furnishings, to more modern motels. A variety of homes and apartments are available as vacation rentals. Four RV Parks are located in or near town while the surrounding national forests offer established campgrounds and dispersed camping opportunities.

The tourist information center is on your right as you enter town at 414 Green Street. Silverton Grocery at 717 Greene Street stocks the basics needed to assemble a meal. Those looking for the wider selection should purchase groceries in Ridgway or Durango.

The Coffee Bear (1309 Green Street) will satisfy your caffeine habit and has a good variety of baked goods, sandwiches and snacks. Outdoor World (1234 Greene Street) offers a nice selection of hiking and fishing gear along area maps and guidebooks.

Telluride, Colorado

Location: On Highway 145, 67 miles southwest of Montrose, CO, and 75 miles northeast of Cortez, CO.

Telluride (8,745-ft), Ouray's larger and classier neighbor, is tucked at the head of a stunning box canyon and surrounded by steep valley walls and peaks rising over 13,000-ft. Like Ouray, the town started as a mining camp in the late 1800's. At the turn of the century and the height of the mining boom the town had almost 5,000 residents and more millionaires per capita than New York City.

By the mid 1950's the boom had turned to bust with most of the mines shuttered and its residents gone. The opening of the Telluride Ski Resort in 1972 changed the town's fortunes. White gold, in the form of snow, transformed the town into a world-class ski resort with a full complement of accommodations, restaurants and retail establishments.

Thankfully the town planners opted to preserve the Victorian charm of the town center, now listed as a National Historic District. An expanded ski area and modern mountain village was built close to Telluride but hidden from view by a 9,000-ft. ridge. The town and the mountain village are linked by a free gondola.

Around Town

Visitors flock to Telluride in the summer, drawn by the area's natural beauty, diverse outdoor activities and festivals. Hikers can literally roll out of bed and walk to trailheads in town leading to some of the region's best hikes. Ten miles to the southwest lies the Lizard Head Wilderness, encompassing three fourteeners and several other summits over 13,000-ft.

If you like Victorian architecture take a stroll along the town's backstreets to see restored structures as well as recently built houses in keeping with the town's historic character. Another nice walk is the 4.25 mile San Miguel River trail, a walking and bicycle path that meanders through town along the river past the park and campground to the Pandora Mine.

Bridal Veil Falls, the tallest freefalling waterfall in Colorado, is a favorite destination located 4 miles east of Telluride. Head east on Colorado Avenue to the parking lot just past the Pandora Mine. Follow the 4WD road or trail that switchbacks uphill for 1.2 miles to the base of the falls. This vantage point provides great views of the waterfall plunging 365-ft. from just beneath the historic Bridal Veil power plant to a stream feeding the San Miguel River. The viewpoint is often enveloped in mist from the water thundering over the rock face and hitting a small pool at the base of the falls.

You can follow the road from the remaining 0.8 miles to a gate blocking further vehicle access up the Bridal Veil Basin. This section of the road enjoys wonderful views of the steep cliffs forming the head of the Telluride valley and the town in the distance. Along the way dramatic views open to the power plant perched atop a rock ledge just above the falls. The building, restored in the 1990's, is listed on the National Register of Historic places. For a closer view of the plant duck through the gate and follow the seldom used mining road for a few minutes to a viewpoint just above the power plant building. (The building and the area around the plant it is private property.)

A hike to Bear Creek Falls is another popular walk. The 2.3 mile trail (one-way) starts at the south end of Pine Street and follows a good trail through the 325-acre Bear Creek Preserve to a great viewpoint showcasing the falls. Total elevation gain is just over 1,380-ft. Hikers with the time and energy can continue up the dramatic Bear Creek canyon on the Wasatch trail.

Nearby Attractions

A variety of activities are available if you want to take a day off from hiking. A short scenic drive along the San Juan Skyway on Highway 45 south of Telluride leads past Trout Lake to Lizard Head Pass (10,222-ft.) where you can enjoy views of Lizard Head's distinctive lone spire rising 400-ft. above its rocky pedestal. Be sure to take a side trip to Trout Lake and the little mining town of Ophir along the way.

Driving north along the San Juan Skyway leads to Placerville, where the route turns right (east) on Highway 62 over Dallas Divide (8,983-ft.) to Ridgway. The drive between Dallas Divide and Ridgway offers panoramic views of the Mount Sneffels Range and the jagged ridges of the Uncompahgre Wilderness rising to the east.

Ridgway, a small town set in the beautiful Uncompahgre Valley, is home to a number of art galleries, antique stores and interesting retail establishments.

A full day needs to be allocated to drive the entire San Juan Skyway. At Ridgway the route turns right on U.S. 550, heading south toward Ouray and Silverton. This section of the route, which features amazing scenery littered with mining relics, climbs over 11,018-ft. Red Mountain Pass on its way to Silverton. My recommendation is to drive this route as part of an extended trip with overnight stops in Ouray and Silverton. Archaeology buffs will also want to take a side trip to Mesa Verde near Cortez, to view the cliff dwellings.

Several 4WD roads lead to ghost towns and stunning views. The easiest is the 5-mile road to Alta Lakes and Alta Ghost town. Be sure to check at the visitor center regarding road conditions and the skill level required to navigate the roads. Mountain bikers will find plenty of trails and 4WD roads of varying lengths and difficulties.

Food, Lodging and Services

Telluride features a full complement of accommodations, restaurants and shops. The town's main street, Colorado Avenue, and the adjacent side streets are lined with an eclectic collection of galleries, boutiques, specialty stores, restaurants and gift shops. Numerous outdoor stores such as the Jagged Edge Mountain Gear (223 E Colorado Ave) and Telluride Sports (150 W. Colorado) cater to climbers, hikers and fisherman.

Clark's Market at 700 W Colorado and the Village Market, at 157 Fir Street, stock just about everything you need to cook the most elaborate of meals. Baked in Telluride, at 127 Fir Street, turns out delicious goodies as well as sandwiches and snacks. Caffeine addicts can get their daily fix at Coffee Cowboy at 131 E. Colorado or at High Alpine Coffee in the back of Between the Covers Bookstore, at 224 W Colorado.

The visitor center (telluride.com) and central reservation office is located at 236 W. Colorado Avenue. Between the Covers at 224 W Colorado is the place to go for maps, guidebooks and leisure reading material.

Lake City, Colorado

Location: *On CO-149, 55 miles southwest of Gunnison and 119 miles northwest of Alamosa.*

Lake City (8,663-ft.) is a remote little Victorian town situated at the confluence of the Lake Fork of the Gunnison River and Henson Creek and surrounded by the Uncompahgre and Gunnison National Forests and the Gunnison BLM district. The town is located along CO-149, 55 miles south of Gunnison and 74 miles north of South Fork.

With close to one thousand square miles of public land nearby there is no shortage of excellent hiking opportunities. Trails climb the area's five 14,000-ft. peaks, wander through wildflower-filled meadows and traverse vast expanses of alpine tundra. Since this remote corner of the state is still relatively unknown hikers can enjoy a degree of solitude not possible in other areas of the state.

Around Town

In the late 1800's Lake City served as a supply hub and smelting center for miners in the nearby San Juan Mountains. In its heyday the town saw the construction of more than 500 structures. Mining activity and the population of the town and Hinsdale County peaked around 1900. Over the next century mining activity waned and the town went through a period of decline.

Today the charming Victorian town, a designated national historic district, is a hub for outdoor enthusiasts exploring the area's stunning mountain terrain. Over 200 of Lake City's original Victorian structures, including commercial buildings, churches, homes, cabins and public buildings, still stand, many restored to their former glory.

Highly recommended is an evening stroll along the town's wooden sidewalks and backstreets to see the restored structures from the 1870's and

1880's. Also of interested are the nicely preserved circa 1930-1950 motor court cabins. A pamphlet with a map of the self-guided tour of the historic district is available at the Lake City Visitor Center and the Hinsdale County Museum, at the corner of Second and Silver Street. The museum, run by the Hinsdale County Historic Society and chronicling the area's history, is also worth a visit.

Other short walks around Lake City include the Henson Creek trail and the River Access trail system. A pamphlet and map describing the walking trails is available at the Visitor Center.

For a glimpse of mining life take a tour of the Hard Tack Mine. The underground mine tour describes the tools and techniques used by hard rock miners and includes exhibits explaining local mining history and equipment along with a rock gallery showcasing the mine's huge collection of rocks and minerals. The Hard Tack is located on County Road 20 (the Henson Creek Road) toward Engineer's Pass, just 2.5 miles outside of town.

The Ute-Ulay Mine/Henson Ghost Town, located 3.5 miles out County Road 20, features a shelf-guided walking tour of the 12-acre property. The walk takes visitors by mining structures, a boarding house and an interesting dam. Signs along the way describe the history of the area.

If your dogs are tired from hiking take a drive along the Silver Thread Scenic Byway. The route heads south from Lake City on CO-149 to Windy Point, located just before Slumgullion Pass. From this vantage point panoramic views encompass four 14,000-ft. peaks, Redcloud Peak (14,034 ft.), Sunshine Peak (14,001 ft.), Uncompahgre Peak (14,309-ft.), and Wetterhorn Peak (14,015-ft.), towering above the town to the northwest. Below is Lake San Cristobal and to the north the Slumgullion Earthflow, comprised of two major earthflows. The first flow occurred about 700 years ago when a huge mass of volcanic rock slumped down the valley, damming the Lake Fork of the Gunnison River and creating Lake San Cristobal. The second slide, visible from Windy Point, started 300 years ago and is still moving down the hillside. The bizarre angle of the trees growing along the hillside illustrates the continued movement of the slide.

The byway continues over Slumgullion Pass heading south to Creede, along the way passing through incredibly beautiful landscape. A few miles north of Creede is the turnoff to the Rio Grande Reservoir. The reservoir is stocked with fish and open to boats.

Creede, located near the headwaters of the Rio Grande, is a nicely preserved rustic mining town. The historic structures along the town's main drag, Historic Street, are now home to a few restaurants and shops. Beyond Creede the road parallels the Rio Grande beneath towering cliffs, ending in South Fork.

The byway also heads north from Lake City, again following CO-149 to Blue Mesa Lake and the Curecanti National Recreation Area, located on Highway 50 to the west of Gunnison. There are a number of short hikes in Curecanti, including the Dillon Pinnacles, Pine Creek and Never Sink, that are good rainy day destinations. Stop at the Elk Creek Visitor Center along Highway 50 for more information.

Just two miles south of town on US-149 is the turnoff for County Road 30 (CR 30) leading to Lake San Cristobal. This beautiful lake is a great place for fishing, boating, kayaking and canoeing. The Red Gulch Day Use area at the south end of the lake includes picnic facilities. The county-owned Wupperman Campground is located on the east side of the lake.

Four wheel drive enthusiasts will want to check out the Alpine Loop National Backcountry Byway. The byway is composed of several jeep roads that link Lake City with Ouray and Silverton to the west. The byway's network of roads travel through stunning scenery, visit ghost towns and cross passes up to 12,880-ft. Check with the Lake City Visitor Center at 800 Gunnison Avenue for information on road conditions and technical skills required to navigate the route and the areas other 4WD roads.

Food, Lodging and Services

For a small town Lake City has a nice selection of accommodations, restaurants and retail shops. Accommodations include B&B's, small motels, lodges and cabins in town and at Lake San Cristobal. There are also a variety of homes and apartments available as vacation rentals.

People who prefer camping will find five campgrounds in the Uncompahgre and Gunnison National Forests near Lake City. There is also the county-owned Wupperman Campground at Lake San Cristobal, located on the east side of the lake. For a list of other public camping facilities go to the Lake City website (lakecity.com/camping/). There are also a number of private campgrounds and RV parks in the area.

Your first stop in town should be the Visitor Center on 800 Gunnison Avenue, where you can pick up a map, learn about current conditions and get advice on recreation activities and nearby attractions. For groceries visit the Country Store Grocery at 916 N State Highway 149, which carries the basics needed to assemble a meal, and the Country Grocery Store at 916 N State Highway 149.

A wonderful selection of baked goods and fresh bread is available at the Lake City Bakery, at 922 N Highway 149. The Chillin Internet Coffee Shop and Cafe, 205 North Gunnison Ave, is the best place in town for a caffeine injection. For a complete list of local retail shops and services visit the Lake City Chamber of Commerce (lakecity.com).

List of Hikes and Locator Maps

Hikes with distances and difficulty rating

Ouray Hikes

1. Blue Lakes/Blue Lakes Pass: 6.3-11 miles (RT), moderately strenuous
2. Bridge of Heaven: 8 miles (RT), strenuous
3. Bear Creek: 4.4-8.0 miles (RT), moderate
4. Wetterhorn Basin: 5.8-9 miles (RT), moderate
5. Blaine Basin: 6.8 miles (RT), moderate
6. Upper Cascade Falls: 4.4-5.9 miles (RT), moderately strenuous
7. Portland: 3.5 miles (RT), easy
8. Alpine Mine Overlook: 5.6 miles (RT), moderately strenuous
9. Richmond Pass: 5.6 miles (RT), strenuous
10. Governor Basin: 5.8-7.6 (RT), moderately strenuous
11. Hayden South: 5.0-6.6 (RT), strenuous
12. Ouray Perimeter Trail: 5.9 (loop), moderate
13. Baldy Trail: 6.8-7.9 (RT), moderate
14. Oak Creek: 6.0-7.0 (RT), strenuous

Silverton Hikes

15. Ice Lakes: 7.0-8.2 miles (RT), moderately strenuous
16. Columbine Lake/Pass: 7.0-8.9 miles (RT), strenuous
17. Porphyry Basin: 5.0 - 7.0 miles (RT), moderate
18. Highland Mary Lakes: 6.0-7.7 miles (RT), moderately strenuous
19. Crater Lakes: 11 miles (RT), easy-moderate
20. Colorado Trail: Little Molas Lake to Lime Creek: 7.4-10.1 miles (RT), easy-moderate
21. Spencer Basin: 4.2 – 7.7 miles (RT), moderately strenuous
22. Pass Creek – Engineer Mountain: 4.8 – 12.8 miles (RT), strenuous
23. Rico-Silverton: 5.2 miles (RT), moderately strenuous

Telluride Hikes

24. Sneffels Highline: 8.0-12.7 mile (loop), strenuous
25. Lewis Lake and Mine: 8.0-8.8 miles (RT), moderately strenuous
26. Blue Lake in Bridal Veil Basin: 6.0 miles (RT), moderate
27. Bridal Veil Falls: 4.0 miles (RT), moderate
28. See Forever/Wasatch/Bear Creek Loop: 5.0-8.4 mile (loop), strenuous
29. Wasatch: 12.3 miles (RT), strenuous
30. Bear Creek Falls: 4.6 miles (RT), easy-moderate
31. Lake Hope: 4.5-5.9 miles (RT), moderate
32. Lizard Head: 7.6-11.7 mile loop, strenuous
33. Cross Mountain: 6.6 miles (RT), moderately strenuous
34. Old Railroad Grade: 2.3 miles (one way), easy

35. Navajo Lake: 9.2 miles (RT), moderately strenuous
36. Kilpacker Trail to Navajo Lake: 11.8 miles (RT), moderately strenuous
37. Liberty Bell/Marshall Basin Loop: 6.0-10.6 miles (loop), strenuous
38. Swamp Canyon: 6.0-7.6 miles (RT), moderately strenuous
39. Ajax Peak: 5.6 miles (RT), strenuous
40. Hawn Mountain: 4.9-5.0 miles (loop), moderately strenuous
41. Iron Mountain: 8.0 miles (RT), moderately strenuous

Lake City Hikes

42. Handies Peak: 2.3-5.4 miles (RT), strenuous
43. Uncompahgre Peak: 7.8 miles (RT), strenuous-difficult
44. Cataract Lake: 4.2-10.0 miles (RT), moderately strenuous
45. Grizzly Gulch: 8.0 mile (RT), killer
46. Redcloud and Sunshine Peaks: 9.0 -11.8 miles (RT), killer
47. Devils Lake: 14.0 miles (RT), strenuous
48. Powderhorn Lake: 7.8-9.6 miles (RT), moderate
49. Cooper Lake: 7.6 miles (RT), moderately strenuous
50. Crystal Lake: 8.2 miles (RT), moderately strenuous
51. Waterdog Lake: 7.8 miles (RT), strenuous
52. Spring Creek Pass East to Snow Mesa: 6.4-10.0 miles (RT), moderately strenuous
53. Spring Creek Pass West to Jarosa Mesa: 8.8 miles (RT), moderately
54. Cannibal Plateau: 5.0 miles (RT), moderately strenuous

1. Blue Lakes Pass ★★★★★

Distance: 6.3 - 11.0 miles (RT)

This popular hike visits three scenic lakes nestled in beautiful glacial basins set amid rugged ridges and peaks. Beyond the lakes the trail climbs to a dramatic pass on the ridge south of Mt. Sneffels (14,150-ft).

Distance: 6.3 miles (RT) to Lower Blue Lake
8.2 miles (RT) to Upper Blue Lake
11.0 miles (RT) to Blue Lakes Pass
Elevation: 9,350-ft. at Trailhead
10,940-ft. at Lower Blue Lake
11,750-ft. at Upper Blue Lake
13,000-ft. at Blue Lakes Pass
Elevation Gain: 1,590-ft. to Lower Blue Lake
2,400-ft. to Upper Blue Lake
3,650-ft. to Blue Lakes Pass

Difficulty: moderately strenuous
Basecamp: Ouray
Area: Mt. Sneffels Wilderness, Uncompahgre NF
Best Season: July - September
USGS Map(s): Mount Sneffels, Telluride

Why Hike Blue Lakes

Turquoise lakes nestled in dramatic glacial cirques, wildflower-filled meadows ringed by craggy peaks and a pass with see-forever views puts Blue Lakes atop my "to do list" on every trip to southwest Colorado.

The hike, one of the few in the Mount Sneffels Wilderness, culminates at spectacular Blue Lakes Pass (13,000-ft.) located on a steep ridge extending south from Mt. Sneffels (14,150-ft). Along the way the trail visits three scenic lakes cradled in beautiful glacial basin set amid rugged 13,000-ft. peaks.

For an easy day Lower Blue Lake, lying in a pretty cirque dominated by Dallas Peak, makes a worthy destination. Still have energy to burn? Continue on the steep trail leading to the upper lakes, set beneath the western flanks of Mt. Sneffels in wildflower filled meadows ringed by jagged ridges. Beyond the lakes a demanding trail ascends 1,250-ft. in 1.4 miles to the panoramic viewpoint at the pass.

Trailhead to Lower Blue Lake

Distance from Trailhead: 6.3 miles (RT)
Elevation at the Lower Blue Lake: 10,940-ft.
Elevation Gain: 1,590-ft.

The Blue Lakes trail starts at the north end of the trailhead parking lot (see driving directions below), passes through a gate and soon reaches a signed "Y" intersection. Here the trail branches right and ascends on moderate grades through a forest of Engelmann spruce and pines along the right (west) of East Fork Dallas Creek. (The trail to the left leads to Blaine Basin.) Occasional openings in the trees provide tantalizing views of surrounding peaks.

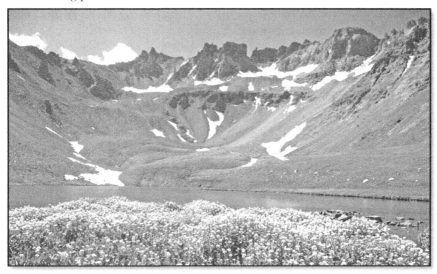

At 1.4 miles the grade moderates and the path soon begins passing through intermittent meadows with vistas of the rugged peaks lining the lower basin. After crossing a creek at 1.8 miles the grade steepens and the trail crosses an avalanche chute with views of Mt. Sneffels to the east. You'll know when you are less than 1/3 of a mile from the lower lake when you see a waterfall tumbling down a rocky cleft on your left (southeast).

Past the waterfall the trail climbs on moderately steep grades to a signed junction with a short spur trail leading straight ahead (south) to Lower Blue Lake. The trail branching to the left (east) continues to the upper lakes. Acclimated hikers will reach this point in about 1 1/2 hours (3.2 miles, 1,500-ft. elevation gain).

Pretty Lower Blue Lake (10,940-ft.) lies nestled in a scenic bowl beneath a cirque of jagged peaks dominated by Dallas Peak (13,809-ft.) to the southwest. Mount Sneffels (14,156-ft.) rises to the east. Steep scree slopes spill down the cirque's rugged walls to the southern and western shoreline of the lake. Nice campsites, sheltered by trees, are located on the lake's north and northwest shore.

Lower Blue Lakes to Upper Blue Lake

Segment Stat: 2.4 miles (one-way) with a 810-ft. elevation gain
Trailhead to Upper Blue Lake: 8.2 miles (RT)
Elevation Upper Blue Lake: 11,750-ft.
Elevation Gain to Upper Blue Lake: 2,400-ft.

To reach the upper lakes return to the junction and turn east. Drop down to the East Fork of Dallas Creek and find a place to cross. Several large logs and rock will help keep your feet dry. The continuation of the trail is on the left (north) side of the creek draining the upper lakes. Finding the trail on the other side of the creek can be little confusing due to erosion and use trails leading to more campsites.

The path now climbs steeply up the headwall of the lower basin, en route crossing back to the west side of the creek. As you climb trees give way to alpine tundra sprinkled with wildflowers in mid-July to early August. At the top of the headwall the trail reaches a fantastic viewpoint showcasing the lower lake basin.

Beyond the viewpoint the climb moderates as the trail passes to the west and above middle Blue Lake, reaching Upper Blue Lake after 0.9 miles and a 700-ft. elevation gain. (Total hiking distance: 4.1 miles / 2,350-ft. of elevation gain.)

The upper lake is set amid meadows dotted with wildflowers. A scenic ridge with steep scree slopes tinted bronze, rust and gold extends from Dallas Peak to Gilpin Peak (13,694-ft.), forming the southern wall of the upper basin. The ridge between Gilpin Peak and Mt Sneffels creates the eastern wall.

While the upper basin is a great destination and the perfect place to relax and take in the scenery, hikers with the time (and good weather) will want to climb to Blue Lakes Pass (13,000-ft). The pass is situated 1,250-ft. above the upper Lake on the ridge extending between Mt. Sneffels and Gilpin Peak.

Upper Lakes to Blue Lakes Pass

Segment Stats: 1.4 miles (one-way) with a 1,250-ft. elevation gain
Trailhead to Blue Lakes Pass: 11.0 miles (RT)
Elevation Blue Lakes Pass: 13,000-ft.
Elevation Gain to Blue Lakes Pass: 3,650-ft.

To reach the pass follow the well-defined trail around the left (east) side of Upper Blue Lake to a series of long, steep switchbacks. As you ascend fields of wildflowers give way to dirt and talus. Footing is generally good except for a few eroded sections with some exposure.

Take occasional breaks from the climb to admire the wonderful views of the jagged ridge towering above the sapphire blue lakes of the upper basin. Reach the top of the pass in 1.4 miles (total distance: 5.5 miles with 3,650-ft. of elevation gain from the trailhead).

The pass offers splendid views of the peaks and ridges defining the Blue Lakes basin. To the south is Yankee Boy Basin dominated by Gilpin Peak (13,694-ft.), Potosi (13,786-ft.) and Teakettle Mountain (13,819-ft.). In the distance a series of peaks and ridges form the northern wall of Yankee Boy Basin..

On the north side of the pass a faint trail marks the start of a Class 3 route climbing Mt. Sneffel's southwest ridge. This route should only be used by parties with prior climbing experience. Most people climb Mt. Sneffels (14,156-ft.) from a well-defined Class 2 route that begins in Yankee Boy basin.

Once you are done soaking in the scenery retrace your steps to the trailhead. Parties with a pre-positioned second vehicle can continue over the pass and down to a 4WD road in Yankee Boy Basin (1.4 miles).

Note: This is a popular trail that is best hiked on a weekday if you wish to encounter fewer people on the trail.

Driving Directions

From Ouray: It takes 45-50 minutes to drive the 24 miles from Ouray to the Blue Lakes trailhead. The drive is quite scenic with views dominated by 14,150-ft. Mt. Sneffels and its neighboring peaks and ridges, almost all over 13,000-ft.

From the center of Ouray take Highway 550 heading north for just over 10 miles to Highway 62 in Ridgway. Turn left (west) on Highway 62. Drive 4.8 miles and then take a left onto County Road 7, marked Dallas Creek (the road use to be marked East Dallas Creek). It is easy to miss the turn while you are admiring the scenery to the south of the highway. In two miles CR-7 bears right where it meets CR-7A. Continue for a total of 9 miles on CR-7 through a beautiful valley to the parking area at the trailhead. Note: CR-7 turns into Forest Road 851.1 at the forest boundary.

From Telluride: From Telluride the trailhead is a 90 minute/44 miles drive. Drive west on West Colorado Avenue to Highway 145. Head west on Hwy 145 for 12.7 miles to where it dead ends at Highway 62 in Placerville. Turn right (east) onto Highway 62 and drive 18.6 miles to County Road 7, marked Dallas Creek. Turn right onto CR-7. In two miles CR-7 bears right where it meets CR-7A. Continue for a total of 9 miles through a beautiful valley to the parking area at the trailhead. Note: CR-7 turns into Forest Road 851.1 at the forest boundary.

Road Conditions: Passenger car accessible if driven carefully. CR-7 is a dirt/gravel road that becomes rougher as it climbs to the National Forest boundary. Beyond this point the road maintenance deteriorates and you will need to dodge potholes and rocks.

2. Bridge of Heaven ★★★★
Distance: 8.0 miles (RT)

This well-engineered trail ascends 3,000-ft. to a knife-edge ridge with spectacular, panoramic views.

Distance: 8.0 miles (RT)
Elevation: 9,300-ft. at Trailhead
12,300-ft. at Bridge of Heaven
Elevation Gain: 3,000-ft.
Difficulty: strenuous

Basecamp: Ouray, Ridgway
Area: Uncompahgre NF
Best Season: July - September
USGS Map(s): Ouray

Why Hike Bridge of Heaven

Choose a promising day and take a walk to heaven. The aptly named Bridge of Heaven trail leads to a lofty vantage point on a narrow 12,300-ft. ridge with spectacular, panoramic views of the Cimarron Range to the northeast, the Sneffels Range to the west and Ironton and Red Mountain Pass to the south.

Getting to heaven takes some effort. The trail ascends 3,000-ft. in 4.0 miles. Thankfully a well-engineered trail makes the climb easier that it sounds. Trailhead access is another issue. Four-wheel drive is required to cross Dexter Creek and negotiate the final 2.2 miles of rough road ascending 700-ft. to the trailhead parking area.

Trailhead to First Viewpoint

Distance from Trailhead: 3.4 miles (RT)
Elevation at Viewpoint: 10,385-ft.
Elevation Gain: 1,085-ft.

From the trailhead parking area (see driving directions), walk about 100 yards up the road to the Horsethief trailhead on the right (south side) of the road. The trail immediately starts uphill on a series of well graded switchbacks through a mixed forest of spruce and aspen. After ascending for about 15 minutes sporadic openings in the trees reveal views of Whitehouse Mountain to the west and Ridgway to the north.

At 1.7 miles reach a marked trail junction on a grassy hillside with a sign pointing to a faint trail heading downhill toward Ouray. This is the old Horsethief trail that starts at the northern end of Ouray (the trail was repaired and rerouted in 2004). To the right of the junction is a grassy knoll with wonderful views of Yankee Boy Basin and prominent peaks of the Sneffels range across the valley to the west. To the south you can see the town of Ouray along with the peaks flanking the San Juan Skyway (aka the Million Dollar Highway) including Mt. Hayden, Mt. Abrams and, the aptly named, Red Mountain. The viewpoint is a good destination for people

hiking with young children or hikers with limited time looking for a short hike with great views.

First Viewpoint to Bridge of Heaven

Segment Stat: 2.3 miles (one-way) with a 1,915-ft. elevation gain
Distance - Trailhead: 8.0 miles (RT)
Elevation at Bridge of Heaven: 12,300-ft.
Elevation Gain - Trailhead to Bridge of Heaven: 3,000-ft.

The trail now travels on mostly open slopes along the south side of a ridge with nice views, passing in and out of isolated pockets of trees. Along the way a few switchbacks ease the ascent. For a brief period the trail crosses to the north side of the ridge revealing the highly eroded hillsides of the Dexter Creek drainage and the western most peaks of the Cimarron range to the northeast, including distinctive Courthouse Mountain.

At 3.5 miles the trail breaks out of the trees for the last time, crosses a small depression and then begins climbing a series of steep switchbacks up a grassy hillside. Expansive and ever improving views of the Cimarron Range, the Sneffels Range, Ironton and the Red Mountain Pass area divert your attention from the stiff climb.

At the top of the hill follow the trail a short distance to a wooden stake marking the Bridge of Heaven, a narrow 20-ft.-long section of the ridge, at 12,300-ft. To get the best views from this amazing vantage point take a short side trip up the dirt knoll on the west side of the Bridge.

From the knoll the magnificent panorama of the Sneffels range and the peaks forming the south and western walls of Yankee Boy Basin fill the skyline to the west. To the south views extends along the San Juan Skyway from Mt. Hayden to the Red Mountains. To the northeast the sculpted peaks of the Cimarron range paint the horizon. To the north is the town of Ridgway. Keep an eye out for bighorn sheep on the rocky ridges below the Bridge.

Across the Bridge to the east the Horsethief trail drops down into a grassy bowl and then continues its southeastern course towards Difficulty and American Flats. These destinations are beyond the range of a day hike.

After soaking in the scenery retrace your footsteps. The well maintained trail makes it easy to enjoy the views all over again on the descent.

Driving Directions

From Ouray: Drive 2.0 miles north from the center Ouray on Highway 550 to County Road 14 and turn right. A sign at the turnoff points to the Bachelor-Syracuse Mine tours. Follow County Road 14, a good gravel road, for 1.0 mile as is winds its way past Lake Lenore and reaches the junction with County Road 14A. Stay on County Road 14 by bearing right at this junction. (CR-14A goes left.) CR-14 continues for 1.5 miles until it reaches a ford with Dexter Creek. (Note: you will first cross Dexter Creek on a bridge at .7 miles. Beyond this point the road becomes a bit rougher). Passenger cars should not ford the creek but instead find parking near the Dexter Creek trailhead, located right before the ford. (Parking before the ford will add 2.2 miles round trip and over 700-ft. of climbing to the hike.)

If you have a 4WD cross the creek and continue up the road for another 1.1 miles to the trailhead parking area on the left. The parking lot is an open area with piles of rock from the Wedge mine. (Note: Please respect the private property on both signs of the road.) The trailhead is located about 100 yards up the road on the right (south). If it is not possible to park at the Wedge Mine continue up the road a short distance (past the trailhead) to an open field and park.

3. Bear Creek National Recreation Trail

★★★★★

Distance: 4.4 - 8.0 miles (RT)

A dramatic trail carved into a steep cliff face high above Bear Creek is just one of the highlights of this hike up a beautiful canyon to two scenic mine sites.

Distance: 4.4 miles (RT) to Grizzly Bear Mine
8.0 miles (RT) to Yellow Jacket Mine
Elevation: 8,470-ft. at Trailhead
10,030-ft. at Grizzly Bear Mine
11,130-ft. at Yellow Jacket Mine
Elevation Gain: 1,560-ft. to Grizzly Bear Mine
2,660-ft. to Yellow Jacket Mine
Difficulty: moderately strenuous

Basecamp: Ouray, Silverton
Area: Uncompahgre NF
Best Season: July - September
USGS Map(s): Ouray, Ironton and Handies Peak

Why Hike the Bear Creek National Recreation Trail

No matter how many times I hike Bear Creek I still marvel at the effort and ingenuity that went into building this trail. In the 1870's miners discovered large quantities of gold and silver in Bear Creek basin southeast of Ouray. Accessing the claims proved difficult. A deep gorge, formed by sheer vertical walls rising high above the rugged creek, guarded the entrance to the basin. Building a trail in the steep rocky terrain along the creek bottom was not an option. Instead the miners blasted a narrow ledge into the cliff 700-ft. above the gorge.

Today, the Bear Creek National Recreation Trail follows this amazing route up beautiful Bear Creek Canyon. A series of long switchbacks with wonderful views of the Mt. Sneffels range climb 1,000-ft. up the east side of the Uncompahgre Gorge to reach the traverse of the ledge high above Bear Creek. Beyond Bear Creek's gorge the trail wanders through forests and alpine meadows beside the creek's tumbling cascades, visiting two scenic, abandoned mines along the way.

In places the trail is narrow with some exposure. This is not a good trail for small children or anyone with a fear of heights.

Trailhead to the Grizzly Bear Mine

Distance from Trailhead: 4.4 miles (RT)
Elevation at Grizzly Bear Mine: 10,030-ft.
Elevation Gain: 1,560-ft.

The Bear Creek National Recreation Trail starts on the west side of Highway 550, 2.5 miles south of Ouray. (See driving directions.) From the park area on the east side of the road, carefully cross to the west side of the road and then follow the trail as it climbs over a road tunnel to the north of the parking lot. In a short distance reach the trailhead registry and the beginning of a series of long, moderately steep switchback ascending the east side of the Uncompahgre Gorge, a deep mountain canyon formed by the Uncompahgre River.

The lower sections of the switchbacks climb through a mixed conifer forest, passing some impressive old white firs. As the trail gains elevation the trees give way to open slopes. Here the trail ascends through rock slides composed of slate and quartzite. In places the trail is narrow with some minor exposure. Terrific views open to the Mt. Sneffels range across the valley to the west and the town of Ouray to the north.

Reach the top of the switchbacks in slightly under a mile having gained 1,000-ft. The grade now moderates as the trail enters the Bear Creek drainage, heading east across a talus slope high above Bear Creek. Views to the south extend to Red Mountain pass. A section of the San Juan Skyway (Million Dollar Highway) is visible in the distance.

Soon the trail levels off following the contours of the canyon's steep walls on a narrow ledge carved into the talus cliff. Footing is generally good except for a few short eroded sections.

One can only image the effort required to build and maintain this route. As you hike along the ledge note how sections of the trail are supported by logs and rubble fill. Across the canyon look for mines dug in the steep canyon walls. The walk along the ledge (0.8 miles) ends where it crosses a rocky drainage.

The trail now ascends moderately on dry slopes with intermittent pockets of trees. About 0.2 miles before the Grizzly Bear Mine the trail enters a nice stand of aspens. Keep an eye out for a metal sided shed on your left. Shortly thereafter mining equipment and a collapsed wood building with a corrugated aluminum roof lie scattered along the side of the trail. This is the Grizzly Bear mine (10,020-ft.), located 2.2 miles and 1,560-ft. up from the trailhead.

The mine is a nice destination and a good turn around point for hikers with limited time (and energy). Otherwise, after exploring the area continue the hike to the Yellow Jacket mine, located 1.8 miles ahead.

Grizzly Bear Mine to the Yellow Jacket Mine

Segment Stat: 1.8 miles (one-way) with a 1,100-ft. elevation gain
Distance - Trailhead to Yellow Jacket Mine: 8.0 miles (RT)
Elevation at Yellow Jacket Mine: 11,130-ft.
Elevation Gain - Trailhead to Yellow Jacket Mine: 2,660-ft.

The trail to the Yellow Jacket mine ascends on a moderate grades above the left (north) side of Bear Creek through intermittent forests of mix conifers and aspens. At 2.7 miles rock-hop across a tributary of Bear Creek. Look for a post marking the continuation of the trail on the other side. Shortly after crossing the stream the path traverses a pretty, wildflower-filled meadow with views of peaks to the north and east.

The trail now continues its moderate t moderately-steep ascent, aided by occasional switchbacks, through meadows and trees. Reach the Yellow Jacket mine (11,130) at 4.0 miles having gained over 2,660-ft. The site, flanked by steep grassy meadows and talus slopes, is littered with mine debris and includes the ruins of a photogenic wood building. To the west distant views of the Mt. Sneffels range fill the skyline.

Slightly beyond the mine site a signposts points the way to the Horsethief trail, which ultimately leads to the Bridge of Heaven and Engineer Pass. Both destinations are too far for a day hike.

To complete your hike, return the way you came.

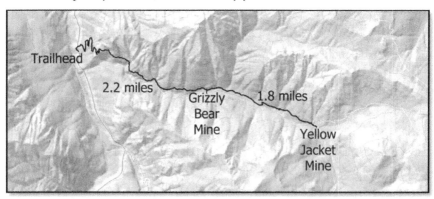

Driving Directions

From Ouray: Take Highway 550 (aka the Million Dollar Highway) 2.5 miles south of Ouray. The trailhead parking lot is on the east side (left) of the road immediately after the road passed through a small tunnel. The trailhead is on west side (right) of the road.

4. Wetterhorn Basin ★★★★★

Distance: 5.8 - 9.0 miles (RT)

This trail wanders through wildflower-filled meadows and then climbs a gorgeous alpine basin to West Fork Pass. From the pass the trail drops into scenic Wetterhorn Basin with great views of Wetterhorn Peak (14,015-ft.).

Distance: 5.8 miles (RT) to West Fork Pass
9.0 miles (RT) to Wetterhorn Basin
Elevation: 10,760-ft. at the Trailhead
12,517-ft. at West Fork Pass
11,850-ft. at Wetterhorn Basin
Elevation Gain: 1,757-ft. to West Fork Pass
-667-ft. to Wetterhorn Basin
Difficulty: moderate

Basecamp: Ouray, Ridgway
Area: Uncompahgre Wilderness, Uncompahgre NF
Best Season: July - September
USGS Map(s): Courthouse Mountain, Wetterhorn Peak

Why Hike Wetterhorn Basin

Heading south on Highway 550 near Ridgway a panorama of the alluring summits and jagged ridges of the Uncompahgre Wilderness fill the eastern skyline, enticing hikers to explore. Several trails penetrate this wilderness from the north, traveling up pretty valleys to scenic passes with dramatic mountain views.

In my opinion the Wetterhorn Basin trail is the finest hike entering the area from the north. The trail gently ascends the beautiful West Fork Cimarron River valley, wandering through scenic meadows beneath Fortress (13-241-ft.), Redcliff (13,642-ft.) and Coxcomb (13,654-ft.) peaks to the head of the valley. Here it climbs a gorgeous alpine basin to West Fork Pass (12,517-ft.).

Just beyond the pass viewpoints showcase stunning Wetterhorn Peak (14,015-ft.) and the emerald green meadows of Wetterhorn Basin. A great lunch spot on the ridge just below the pass offers panoramic views of the basin, the peaks towering above Cow Creek drainage to the southwest and the Sneffels range to the west. Alternatively, hike into the basin to the base of Wetterhorn Peak for a more intimate view.

Trailhead to West Fork Pass

Distance from Trailhead: 5.8 miles (RT)
Elevation at the Pass: 12,517-ft.
Elevation Gain: 1,757-ft.

Few trails boast the stunning views seen from the start of the Wetterhorn Basin hike. From the 4WD trailhead (see driving directions below) Redcliff and Coxcomb Peaks dominate the view at the head of the valley, rising above flower-filled meadows and spruce-fir forests. Our destination is the pass to the west of Coxcomb.

The well-defined trail stays to the left (east) of the West Fork of the Cimarron River, ascending on easy grades through open meadows before entering the forest at 0.7 miles. As the trail continue up the valley, openings in the trees offer intermittent views of the valley. Along the way the trail crosses side steams and avalanche chutes, emerging at a beautiful alpine basin at the head of the valley at 1.6 miles (11,370-ft.).

Cross a small stream and head west across the basin to a series of switchbacks ascending the valley's western slopes through grassy meadows sprinkled with columbines, Indian paintbrush and buttercups. As you climb the trail crosses to the west side of the West Fork, now just a pretty stream cascading down the hillside.

Across the valley Precipice, Fortress, Redcliff and Coxcomb peaks punctuate the ridge forming the valley's eastern wall. To the north views open to distinctive Courthouse Mountain and Chimney Rock.

The grade abates briefly before ascending a steep slope of talus and boulders. Beyond the boulders the trail climbs a grassy knoll dotted with wildflowers, reaching West Fork Pass (12,517-ft.) in 2.9-miles after gaining 1,757-ft.

Coxcomb Peak rises to the east of the pass. To the south enjoy great views of the peaks and ridges towering above the Wetterhorn and Cow Creek drainages – but not of Wetterhorn Peak.

Pass to Wetterhorn Lookout

Segment Stat: 0.5 miles (one-way) with a net 261-ft. elevation loss
Distance - Trailhead to Lookout: 6.8 miles (RT)
Elevation at the Lookout: 12,256-ft.
Elevation Gain - Trailhead to Lookout: +1,857-ft./-261-ft.

To see Wetterhorn Peak climb a short distance up the ridge to the west of the pass or follow the obvious use trail contouring to the west just below the south side of the pass. The idea is to get above or to the right (west) of a ridge extending from Coxcomb Peak that is blocking the view of Wetterhorn Peak.

For more expansive views I recommend hiking down the south side of the pass for about 0.3 miles (losing about 330-ft.) and then heading right (west) across a rocky meadow to an obvious use trail climbing steeply up a ridge jutting into the basin. From the end of the ridge enjoy stunning views of Wetterhorn Peak towering above the emerald green basin and bird's eye views into Cow Creek and Wetterhorn creek drainages to the south. The Mt. Sneffels range graces the skyline to the west.

Pass to Wetterhorn Basin

Segment Stat: 1.6 miles (one-way) with a +100-ft./-750-ft. elevation gain/loss
Distance - Trailhead to Wetterhorn Basin: 9.0 miles (RT)
Elevation at Wetterhorn Basin: 11,850-ft.
Elevation Gain - Trailhead to the Basin: 1,857-ft. / -750-ft.

For a more intimate view of Wetterhorn Peak follow the trail down the south side of the pass into the basin. The trail drops over 750-ft. then climbs about 100-ft. to Wetterhorn Creek in 1.6 miles. (Total round trip from the trailhead to the creek is 9-miles.) From this vantage point pyramid-shaped Wetterhorn Peak pierces the skyline to the east while distinctive Coxcomb Peak looms to the north.

Driving Directions

From Ouray: Head north from Ouray on US Highway 550 for just under 12 miles and turn right (east) onto Owl Creek Road (CR10 - Ouray County 10). The turn is 1.8 miles past the turnoff to Ridgway (Highway 62). Follow the signs to Owl Creek Pass (14.9 miles). Along the way CR 10 turns into CR 8 and then FR 858 after crossing into the Uncompahgre National Forest. The drive offers fine views of Courthouse Mountain and Chimney Rock. Continue over the pass for 0.3 miles to FR 860 (West Fork Road). Turn right and follow FR 860 for 3.3 miles to the trailhead with ample parking. High clearance/4WD is required for the last 1.5 miles of the road which is very rocky and includes a creek crossing that can be problematic.

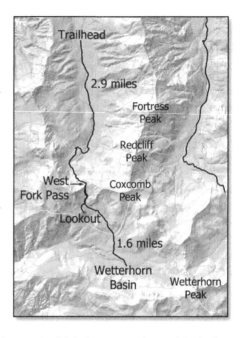

5. Blaine Basin ★★★★

Distance: 6.8 miles (RT)

This is a good hike for people looking for solitude and dramatic, up-close views of the north face of Mt. Sneffels (14,150-ft.). Don't let the crowded parking lot deter you. Most hikers are headed for the Blue Lakes basin. You will have the Blaine Basin trail mostly to yourself.

Distance: 6.8 - 8.2 miles (RT) to Blaine Basin
Elevation: 9,350-ft. at Trailhead
11,200-ft. at Blaine Basin
Elevation Gain: 1,850-ft. to Blaine Basin
Difficulty: moderate

Basecamp: Ouray, Ridgway
Area: Mt. Sneffels Wilderness, Uncompahgre NF
Best Season: July - September
USGS Map(s): Ouray
See Page 19 for Map

Why Hike Blaine Basin

Looking for a little solitude? Then take a hike to Blaine Basin.

This lightly used trail does not require a lot of effort and culminates in a scenic wildflower-filled basin with great views of Mt. Sneffels (14,156-ft.),

Kismet (13,694-ft.) and Cirque Mountain (13,868-ft.). Along the way the trail wanders through forests, passes a pretty waterfall and crosses Wilson Creek three times.

Looking for more of a challenge? Then climb the steep, off-trail route to a high bench between Mt. Sneffels and Blaine Peak for close-up views of Sneffels and a bird's-eye view of the basin.

Be forewarned, the trailhead parking area is often overflowing down the access road. Don't let the crowded parking lot deter you. Most hikers are headed up the Blue Lakes trail. You will likely have the Blaine Basin trail mostly to yourself.

Trailhead to Blaine Basin

Distance from Trailhead: 6.8 miles (RT)
Elevation at Blain Basin: 11,200-ft.
Elevation Gain: 1,850-ft.

This hike shares the trailhead parking area with the Blue Lakes trail (see driving directions). Walk through the gate at the northern end of the parking lot and in a short distance reach a "Y" intersection. Turn left at the sign pointing toward Blaine Basin (about 300-ft. from the gate.) The trail to the right goes to Blue Lakes.

In a few hundred yards the trail, an old logging road, crosses the East Fork Dallas Creek on a wood bridge. Follow the road as is ascends on moderate grades through spruce-fir forest, ignoring two minor roads branching to the right.

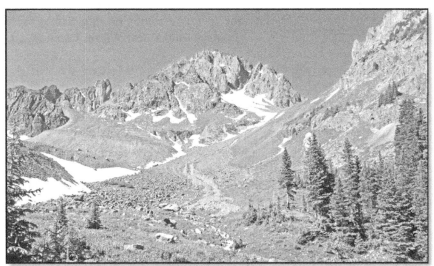

At 0.6 miles the trail crosses a low ridge and enters the Wilson Creek drainage. The grade abates as the path traverses aspen groves and meadows to meet Wilson Creek at 0.6 miles. Backtrack a brief distance from the

crossing to find a rock cairn marking a trail heading right and leading to a makeshift bridge, constructed of logs, crossing the creek. Across the creek rejoin the road switchbacking up the hill to the right.

Beyond the crossing reach a trail junction and turn right (east/southeast) on the trail signed for Blaine Basin. The trail to the left is the East Dallas trail that descends to the East Dallas Road.

For the next 0.8 miles the trail meanders through forest with intermittent meadows, paralleling the creek and crossing its two more times at 1.6 miles and 2.0 miles. Just after the third crossing look for a pretty waterfall cascading down the cliff face to the right (southwest) of the trail.

At 2.2 miles a sign marks a junction where the trail curves to the left (east). Ignore the unmarked trail to the right that leads to the base of the falls. Past the sign the path starts ascending on moderately-steep grades, reaching a signed junction with the Dallas Trail, branching left, at 2.3 miles. Continue straight ahead on the Blaine Basin trail.

The rocky trail now climbs a steep slope through trees. Near the top of the slope the trail ascends through a small meadow and then turns right (south) toward the creek. Follow the trail as it climbs on moderate grades through trees and emerges in a beautiful meadow near Wilson Creek at 3.0 miles. This is lower Blaine Basin.

The meadow provides the first views of the north face of Mt. Sneffels (14,150-ft.), rising to the southwest. For even better views follow the trail as it crosses the creeks and climbs gently through meadows filled with wildflowers in season. Soon the trail starts climbing steep switchbacks up a hillside scattered with small trees, passing a sign for Blaine Basin at 3.2 miles. The smaller trees indicate the path of avalanches thundering down Sneffel's north face.

After a short climb reach the upper basin (11,120-ft.) at 3.4 miles. The trail ends at a lovely viewpoint. In season the fields of the upper basin are filled with a spectacular display of wildflowers. Mt. Sneffels towers above the scenic basin with Kismet (13,694-ft.) and Cirque Mountain (13,680-ft.) rising to east of Sneffels. To the right (west) is Blaine Peak (12,910-ft.). Glacial moraines clearly illustrate the paths of ancient glaciers that once filled the basin.

A faint use trail is visible climbing steeply up the slope to a high bench between Mt. Sneffels and Blaine Peak. If time, energy and weather permit, the off-trail route to the bench offers up close views of Sneffels and bird's-eye views of the basin.

Route to the Bench

Segment Stat: 0.7 mile (one-way) with 880-ft. elevation gain
Distance from Trailhead: 8.2 miles (RT)
Elevation at the Bench: 12,080-ft.
Elevation Gain: 2,730-ft.

To reach the bench, walk a short distance up the valley and then cross to the right (west) side of a rocky gully. On the other side of the gully continue ascending the valley until you find a good place to climb the grassy slopes to the use trail seen from the lookout. Follow the use trail as it switchbacks up the grassy slope to the south of Blaine Peak.

The trail fades as it reaches a gully carrying meltwater from the north slopes of Mt. Sneffels. Under good conditions you can cross the gully and find a trail on the other side that continues to the Blaine Mine. On my recent trip to the basin ice and loose rock filled the gully, preventing a safe crossing. In this case I simply climbed the grassy slopes to the right (northwest) of the gully until I reached the high bench overlooking Blaine Basin. From the bench enjoy lovely, up-close views of Mt Sneffel's north face and Cirque Mountain to the southeast. This side trip gains almost 900 feet in just 0.7 miles, adding 1.4 miles to the round trip hiking distance.

Many people will be happy simply exploring the scenic upper basin and taking pictures of the wildflowers. When you are done enjoying the basin retrace your steps to the trailhead parking area.

Driving Directions

From Ouray It takes 45-50 minutes to drive the 24 miles from Ouray to the Blue Lakes/Blaine Basin trailhead. The drive is quite scenic with views dominated by 14,150-ft. Mt. Sneffels and its neighboring peaks and ridges, almost all over 13,000-ft.

From the center of Ouray take Highway 550 heading north for just over 10 miles to Highway 62 in Ridgway. Turn left (west) on Highway 62. Drive 4.8 miles and then take a left onto County Road 7, marked Dallas Creek (the road use to be marked East Dallas Creek). It is easy to miss the turn while you are admiring the scenery to the south of the highway. In two miles CR-7 bears right where it meets CR-7A. Continue for a total of 9 miles on CR-7 through a beautiful valley to the parking area at the trailhead. Note: CR-7 turns into Forest Road 851.1 at the forest boundary.

From Telluride: From Telluride the trailhead is a 90 minute/44 miles drive. Drive west on West Colorado Avenue to Highway 145. Head west on Hwy 145 for 12.7 miles to where it dead ends at Highway 62 in Placerville. Turn a right (east) onto Highway 62 and drive 18.6 miles to County Road 7, marked Dallas Creek. Turn right onto CR-7. In two miles CR-7 bears right where it meets CR-7A. Continue for a total of 9 miles through a beautiful valley to the parking area at the trailhead. Note: CR-7 turns into Forest Road 851.1 at the forest boundary.

Road Conditions: Passenger car accessible if driven carefully. CR-7 is a dirt/gravel road that becomes rougher as it climbs to the National Forest boundary. Beyond this point the road maintenance deteriorates and you will need to dodge potholes and rocks.

6. Upper Cascade Falls ☆☆☆
Distance: 4.4 - 5.9 miles (RT)

This great half day hike climbing high above the eastern side of Ouray features panoramic views of the Uncompahgre Valley, Cascade Falls and the Amphitheater.

Distance: 4.4 miles (RT) to Upper Cascade Falls
5.9 miles (loop) with return via the Portland Trail
Elevation: 8,500-ft. at Trailhead
10,030-ft. at Upper Cascade Falls
Elevation Gain: 1,530-ft. to Upper Cascade Falls
Difficulty: moderately strenuous

Basecamp: Ouray
Area: Uncompahgre NF
Best Season: July - September
USGS Map(s): Ouray

Why Hike Upper Cascade Falls Trail

Scenic views of the amphitheater rock formation, Upper Cascade Falls and Ouray along with a good workout are the rewards of this half day hike, located just a mile south of Ouray. Links to the Portland and the Lower Cascade Falls trails create interesting options to extend the trip. The length of the hike, its close proximity to town and good views make it a nice option if the weather is expected to turn for the worse later in the day.

Trailhead to Upper Cascade Falls

Distance from Trailhead: 4.4 miles (RT)
Elevation Upper Cascade Falls: 10,030-ft.
Elevation Gain: 1,530-ft.

The trail to Upper Cascade Falls starts at the southeast end of a small parking area at the top of the Amphitheater Campground (see driving directions below). Follow the trail for 0.2 miles as it contours along the hillside to a trail junction. At the junction turn left on the Upper Cascade Falls trail toward the Chief Ouray Mine. The trail to the right, the Portland Trail, can be used as a return leg of an extended loop hike.

Climb through scrub oaks and mixed conifers to a second junction, located just over 0.5 miles from the trailhead. Stay on the Upper Cascade trail heading toward the Chief Ouray Mine. The trail to the left heads downhill toward the campground and Lower Cascade falls. This section of the trail enjoys nice views to the west and southwest toward Potosi Peak and Hayden Mountain.

Beyond the junction the grade steepens. Openings in the foliage offer tantalizing views of the sculpted walls of the amphitheater circling the eastern end of the basin. After hiking 0.3 miles reach a second junction with the Portland trail, which branches right. We bear left, following the signs toward Chief Ouray Mine.

The trail now ascends a dry hillside on steep switchbacks, gaining over 1,100-ft in just under a mile. As you climb enjoy wonderful views of the amphitheater. Hayden Mountain and the peaks and ridges around Potosi Peak dominate the scene to the west and southwest.

At the top of the switchback the path traverses a rocky ledge and crosses a ridge. Vantage points along the path offer views of Twin Peaks and the Sneffels range to the west and the town of Ouray 2,300-ft below.

After crossing the ridge the trail curves northeast (right) and descends through trees for 0.3 miles to cross the creek at Upper Cascade Falls. Opening in the trees provide views of the Chief Ouray bunkhouse building across the drainage. (The bunkhouse is a light blue metal building.)

There are actually two waterfalls, one above the trail and one below. The waterfall below the trail can be heard buy not seen.

After enjoy the secluded area around the falls you can either return the way you came or walk another 0.2 miles to the mine buildings. This section of the trail is not recommended for people with a fear of heights.

Return via the Portland Trail

Distance from Trailhead: 5.9 mile (loop)
Ending Elevation: 8,500-ft. at the trailhead
Elevation Gain/Loss: -1,530-ft.

Return the way you came or extend the hike by turning left (east) onto the Portland Trail. The junction is located at the base of the switchbacks. Returning via the well signed Portland Trail adds 1.5 miles to the hike and is highly recommended. The trail features wonderful views of the amphitheater and the peaks rising to the south and west of Ouray. See the Portland Trail description for more information.

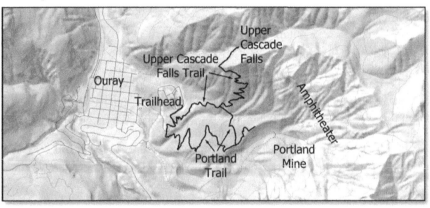

Driving Directions

From Ouray: Drive south from Ouray on Highway 550 for just over a mile to the Amphitheater Campground and turn left onto the campground access road. The turnoff is past the second switchback leaving town. Follow the paved road into the campground for 1.25 miles, keeping left at all intersections. The trailhead, marked for the Upper Cascade trail, is located at the top of the campground. A good hand-drawn map on a signpost at the trailhead shows the interconnecting trail system that includes the Portland Trail, the Upper and Lower Cascade Falls Trails and the Portland Mine Road.

If walking from Ouray, walk up 8th Ave to Lower Cascade Falls, turn right (south) on the Perimeter trail for 0.2 miles to a junction. Turn left and ascend for 0.6 miles to the Cascade/Portland trail (the second junction at 0.5 miles in the description) and then turn left toward Upper Cascade Falls.

7. Portland Trail ✩✩✩

Distance: 3.5 - 4.2 miles (RT)

This short, easy loop hike explores the basin below a huge amphitheater of eroded cliffs rising above the eastern side of Ouray and features scenic viewpoints to appreciate the formation along with the peaks rising to the south and west of town.

Distance: 3.5 miles (loop) with return via Upper Cascade Trail or 4.2 miles (RT)
Elevation: 8,500-ft. at Trailhead 9,250-ft. at high point on the Portland Trail
Elevation Gain: 750-ft. to high point on the Portland Trail
Difficulty: easy

Basecamp: Ouray
Area: Uncompahgre NF
Best Season: July - September
USGS Map(s): Ouray
See Page 36 for Map

Why Hike the Portland Trail

The Amphitheater, a huge sculpted gray cliff face formed from highly eroded volcanic rock, rises above a large bowl-shaped valley on the eastern side of Ouray. A short, easy loop hike, combining the Portland Trail with a portion of the Upper Cascade Falls Trail, explores the basin below the amphitheater and features scenic viewpoints to appreciate the formation along with the peaks rising to the south and west of Ouray. The walk is a good option for those with limited time or on a day when the weather precludes hiking at higher elevations.

The Portland Trail can be extended into a longer hike when combined with the Upper Cascade Falls Trail. See the description of the Upper Cascade Falls trail for more information.

Portland Trail Description

Distance: 4.2 miles (RT)
Elevation at Overlook: 9,250-ft.
Elevation Gain: 750-ft.

There are several different access points to get on the Portland trail. I prefer starting at the Upper Cascade Falls trailhead, located at the top of the Amphitheater Campground (see driving directions).

Follow the trail, which starts at the southeast end of the small trailhead parking area, for 0.2 miles as it contours along the hillside to a trail junction. Turn right at the junction on the Portland trail. The trail to the left, the Upper Cascade Falls trail, will be used as a return leg of the loop hike.

From the junction the trails descends to cross a normally dry drainage, climbs out the other side and starts ascending the basin on a series of gentle switchbacks. About a half a mile beyond the trailhead you will come to second trail junction. Continue heading northeast in the direction of the scenic overlook indicated on the sign. [The Portland trailhead, pointing to the southwest on the sign, leads to a second trailhead on the Portland Mine Road. This is a good starting point if the campground is closed (see driving directions below)].

Beyond the junction the trail climbs through mixed conifers and small sections of scrub oak. Openings in the foliage feature nice views to the west and southwest toward Hayden Mountain and the peaks and ridges around Potosi Peak. About 1.7-miles from the campground trailhead an opening provides views across the drainage to a mining operation at the southern end of the Amphitheater.

At 2.0 miles a sign points to a scenic overlook with great views of the amphitheater towering above the basin and Hayden Mountain. Shortly after the overlook (0.1-mile) reach a three-way trail junction.

At the three way intersection you have several options. I recommend going left in the direction of the Amphitheater Campground to complete the loop hike. The trail drops down to cross a normally dry drainage and then ascends to meet the Upper Cascade Falls trail in 0.6 miles. Go left on the Cascade Falls trail toward the Amphitheater Campground. (The trail to the right climbs 1,100-ft in just under a mile on its way to Upper Cascade Falls and the Chief Ouray Mine.) At the next two junctions follow the signs back to the Campground and the trailhead parking area. See the Upper Cascade description for more information.

Another option is to take a side trip to the Portland Mine. To visit the mine head right at the three way junction, following the trail to the mine. The route drops about 150-ft. to cross Portland Creek and then climbs to join the Portland Road in 0.5 miles. Follow the road east to the mine.

Finally, you can simply turn around at the three-way junction and return the way you came. The out-and-back hike is 4.2 miles (RT) from the campground or 3.8 miles (RT) from the trailhead on the Portland Road (see driving directions).

Driving Directions

From Ouray: Drive south from Ouray on Highway 550 for just over a mile to the Amphitheater Campground and turn left onto the campground access road. The turnoff is past the second switchback leaving town. Follow the paved road into the campground for 1.25 miles, keeping left at all intersections. The trailhead, marked for the Upper Cascade Trail, is located at the top of the campground. A good hand-drawn map on a signpost at the trailhead shows the interconnecting trail system that includes the Portland Trail, the Upper and Lower Cascade Falls Trails and the Portland Mine Road.

If the access gate to the campground is closed you can reach the Portland trail by walking up the campground road or use two alternative access points. The first access point is reached using the Baby Bathtubs trail. After turning left onto the campground road look for a parking area on your left, right before a bridge. The Baby Bathtubs trail starts on the right side of the road just past the bridge. Follow this trail for just over 0.3 miles to where it meets the Portland trail.

The second access is on the Portland Road. From the Amphitheater Campground road junction at U.S. 550 turn into the campground, follow the road for about 100 yards and turn right on the Portland Road, an unmarked dirt road. Follow the Portland Road for about 0.25 miles to the Portland Trailhead (the first road to the left). This section of the Portland trail crosses a small foot bridge over Portland Creek and ties into the loop trail system in a few hundred yards.

8. Alpine Mine Overlook ☆☆☆
Distance: 5.6 miles (RT)

Hikers completing the stiff climb to an overlook 3,000-ft. above Ouray are rewarded with panoramic views of Ouray, the amphitheater and the sea of peaks and ridges rising to the east of town.

Distance: 5.6 miles (RT) to Alpine Mine Overlook
Elevation: 8,750-ft. at Trailhead 10,930-ft. at Alpine Mine Overlook
Elevation Gain: 2,180-ft. to Alpine Mine Overlook
Difficulty: moderately strenuous

Basecamp: Ouray
Area: Uncompahgre NF
Best Season: July - September
USGS Map(s): Ouray, Ironton

Why Hike to the Alpine Mine Overlook

Perched 3,130-ft. above Ouray, the Alpine Mine Overlook features 180-degree panoramic views of the Ouray area and the wall of cliffs and mountains rising to the east. Hayden Mountain and the peaks looming above the Million Dollar Highway dominate the scene to the south and southeast.

The half-day hike to the overlook is a good workout and a great way to acclimate, climbing over 2,000-ft. in just under 3-miles. Along the way hikers are treated to close-up views of Hayden Mountain and the jagged cliff face defining the western wall of the Weehawken Valley.

Be aware that you will not be alone on this popular hike, located just 3.0 miles to the west of Ouray.

Trailhead to Junction with the Alpine Mine Trail

Distance from Trailhead: 1.5 miles (one-way)
Elevation at Junction: 9,980-ft.
Elevation Gain: 1,230-ft.

The trail to the Alpine Mine Overlook starts at the Weehawken trailhead (see driving direction). Follow the trail as it ascends moderate to moderately steep switchbacks through a forest of aspen and mixed conifers up the hillside to the north of Weehawken Creek. As you climb the trees give way to open meadows interspersed with aspen groves. The meadows provide nice views of Hayden Mountain across Canyon Creek valley. After about a mile of hiking the trees thicken and restrict the views.

Reach a junction with the Alpine Mine trail at 1.5 miles. Before turning right on the Alpine Mine trail continue a few feet up to the Weehawken trail to a clearing that provides nice views of the cliff face forming the western wall of the Weehawken drainage.

Junction to Alpine Mine Overlook

Segment Stat: 1.3 miles (one-way) with a 950-ft. elevation gain
Distance - Trailhead to Overlook: 5.6 miles (RT)
Elevation at Overlook: 10,950-ft.
Elevation Gain - Trailhead to Overlook: 2,180-ft.

Beyond the junction the trail continues its ascent on a series of short, steep switchbacks that gain over 700-ft in 0.7-miles. Toward the top of the switchbacks the trail traverses a steep meadow. At the top of the meadow views open to the sculpted hillside above the trail.

The grade abates a bit as the trail traverses the scree covered slopes of a steep drainage on a narrow footpath with some exposure. Reach the head of the drainage and the site of the Alpine Mine at 2.4 miles. Here you will see mining equipment and remnants of tracks for ore cars. Mine buildings are located in the trees above the trail.

Beyond the mine the path ascends 180-ft. in 0.2 miles to reach the top of a ridge and the high point of the trail at 10,950-ft. Follow the trail along the top of the dry ridge interspersed with mixed conifers to the first lookout point featuring great views to the southwest of Potosi Peak and the sculpted cliff face towering above Weehawken Creek. Hayden Mountain and the peaks and ridges along the Million Dollar Highway rise to the southeast.

Continue along the ridge to a sign marking the path through the trees to the Alpine Mine Overlook. The overlook features 180-degree panoramic views. Ouray lies deep in the valley below with a wall of cliffs and mountains rising to the east. The Amphitheater rock formation towers above the southeast end of town. Twin Mountains dominates the view to the north while the peaks along the Million Dollar Highway and Hayden Mountain fill the skyline to the south.

The overlook is quite exposed with sheer drop-offs. Care should be taken while ogling the scenery. This is not a good place for small children.

After admiring the view return the way you came.

Driving Directions

From Ouray: Drive south on US Highway 550 for approximately 0.25 miles. Turn right onto Colorado State Highway 361 (Camp Bird Road) and continue for another 2.7 miles to the Weehawken Trailhead on the right side of the road.

9. Richmond Pass ★★★★

Distance: 5.6 miles (RT)

Terrific views of the high peaks towering above the Million Dollar Highway and Yankee Boy Basin are the rewards of this steep climb to a scenic pass to the south of Hayden Mountain.

Distance: 5.6 miles (RT)
Elevation: 9,910-ft. at Trailhead
12,693-ft. at Richmond Pass
Elevation Gain: 2,783-ft.
Difficulty: strenuous

Basecamp: Ouray
Area: Uncompahgre NF
Best Season: July - September
USGS Map(s): Ironton

Why Hike to the Richmond Pass

Fit, acclimated hikers will love this steep trail climbing to Richmond Pass, a scenic saddle on the ridge to the south of Hayden Mountain near Ouray, Colorado. The first section of the hike ascends through beautiful groves of aspen that give way to spruce-pine forest interspersed with small meadows. Across the valley views open to the colorful Red Mountains and the Brown Mountain ridge, anchored by Abrams Mountain to the north. Soon the Twin Sisters and nearby summits to the west of Silverton, Colorado join the scene.

After 1.7 miles the path climbs above the timberline and continues the steep ascent up beautiful tundra-clad slopes. The stunning views now expand to include a sea of peaks to the northeast, including the 14,000-ft. summits in the Uncompahgre Wilderness. Ahead views open to the pass, a saddle on the ridge between Hayden Mountain to the north and Peak 13,011-ft. to the south.

As the trail crests the pass the high peaks towering above Yankee Boy Basin, including Gilpin Peak, Mount Sneffels (14,150-ft.), Cirque Mountain, Teakettle Mountain and Potosi Peak, spring into view. A short walk to an overlook on the west side of the pass yields more great views of the basin along with Chicago Peak and the summits surrounding the Imogene Pass area.

Surefooted hikers can extend the hike by climbing north from the pass to the summit of Hayden Mountain South. With a prearranged car shuttle a longer point-to-point hike descends down the west side of the pass to an old mining road that leads to the Imogene Pass jeep road. The Imogene Pass road is very rugged, requiring a high clearance, 4WD vehicle.

The unmarked trailhead for this hike, located along Highway 550 near the southern end of Ironton Park, is easy to miss. Pay close attention to the driving directions (below). Highway 550 south of Ouray is a narrow, curvy road with spectacular views. It is easy to drive by the unmarked turn while you are admiring the scenery.

Trailhead to Richmond Pass

The Richmond Pass trailhead is located along Highway 550 at the south end of the Ironton Park area near Ouray, Colorado. (See driving directions below.) From the parking area walk 200-ft. west up an old road paralleling the highway to a trailhead sign listing the mileage to Richmond Pass, 2.4 miles, and the Richmond Basin Road, 3.7 miles. (My GPS measurements found the trail to be a little longer.)

Beyond the sign the road curves to the right and soon becomes a trail. A short distance beyond is a trail register. Past the register the trail starts climbing through aspen on a series of moderately-steep to steep switchbacks.

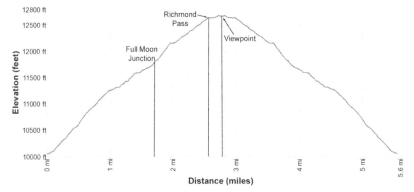

After walking a half mile openings in the trees offer views of Red Mountain No 2 (12,219-ft.) and No 3 (12,890-ft.) to the south. Brown Mountain (13,339-ft.) rises across the valley to the east. As you ascend the aspen give way to evergreens and small meadows with ever improving views of the colorful Red Mountains.

After hiking 1.2 miles reach a small sign in a meadow pointing right toward the continuation of the trail. Ignore the old, faded pack trail heading left (west) near the sign. From the meadow distant views open to the Twin

Sisters, two distinctive peaks rising to the southwest. Closer at hand are the 13,000-ft. peaks at the head of McIntyre Gulch, the valley to the southwest.

At 1.7 miles we leave the last of the trees behind and reach the top of the switchbacks. To the northeast are fine views of Abrams Mountain (12,801-ft.), the northern most peak along the Brown Mountain Ridge. Here a trail sign marks the junction with the Full Moon trail, a faint track heading right (northeast). We bear left (west) on the Richmond Trail.

Keep an eye on the weather as you continue the hike. You are now above the timberline and completely exposed. Turn around if thunderstorms are threatening.

The trail now climbs steeply along a dirt/scree covered slope before leveling out at 2.0 miles atop a tundra clad ridge separating McIntyre Gulch, to the south, and Full Moon Gulch, to the north. The pass is now in sight, the saddle at the head of the ridge between Hayden Mountain (13,206-ft.) to the north and Peak 13,011 to the south. From this vantage point enjoy fabulous views of the Red Mountains across the valley to the southeast.

The trail now become a little faint as it drops into a small bowl. Rock cairns make the trail as it travels through the bowl. Look ahead to see a stake marking where the trail climbs out of the bowl.

Beyond the bowl the steep climb up the ridge is accompanied by stunning views of the rugged peaks at the head of McIntyre Gulch, Hayden Mountain, the Red Mountains and Brown Mountain. A sea of high peaks fills the skyline to the northeast. On a clear day the tops of Wetterhorn and Uncompahgre Peak, two 14,000-ers, are visible. To the southwest the high peaks along the Mineral Creek Valley and beyond dominate the view.

At 2.3 miles the trail curves to the right as it climbs around a low hill. The trail is faint through this section.

Soon you reach a rock cairn with a stake. Here the trail splits. The obvious trail to the right is the lower trail. The path branching left is the high trail, which initially is very faint but becomes clearer as you climb.

The lower trail is slightly longer and used early in the season to circumvent a snow cornice on the ridge. The higher route, which is more direct, is preferred once the snow melts on the ridge top. As you near the pass the higher trail crosses scree covered slopes.

Crest Richmond Pass (12,667-ft.) at 2.6 miles. Here amazing views open to Yankee Boy Basin to the northwest. Gilpin Peak (13,694-ft.), Mount Sneffels (14,150-ft.) and Potosi Peak (13,786-ft.) tower above the basin. Cirque Mountain (13,686-ft.) and Teakettle Mountain (13,819-ft.) rise between Mount Sneffels and Potosi Peak. The Yankee Boy Basin Road (aka County Road 361) is seen snaking up the valley floor.

The Richmond Pass Trail continues over the pass, dropping steeply down the western slopes of Hayden Mountain on an old pack trail. The trail ends at a jeep road which descends to the Imogene Pass Road. A car shuttle is required for this point to point hike. Two use/social trails branch right (north) from the pass, leading to the summit of Hayden Mountain South.

My recommendation is to take the use/social trail branching left from the pass. This trail crosses a bench on an undulating path with more fine views of Yankee Boy Basin. Continue along the bench for 0.2 miles to a viewpoint at the end of the bench at 2.8 miles. Below the bench you will see a mining road climbing Richmond Basin. Chicago Peak (13,385-ft.) rises along the ridge to the west. The viewpoint is an excellent place to have lunch and soak in the views.

From the viewpoint, retrace your steps to the trailhead for a 5.6 mile hike. The views are even better on the way down since you are facing the Red Mountain area.

From the bench it is possible to drop down to the mining road and then descend the road to the junction with the Imogene Pass Road (about 3 miles). From the junction it is a 2.3 mile to the Yankee Boy Basin Road. Again, this option would require a car drop. The length of the point to point hike could be shortened by driving the shuttle vehicle up the Imogene Pass Road to the junction with the Richmond Basin Mining Road. Note: The Imogene Pass Road requires a high clearance, 4WD vehicle. Check with the Ouray Visitor Center on current road conditions before trying this point-to-point hike.

Note: The unmarked trailhead for this hike, located along Highway 550 near the southern end of Ironton Park, is easy to miss. Pay close attention to the driving directions (below). Highway 550 south of Ouray is a narrow, curvy road with spectacular views. It is easy to drive by the unmarked turn while you are admiring the scenery.

Driving Directions

From Ouray: From the center of Ouray (6th Avenue and Main Street), head south on Highway 550-S for 8.7 miles and turn right (northeast) onto an unmarked spur road leading to the trailhead parking area. (The turnoff is 9.1 miles from the Ouray Visitor Center adjacent to the Hot Springs.)

Finding this road might be the hardest part of the hike. To help you locate the turnoff I am including some landmarks and intermediate distances.

As you drive south out of town the road climbs a few switchbacks, travels through a tunnel and then passes the Bear Creek National Recreation Trail parking area, on the left (east), and then the Engineer Pass Jeep Road, also on the left (east), at 3.9 miles.

At 5.3 miles drive through an avalanche shed. Soon the road climbs a few more switchbacks and then levels off as it reaches Ironton Park. Here you will pass a stone building, on the left (east), and Crystal Lake, on the right (west).

At 7.9 miles pass a road and a large parking lot on the left (southwest), just before a large reclamation site. Now you need to really pay attention. Soon you will see the ruins of a wood building, the schoolhouse for the Larson Brother's mine, on the right (northeast).

Travel 0.8 miles past the schoolhouse and turn right onto an unmarked dirt road. This will be the next right turn after the schoolhouse and is very easy to miss if you are not paying attention. You've missed the turn if you pass a large gravel pull-off on the left and then start up some switchbacks.

Follow the spur road for a short distance and then turn left on a dirt track. There will be a pile of mine tailings to the right of the turnoff. The dirt track leads to a small parking area where you will see a sign for the Richmond Trailhead.

The GPS coordinates for the turnoff: 37.988587, -107.649762

10. Governor Basin ★★★✦
Distance: 5.8 – 7.6 miles (RT)

Ascend a scenic jeep road into the heart of Governor Basin, explore the Mountain Top mine ruins and then follow a route to an overlook with impressive views of the high peaks of Yankee Boy Basin.

Distance: 5.8 miles (RT) to
Governor Basin
7.6 miles (RT) to Overlook
Elevation: 10,715-ft. at Trailhead
11,990-ft. at Governor Basin
12,800-ft. at Overlook
Elevation Gain: 1,275-ft. to
Governor Basin
2,085-ft. at Overlook
Difficulty: moderately strenuous

Basecamp: Ouray
Area: Uncompahgre NF
Best Season: July - September
USGS Map(s): Telluride

Why Hike to Governor Basin

I don't often recommend hikes on jeep roads, but I make an exception for Governor Basin. The hike is highly scenic and includes a visit to the Mountain Top mine, where the ruins of a multi-story wood dormitory. Beyond the jeep road a route climbs to a high overlook with breathtaking views of Mount Emma, the San Sophia Ridge, Cirque Mountain, Teakettle Mountain, Potosi Peak and beyond. During late July and early August the meadows of Governor Basin are awash in a magnificent display of wildflowers.

With adequate time, energy and good weather it is possible to explore beyond the viewpoint, scrambling up nearby ridges for views that extend to Mount Sneffels and/or the Telluride area. The area also provides access to Mount Emma, although this class 4 scramble is best left to experienced climbers.

I strongly advise getting an early start on this hike to beat afternoon thunderstorms, a frequent occurrence in area, and to avoid the bulk of the jeep traffic on the road. Hiking the road on a week day, when Jeep traffic is typically lighter, is also a good idea. Avoid the hike during the Ouray Jeep Rally and holiday weekends.

Trailhead to Governor Basin

Distance from Trailhead: 5.8 (round trip)
Elevation at Basin: 11,990-ft.
Elevation Gain: 1,275-ft.

This description assumes you start this hike from the Governor Basin Road pullout just past the intersection with the Yankee Boy Basin Road. (See driving directions below). From the pullout, the Governor Basin road curves to the left, passing the gated road to the Walker/Ruby mine. Beyond the mine the road crosses a wood bridge spanning Sneffels Creek, climbs a few switchbacks and then ascends southwest on moderate grades.

Potosi Peak's (13,786-ft.) rugged slopes tower above the road to the northeast while Stony Mountain (12,698-ft.) rises to the west. Ahead the jagged profile of the San Sophia Ridge fills the skyline.

At 0.7 miles the main road curves to the left, passing a side road blocked by a gate, and soon crosses a creek. The road now narrows and enters the trees as it climbs moderately-steep to steep switchbacks. Openings in the trees offer fine views of Teakettle Mountain and Potosi Peak to the north/northeast. Soon Cirque Mountain joins the scene. The unattractive area along the valley floor the east is the Revenue Mine.

At 1.4 miles the road veers right at a hairpin curve. Ignore the two lesser roads branch left toward Sidney Basin. The grade now moderates and the trees thin. Lovely alpine meadows offer ever improving views of the surrounding peaks.

Reach a second junction at 1.7 miles. The signed road to the left also leads to Sidney Basin, creating a loop with the previously passed roads. We continue straight ahead on the Governor Basin Road.

The trees now give way to meadows and fine views open to Stony Mountain to the north. Mount Emma (13,581-ft.) and Gilpin Peak (13,691-ft.) dominate the view to the west/northwest. Soon the road curves to the left (southwest). Here we have unimpeded views of Governor Basin where the Mountain Top mine's old wood dormitory lies toppled in the basin's meadows beneath the photogenic San Sophia Ridge. As you proceed up the road views open to Mount Sneffels (14,150-ft.) towering above Stony Mountain's west ridge.

At 2.2 miles reach an area with several road junctions. The roads branching left lead to the Virginius Mine, which is on private property. Please do not trespass. We bear right, staying on the main road that descends on moderate grades into the basin, passing some reclamation work and then crossing a creek at 2.7 miles. The reclamation area is an eyesore. Thankfully the great view of the San Sophia Ridge diverts your attention.

Beyond the creek the road climbs gradually to a "Y" intersection. The spur road branching right leads to a tailings pile near the dilapidated wood dormitory of the Mountain Top Mine at 2.9 miles. A gated mine tunnel, rail tracks, a metal building and various piles of debris are located atop the tailings pile. For many parties the Mountain Top Mine site is a good turn around point. If so, after investigating the ruins retrace your steps to your vehicle for a 5.8 mile round-trip hike.

Route to the Overlook

Segment Stat: 1.1 miles (one-way) with an 810-ft. elevation gain
Distance - Trailhead to Overlook: 7.6 miles (RT)
Elevation at Overlook: 12,800-ft.
Elevation Gain - Trailhead to Overlook: 2,085-ft.

If you wish to continue exploring Governor Basin, return to the "Y" intersection (3.2 miles) and take the road branching left. The road now climbs on moderately steep grades. Pay attention as you climb. You will follow the road as it curves to the right, then to the left, then to the right and back again to the left. As you curve to the left for the second time watch for a green metal stake that is leaning against a rock along the right side of the road at 3.4 miles. This should be short distance beyond a small creek, which may be dry. There is supposed to be a trail here, but it is very faint and hard to find.

Turn right at the stake and head up the grassy hill, staying to the left of the creek. As you climb note the dark rock outcropping ahead. Below this feature you should soon see a faint, boot-beaten path that heads right (north) up a grassy slope. This is the route to the overlook.

Follow the trail, which becomes more obvious as you ascend steeply up the hillside. To the southeast are fine views of Peak 13,337 towering above the Virginus mine and the San Sophia Ridge.

Reach a grassy ridge at 3.7 miles. Here the route makes a sharp left. There should be another stake marking this turn. Be sure to look around and identify some landmarks so that you don't miss the turn on the return trip. From this vantage point Cirque and Teakettle Mountains rise beyond the ridge.

Continue climbing, stay to the left of a gully. As you crest a low rise the grade briefly abates. Ahead, on the right, is a small tailing pile. Follow the boot beaten path that crosses a small creek and ascends past the tailings pile. You are now on an obvious road that heads southwest towards the San Sophia Ridge.

At 3.8 miles the boot beaten path turns right (north/northwest), paralleling the San Sophia Ridge as it climbs up meadows and then rocky slopes. Intermittent cairns mark the route. At 4.0 miles reach a saddle at the base of a scree slope spilling down the ridge. Turn right here and ascend a short distance to an overlook atop a bench with breathtaking views of Mount Emma, the San Sophia Ridge, Cirque Mountain, Teakettle Mountain, Potosi Peak and beyond. Mendoza Peak (13,275-ft.) and Peak 13,337 punctuate the ridge rimming the south side of Governor Basin. Stony Mountain, dwarfed by the surrounding peaks, rises along the ridge to the northwest.

Hikers with the time, energy and good weather may want to continue heading north, crossing the next basin and climbing to a pass on the ridge to the left (west) of Peak 13,027. From the saddle near the overlook, this side trip descends slightly and then ascends through tundra and scree covered slopes to the pass. Here views open to Mount Sneffels towering above Yankee Boy Basin. Extending the hike to the pass adds about a mile to the trip.

Beyond the pass a faint path diagonals across loose, unstable scree, heading for the ridge crest. Unfortunately the trail peters out before reaching its destination. Seasoned scramblers will now chart their own course, heading slightly left to reach a spot atop the ridge between rock outcroppings. Views from the ridge extend down Mill Creek Basin (east of Telluride) to Deep Creek Mesa and the high peaks of the Lizard Head Wilderness.

When you are done enjoying the views retrace your steps back to the trailhead. As you descend the road, listen for jeeps coming up the road. It is hard to see around some of the curves. Step off the road to allow approaching vehicles adequate room to negotiate the narrow rugged track.

Driving Directions

From Ouray: From the center of Ouray (6th Avenue and Main Street), head south on Highway 550-S for 0.6 miles. At the south end of town the road climbs a switchback. As you round the hairpin curve on the first switchback watch for a signed road off to the right. This is County Road 361 leading to Camp Bird Mine and Yankee Boy Basin.

Turn right onto County Road 361 and follow the road for 4.7 miles to the large Camp Bird Mine complex. Bear slightly right to stay on the main road marked for Yankee Boy Basin and Imogen Pass. You will now drive past the mine and under a rock overhang. In 1.3 mile reach the junction with the Imogene Pass road on the left. Continue straight ahead, passing the old Sneffels town site, the Revenue Mine and the large ruins of the Atlas Mill (all on the left). Drive 0.8-miles to a "Y" intersection and bear left on the signed road for Governor Basin. (The continuation of the Yankee Boy Basin road to the right is marked for high clearance/4WD vehicles).

A short distance down the Governor Basin road is a pullout on the left. I recommend parking here.

You can drive further up the dirt Governor Basin road if you have a high clearance/4WD vehicle. To continue, follow the road as it curves to the left past the Walker/Ruby mine and then crosses Sneffels Creek on a wood bridge. Beyond the bridge continue along the main road to a "Y" intersection. Ignore the road branching right with the locked gate. Instead bear left on the main road. Beyond this junction the road crosses a creek (watch you don't scrape your under carriage here) and becomes narrower and bumpier. There are potential places to park at 1.1, 1.4, 1.7 and 2.2 miles. Just make sure you are well off the road when you park. Adjust the hiking description above to account for the distance you drive up the road beyond the recommended parking area.

The Yankee Boy Basin road is a graded dirt road and typically passible for vehicles with reasonable clearance. As you drive up the road it gets rougher. Passenger vehicles with good clearance can typically make it to the Imogene Pass turnoff and, if driven carefully, the 0.8 miles beyond to the Governor Basin Road. Beyond this point is for high clearance/4WD vehicles only. Before setting out stop at the Ouray Visitor Center to check on current road conditions.

11. Hayden Trail ★★★★

Distance: 5.0 – 6.6 miles (RT)

Great views of the peaks rising above Ironton Park are the rewards for this stiff climb up the east facing slopes of Hayden Mountain. A traverse below the Hayden Ridge then leads to a route ascending to Peak 12,578 with terrific views of Yankee Boy Basin.

Distance: 5.0 miles (RT) to Overlook
6.6 miles (RT) to Peak 12,578
Elevation: 9,620-ft. at Trailhead
11,970-ft. at Overlook
12,578-ft. at Peak 12,578
Elevation Gain: 2,350-ft. to Overlook
2,958-ft. at Peak 12,578
Difficulty: strenuous

Basecamp: Ouray
Area: Uncompahgre NF
Best Season: July - September
USGS Map(s): Ouray, Ironton

Why Hike the Hayden Trail

This steep trail climbs high above the west side of Ironton Park to the tundra-clad slopes beneath Hayden Ridge. Here views extend south to the Red Mountains and high peaks to the north of Silverton. Across the valley Abrams Mountains anchors the north end of the Brown Mountain ridge while a sea of peaks fills the skyline above the Engineer Pass road.

A traverse through scree and then tundra-clad slopes below the ridge leads to a route ascending the ridge crest to Peak 12,578. Here the high peaks soaring above Yankee Boy Basin dominate the view to the west.

The stiff climb and views from this trail are similar to the Richmond Pass trail to the south. If I only had time for one of these hikes I would choose Richmond Pass. The trailhead for Richmond Pass is harder to find but after surmounting this challenge, the trail and the views on the ascent to Richmond pass are better. Footing on a short upper section of the Hayden trail is precarious in places and could cause some parties to stop before climbing to the ridge.

Experienced hikers looking for solitude and a good workout will like this trail. The trail is also recommended to hikers who are looking for some new ground to cover after hiking the more popular trails in the area.

Trailhead to Overlook

Distance from Trailhead: 5.0 (round trip)
Elevation at Overlook: 11,970-ft.
Elevation Gain: 2,350-ft.

The Hayden Trail is accessible via Highway 550 south of Ouray (Hayden South), and a 4wd road off the Camp Bird Mine Road (Hayden North). I prefer the access via Highway 550 since it is a better trail and does not require a 4WD vehicle (see driving directions below). Both trails feature great views, especially if you climb off-trail to the ridge crest.

The Hayden South trail starts at the northeast end of Crystal Lake in Ironton Park. Here a white metal gate blocks access to a gravel road crossing the dam at the north end of the lake. Parking is provided at a large pullout along the road. Follow the trail around the gate to the trail register and trailhead sign. Sign the trail register and then cross the dam on the gravel road. At the end of the dam is a signed trail junction. Bear right on the Hayden Trail. The Full Moon Trail branches to the left.

The trail now ascends through trees up the east facing slopes of Hayden Mountain and soon crosses a gully. After a brief stint climbing along the north side of the gully the path turns right and ascends steep log steps up a dirt/scree covered slope.

Past the steps the stiff climbs continues up switchbacks, traveling through aspen groves and pine trees. After a mile the trees give way to meadows and views open to Abrams Mountain (12,801-ft.) across the valley to the east. The trail is now a boot width wide.

At 1.2 miles the trail crosses a gully that carries snowmelt early in the season. Beyond the gully the grade abates as the path ascends through meadows scattered with clumps of evergreens. Hayden Mountain soon comes into view to the west. Red Mountain No. 1, No. 2 and No. 3 dominate the view to the south. Across the valley Brown Mountain, anchored by Abrams Peak, is now in full view.

At 1.6 miles the steep climb resumes as the trail turns to the right and climbs switchbacks up grassy slopes high above the north side of the gully. Hayden Ridge towers overhead. As you climb the views expand to include Storm Peak (13,487-ft.) and summits rising to the north of Silverton.

The trail turns right (north) at 2.0 miles and the grades abates. Wooden stakes and cairns mark the faint path through and undulating landscape of tundra-clad knolls. The trail is now paralleling Hayden Ridge. Ahead views open to the ridge's sheer rugged cliffs.

At 2.2 miles the trail enters of gully resembling a moonscape of disintegrating gray rock formations. Between the trail and the cliffs is a deep channel draining meltwater from the cliffs. Soon the trail deteriorates as is descends on scree through a rock slide. Loose rock makes the footing precarious in places.

The area has some exposure which some hikers may find uncomfortable. If so, return to the meadows and find a nice place to relax and take in the views.

Thankfully the bad section of the trail is short and we soon return to a faint, boot beaten path through the tundra. Look for stakes to help guide you. Take time to stop here and admire the sea of peak rising across the valley to the east.

At 2.5 miles the path starts descending on easy to moderate grades as it crosses the top of the West Riverside Slide, a massive avalanche chute. This is a good turnaround point for parties that don't want to climb to the ridge crest.

Route to Peak 12,578

Segment Stat: 0.8 miles (one-way) with a 608-ft. elevation gain
Distance - Trailhead to Peak 12,578: 6.6 miles (RT)
Maximum Elevation: 12,578-ft.
Elevation Gain - Trailhead to Peak 12,578: 2,958-ft.

To continue the hike, cross the top of the West Riverside Slide. Beyond the slide, the trail continues its descent to a small ravine, actually a tributary of Silver Gulch, at 2.9 miles. Use care when crossing the steep scree slopes along the side of the ravine. The area is quite treacherous if the ravine is filled with snow. If snow is present, it might be best to turn around or turn left before the ravine and climb steeply up to Hayden Ridge.

Otherwise, cross the ravine and climb the grassy slopes to a minor ridge at 3.0 miles. Look left here and you will see the steep route to Hayden Ridge. To reach the ridge crest simply climb the grassy slopes of the minor ridge for 0.1 miles to Hayden Ridge. Turn left on the ridge and ascend grassy slopes toward Peak 12,578. The last section is a scramble up scree and rock to the white marker at the top of the peak at 3.3 miles

From the summit enjoy fantastic views of Whitehead Mountain, Mount Ridgeway, Teakettle Mountain, Cirque

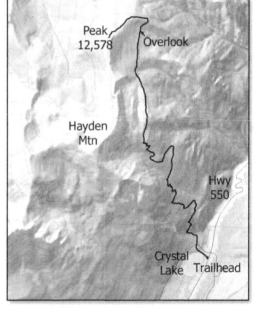

Mountain and Potosi Peak towering above Yankee Boy Basin. The brownish peak in the distance beyond Potosi is Mount Sneffels. Across the valley a sea of summits fill the skyline above the Engineer Pass Road and Bear Creek. Abrams Mountain and Brown Mountain dominate the view to the east while the Red Mountains and the high peaks around Silverton fill the skyline to the south. Closer at hand is Hayden Mountain North (13,139-ft.).

When you are done enjoying the views, descend from the ridge and follow the Hayden Trail back to your vehicle.

Note: The Hayden Trail continues beyond the 3.0 mile point to a saddle and then drops down Squaw Gulch on a steep trail to the Cutler Mine Road, a rough 4WD road that descends to the Camp Bird Mine/Yankee Boy Basin road in one mile. Some call this trailhead Hayden North. Portions of the trail descend steeply down scree covered switchbacks that some hikers find problematic. If you wish to do the point-to-point hike, it is recommended that you climb up from the North trailhead and then descend to the Hayden South trailhead at Ironton Park. The point-to-point hike is 5.6 miles long. Add 2.0 miles round-trip to the hike if you don't have a 4WD vehicle and need to walk the Cutler Mine Road.

Driving Directions

From Ouray to the Hayden South Trailhead: From the center of Ouray (6th Avenue and Main Street), head south on Highway 550-S for 6.4 miles and park at the pullout at the northeast end of Crystal Lake in Ironton Park. As you drive south out of town the road climbs a few switchbacks, travels through a tunnel and then passes the Bear Creek National Recreation Trail parking area, on the left. Soon you will pass the Engineer Pass Jeep Road, also on the left, at 3.9 miles.

At 5.3 miles drive through an avalanche shed. Soon the road climbs a few more switchbacks and then levels off as it reaches Ironton Park. Here you will pass a stone building on the left. A very short distance beyond the stone building the road crossed Red Mountain Creek. On the right (west) side of the road, just past the creek, is a large pullout – park here. The pullout is located at the northeast end of Crystal Lake. A white metal gate blocks a gravel road crossing the dam at the foot of the lake. Beyond the gate is the Hayden trailhead sign and a trail register.

From Ouray to the Hayden North Trailhead: From the center of Ouray (6th Avenue and Main Street), head south on Highway 550-S for 0.6 miles. At the south end of town the road climbs switchbacks. As you round the top of the hairpin curve on the first switchback watch for a road off to the right. This is County Road 361 leading to the Camp Bird Mine and Yankee Boy Basin. Turn right onto County Road 361 and follow the road for 1.7 miles and turn left on the 4WD Cutler Mine Road. There should be a sign for the Hayden Trail at the intersection. Keep left as you ascend the steep, rugged road to avoid McNulty Lane on the right. Bear right at the second fork. The trailhead is located one mile up the road and is marked with a wood sign. There is very limited parking at the trailhead.

12. Ouray Perimeter Trail ★★★★

Distance: 5.9 miles (Loop)

Ouray's scenic Perimeter Trail circumnavigates the town, traversing cliffs, canyons and forested hillsides. Points of interest along the trail include Cascade Falls, the Baby Bath Tubs, the Amphitheater, the Uncompahgre River and Canyon Creek.

Distance: 5.9 miles (Loop)
Elevation: 7,680-ft. - Trailhead
8,530-ft. at High Point
Elevation Gain: 1,600-ft.
Difficulty: moderate

Basecamp: Ouray
Area: Uncompahgre NF
Best Season: July - September
USGS Map(s): Ouray

The Perimeter Trail Loop

The Perimeter Trail offers a good perspective of the Ouray area and is a nice option if the weather is taking a turn for the worse in the high country. The path is accessible from a number of points around the town, permitting the trail to be cut short or done in segments. Connections with other town trails offer interesting ways to extend a hike or use segments of the trail to create scenic loops. Maps and trail descriptions are available at the Ouray Visitor Center, located at the north end of town adjacent to the Hot Springs.

The easiest place to start the Ouray Perimeter Trail is at the Ouray Visitor Center. (See driving directions below.) From the Visitor Center cross to the east side of the Main Street (Highway 550) to a map located next to a large boulder. The trail now heads northwest, passes behind the Skyrocket Townhomes and then ascends a steep wood staircase.

Soon the trail turns right, heading south/southeast, as it ascends along cliffs toward Cascade Falls. As you climb pass the historic Two Kids Mine and enjoy terrific views of Ouray and the rugged peaks towering above the south and west sides of town. Views encompass Twin Peaks, Whitehouse Mountain (13,452-ft.), Mount Abrams (12,801-ft.), Hayden Mountain

(13,139-ft.) and U.S. Mountain (13,036-ft.). Portions of this trail are exposed and may cause discomfort to people with a fear of heights.

At 0.6 miles the trail starts a brief descent that leads to lovely Cascade Falls at 0.7 miles. The falls is the lowest of a series of seven waterfalls on Cascade Creek. After crossing a bridge below the falls the trail enters the trees and climbs steeply up the Lower Cascade Trail. At 0.9 miles reach a junction where the Perimeter trail turns right while the Lower Cascade Trail bears left up the hillside.

The Perimeter trail now follows an undulating course along the slopes beneath the Amphitheater Campground. Openings in the trees offer more great views of the high peaks to the south and west. At 1.2 miles cross the 5th Avenue Trail which offers another option for leaving the trail and returning to town.

Beyond the junction the trail enters the trees and ascends a short distance to the paved Amphitheater Campground Road. Turn right and follow the road for 0.1 miles. Cross the road at 1.5 miles and find the continuation of the Perimeter trail, which coincides with the Baby Bath Tub Trail for the next 0.3 miles. (If you cross a bridge on the road you have gone too far. Turn around and look for the trail on the south side of the road.)

The Baby Bath Tubs segment of the trail features interesting quartz pools (bath tubs) in the streambed. Along the way the trail crosses Little Portland Creek, and then parallels the creek as it climbs to a junction with the Portland Trail. Turn right here and almost immediately cross a bridge over Portland Creek. Follow the Portland Trail for 300-ft. to a "Y" junction. Bear left on the Perimeter trail which climbs uphill through the Three Pines Day Use Area to the Portland Mine Road. Walk a short distance up the road and then turn right. The path now travels through the Potato Patch and reaches the high point of the trail (8,500-ft.) atop a rocky knoll at 2.1 miles.

Below the trail is the dramatic Uncompahgre Gorge. Hayden Mountain towers overhead while Whitehouse Mountain and Twin Peaks dominate the view to the west. The Amphitheater looms over the valley to the northeast.

The descent from the high point is accompanied by great views of Abrams Mountain rising to the south. Reach Highway 550 at 2.4 miles. Carefully cross the highway and then turn left (south) on an old road that reverts to a trail at 2.8 miles. (It is possible to short-cut this section by 0.5 miles by turning right.)

The trail descends to a bridge crossing the Uncompahgre River at 2.9 miles. Cross the bridge and then climb up and cross a stile over a large pipe along a service road (the Ice Park trail). The pipe carries water to the Ouray Hydro-Electric Plant and supplies water to the Ice Park in the Uncompahgre Gorge to your right.

Turn right (north/northwest) and follow the services road for 0.6 miles. Across the river are views of the Ouray Via Ferrata. Just past a small reservoir bear right on a trail that reaches CR 361 (the Camp Bird Road to Yankee Boy Basin) at 3.8 miles. Cross the road and follow the trail to Box Canyon Falls and Park. A detour to the park (fee required) is recommended if time and energy allow.

Stay left and cross the steel suspension bridge over dramatic Canyon Creek Gorge. On the far side of the bridge travel through a tunnel once used to route an old water pipe and then descend steep stone stairs along a cliff face. Railings and fixed pipe along the cliff facilitate the descent.

Beyond the stairs the trail ascends a hillside to meet the South Pinecrest Road at 4.3 miles. This is another good spot to exit the Perimeter Trail.

Turn left and ascend South Pinecrest Road for 0.3 miles to a signed junction for the Oak Creek/ Twin Peaks Trail and the continuation of the Perimeter Trail. Turn right and follow the trail uphill. Soon you will reach a junction where we bear right to stay on the Perimeter Trail.

Follow the path as it drops steeply into Oak Creek Canyon and crosses Oak Creek on a new bridge. Metal stairs facilitate the climb out of the canyon to Henn's Overlook at 5.0 miles. The overlook features fine views of Ouray. The Amphitheater, Cascade Mountain, Cow Mountain and Gold Hill rise above the east side of town.

From the overlook the trail descends to Oak Street at 5.5 miles. Turn left (north) on Oak Street and pass by the campground and trailer park. At 5.7 miles (at the north end of the trailer park) turn right and cross the Uncompahgre River on a bridge. You will now be at the southwest end of the Hot Springs/Visitor Center Parking area. Walk to where you started the hike to complete the 5.9 mile loop.

Driving Directions

From Ouray: The official beginning of the Ouray Perimeter Trail is at the Ouray Visitor Center, 1230 Main Street (Highway 550). The Visitor Center is located at the north end of town along the west side of Highway 550 and shares a parking lot with the Ouray Hot Springs. There is plenty of free parking in the lot.

13. Baldy Trail ★★★

Distance: 6.8 – 7.9 miles (RT)

The moderate hike to Baldy Peak features great views and an interesting perspective of the high peaks of the Ouray Region.

Distance: 6.8-7.9 miles (RT) to Baldy Peak
Elevation: 8,485-ft. at Trailhead 10,603-ft. at Baldy Peak
Elevation Gain: 2,118-ft. to Baldy Peak
Difficulty: moderate

Basecamp: Ouray
Area: Uncompahgre NF
Best Season: July - September
USGS Map(s): Ouray, Wetterhorn

Why Hike the Baldy Trail

The Baldy trail rewards hikers with great, albeit distance views, with only a moderate expenditure of effort. Starting at a relatively low elevation, the trail climbs through trees and meadows and then along ridges with terrific views of the Sneffels and Cimarron Ranges along with the high peaks to the south along Highway 550 and Yankee Boy Basin. Atop Baldy Peak the views get even better. From this modest overlook at 10,603-ft. hikers gain a great perspective of the Mount Sneffels area and the high peaks surrounding the Ouray area.

This hike is good choice for the shoulder seasons. The relatively low elevation of the destination also makes the trail suitable for parties trying to acclimate or if bad weather is threatening the high country.

When the access road is dry, the trailhead is accessible by 2WD vehicles with good clearance. Check with the Ouray Visitor Center for current road conditions before setting out.

Trailhead to Baldy Peak

This trail description assumes you park in the field before the Baldy trailhead. (See driving directions below.) The last 0.3 miles to the trailhead require a high clearance, 4WD vehicle. If starting from the trailhead, subtract 0.3 miles from the one-way mileage in the description.

From the parking area in the field, return to the road junction and turn right. A steep descent down the road leads to a creek. Cross the creek and then ascend the continuation of the road on easy grades to the Baldy trailhead at 0.3 miles.

The trail quickly reaches a junction a short distance beyond the trailhead. Bear left at the junction on the Baldy Trail toward Baldy Peak. (The trail to the left is the Storm Gulch Trail.) Ascend a hillside clad in Gambel oaks and brushy meadows on moderate to moderately-steep switchbacks. The meadows offer views to the timbered hillsides lining the Cutler Creek drainage to the southeast.

At 0.8 miles the trail splits. Bear left at the split. The trail to the right is no longer used and becomes brushy and hard to follow before it rejoins the main trail. After hiking a mile we get our first views of Whitehouse Mountain (13,492-ft.) in the Sneffels range to the southwest. As you climb the trees give way to meadows and low shrubs. Views open to the Hayden Mountain (13,206-ft.) rising to the south of Ouray and the rugged ridge rimming the south side to Dexter Creek.

At 1.5 miles the trail curves to the right (northeast) and ascends a dry hillside to the top of a ridge at 1.8 miles. As you climb, enjoy ever improving views of the Sneffels Range.

Atop the ridge the grade moderates. The path now follows an ascending traverse through meadows and spruce-pine forest along the ridge. Views expand to include Mount Sneffels in the Sneffels Range. The summits in the Uncompahgre Wilderness, including distinctive Courthouse Mountain, Wetterhorn Peak (15,015-ft.) and Uncompahgre Peak (14, 309-ft.), fill the skyline to the east. To the south views extend to the Red Mountains along Highway 550 and the high peaks of Yankee Boy Basin.

At 2.9 miles the trail levels as it reaches a junction. To the right (east) is the Cutler Trail leading to the Storm Gulch trail and an alternative way back to the trailhead. We turn left (west) on the Baldy Peak Trail. Ahead Baldy Peak is the high point along the grassy ridge.

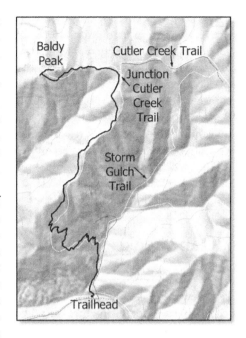

The trail now travels below the south side of the ridge crest. As you proceed enjoy more great views of the Sneffels Ranges, the summits in the Uncompahgre Wilderness and the high peaks to the south.

After walking about a half mile the trail traverses the slopes beneath Baldy Peak and then curves to the right, climbing to a saddle on the ridge to the west of Baldy at 3.6 miles. Here the trail fades. To the right is a grassy hillside leading to the top of Baldy Peak. Chart your own course up the slope to the top of Baldy Peak (10,603-ft.) at 3.7 miles.

The grassy summit features fantastic, albeit distant views. The Sneffels Range fills the skyline to the southwest. Courthouse Mountain, Wetterhorn Peak and the summits in the Uncompahgre Wilderness dominate the view to the east. Looking south, views stretch to Abrams Mountain, Brown Mountain, the Red Mountains and Storm King Peak. Hayden Mountain, Chicago Peak and the high peaks surrounding Imogene Basin tower above the south side of Yankee Boy Basin.

When you are done taking in the views, return to the junction of the Baldy Trail with the Cutler Creek Trail. You now have two options for returning to the trailhead. My preferred option is to retrace my steps on the Baldy Trail.

If you prefer to cover new ground, head east on the Cutler trail for 0.8 miles and the turn right (south) on the Storm Gulch trail. The Cutler trail fades as it enters the trees. It's best to carry a map or GPS to stay on track. The descent on the Storm Gulch trail includes some steep, scree covered slopes. After 1.8 miles the Storm Gulch trail is joined by the Shortcut Trail. From here it is another 0.5 miles back to the Baldy trailhead. Returning via Cutler and Storm Gulch adds a half mile to the round-trip trail distance.

Driving Directions

From Ouray: From the center of Ouray (6th Avenue and Main Street), head north on Highway 550-N toward Ridgway for 2.1 miles and turn right onto the Dexter Creek Road. Follow the Dexter Creek Road for 1.0 mile as it climbs past a subdivision and then curves around past Lake Lenore on the right. At the next junction turn left on County Road 14A and cross a bridge.

Country Road 14A now ascends, passing a few more homes. At 4.1 miles stay right where the road forks. The road to the left is Country Road 14B. You are now in the Uncompahgre National Forest and the road becomes a bit rougher. At 5.0 miles County Road 14B rejoins County Road 14A. The road now descends. Stay on the main road, ignoring any minor roads you pass. At 5.6 miles reach a junction. The road to the left descends steeply crosses a creek and then ascends to the trailhead at 5.9 miles.

The descent and crossing of the creek is only recommended for parties with a high clearance, 4WD vehicle. All other should continue straight ahead at the junction for short distance to an obvious parking area in a large field.

14. Oak Creek ★★★
Distance: 6.0 – 7.0 miles (RT)

Nice views of Hayden Mountain, Whitehouse Mountain and the Uncompahgre River Gorge are the highlights of this hike up pretty Oak Creek Canyon to an overlook on the southern flank of Twin Peaks.

Distance: 6.0 miles (RT) to Overlook
7.0 miles (RT) to Silvershield via Loop
Elevation: 8,150-ft. at Trailhead
10,640-ft. at Overlook
10,760-ft. at High Point
7,640-ft. at Silvershield Trailhead
Elevation Gain: 2,490-ft. to Overlook
+120-ft./-3,120-ft. to Silvershield Trailhead via Loop
Difficulty: strenuous

Basecamp: Ouray
Area: Uncompahgre NF
Best Season: July - September
USGS Map(s): Ouray

Why Hike to Oak Creek

The Oak Creek Trail is a good option if the weather precludes hiking in the high country. The trail, which starts in Ouray, provides a good workout and is a nice choice for parties trying to get acclimated. Fine views of the surround peaks and valleys, a pretty waterfall and some old mine tunnels add interest to the walk. From the overlook great views extend southeast down the Uncompahgre River Gorge. Hayden Mountain towers over the valley to the south while Whitehouse Mountain dominates the view to the west. To the east are the high peaks rising above the Amphitheater.

Continue the Oak Creek hike beyond the overlook by climbing over a low saddle and then descending the wooded hillsides on the north side of Twin Peaks to the Silvershield trail. The Silvershield trail descends to Oak Street, a mile to the north of downtown Ouray.

Trailhead to Overlook

Distance from Trailhead: 6.0 (round trip) or 7.0 mile (loop)
Elevation to Overlook: 10,640-ft.
Elevation Gain: 2,490-ft.

From the trailhead on South Pinecrest Drive in Ouray (see driving directions below), follow the trail as it climbs the hillside and soon passes the junction with the Perimeter trail branching off to the right. We continue ascending the Oak Creek Trail on moderate to moderately-steep switchbacks through oak, juniper and pine trees. Openings in the trees along the first two switchbacks offer views of the Amphitheater rising above the east side of downtown Ouray.

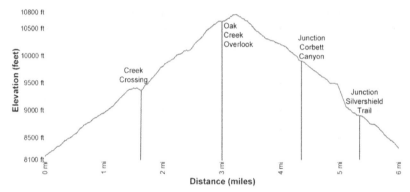

After a half mile views open up Canyon Creek (the Camp Bird Road) to the Hayden Mountain massif rising to the south and United States Mountain (13,036-ft.) towering above the Camp Bird Mine area to the southwest. Also visible are the rugged crags on the ridge extending from Peak 12,099 along the south side of Angel Creek.

Reach a trail junction at 0.9 miles. Here the Twin Peaks Trail branches to the right. We bear left, continuing on the Oak Creek Trail. The path now ascends steeply through clusters of spruce, pine and aspen trees set amid small meadows. Intermittent views open to the jagged cliffs and knob of Sister Peak (10,798-ft.), one of the Twin Peaks, across the valley to the north. Hayden Mountain dominates the view to the south.

At 1.5 miles the climb ends and the path now follows a descending traverse along the south side of Oak Creek. At this point you can't see the creek but you can hear it.

Soon views open to a pretty waterfall along Oak Creek. As the trail approaches the falls it curves to the right. Here views open down the length of Oak Creek Canyon to the cliffs rising above the east side of Ouray.

At 1.6 miles the path crosses the creek just above the waterfall. This area of the creek is a nice place to take a break and is a good destination for anyone looking for a short hike.

Beyond the waterfall the trail climbs a switchback up the north side of the creek and then turns left (west), following an undulating trail through trees above the north side of the creek. Along the way we pass some mine ruins. Use care along the first section of the trail where the path is eroded and the footing is not great. Look for two mine tunnels chiseled into a cliff face along the trail at 2.0 miles.

At 2.4 miles the path reaches a beautiful meadow rimmed by tall aspen and spruce trees. Here the trail curves to the right (north) and climbs steep switchbacks through meadows and clusters of trees. The trail is faint in places but generally not difficult to follow.

At 2.8 miles the grade abates a bit as the trail turns right (east) and crosses a drainage. As the trail climbs out the drainage fine views open to Whitehouse Mountain (13,492-ft.) towering above the valley to the west. Here you can also see up the Uncompahgre River Gorge to Abrams Mountain (12,801-ft.) and beyond.

The path now heads east, reaching the signed Oak Creek Overlook at 3.0 miles. Hayden Mountain towers above the valley to the south while Whitehouse Mountain fills the skyline to the west. Views extend southeast up the Million Dollar Highway and Engineer Pass Road. Across the valley to the east are the high summits rising above the Amphitheater.

The lookout is a great place to take a break or have a picnic lunch. From here you have two options, retrace your steps to the trailhead (6.0 miles round-trip) or continue on the Oak Creek trail to the Silvershield trailhead (7.0 miles including the one mile walk back to downtown Ouray). I personally prefer to return to the Oak Creek trailhead from the Overlook because of the better views.

Oak Creek Trail to the Silvershield Trailhead

Segment Stat: 4.0 miles (one-way) with a 120-ft./-3,120 elevation gain/loss
Loop Distance: 7.0 miles (loop)
Maximum Elevation: 10,760-ft.
Ending Elevation: 7,640-ft.
Elevation Gain/Loss: +2,610-ft. / -3,120-ft.

From the overlook, walk northwest on the Oak Creek trail in the direction of the Silvershield trail. The path climbs on moderate grades to a wooded saddle on the ridge at 3.2 miles (10,740-ft.). From the saddle the trail descends on moderate to steep grades through viewless forest.

At 4.3 miles reach the junction with the Corbett Canyon trail branching left. We turn right, continuing on the Oak Creek Trail. Beyond the junction the trail descends some very steep grades before arriving at the junction with the Silvershield Trail at 5.3 miles. This is the end of the Oak Creek Trail. To the right the Silvershield trail heads toward the Twin Peaks area. We continue straight ahead on the Silvershield Trail toward the trailhead. Soon views open to Gold Hill's rugged cliffs towering above the east side of the Highway 550.

The path now drops steeply down dry hillsides to the Tamara Calhoon Memorial at 5.7 miles. Here a sign provides information about Gold Hill's mining history and a bench offers a nice place to rest and enjoy the views.

Past the memorial the trail descends down dusty slopes to Oak Street at 6.0 miles. Turn right on Oak Street and walk about a mile back to the center of Ouray for a 7.0 mile loop hike.

Driving Directions

From Ouray: From 3rd Avenue and 1st Street in Ouray (corner of the Victorian Inn), head west on 3rd Ave. At the intersection with the Box Canyon Road, 3rd Avenue turns into Oak Street. Follow Oak Street for 0.1 miles as it crosses the bridge over the river and curves to the right. Turn left on Queen Street. Ascend Queen for one block and then turn left on South Pinecrest Drive. Ascend Pinecrest Drive for 0.4 miles to the Oak Creek/Twin Peaks Trailhead.

Alternatively, from Main Street and 7th Avenue in Ouray, head west on 7th Avenue for 0.2 miles and cross the river on a bridge. Beyond the bridge turn left on Oak Street. Follow Oak Street for 0.2 miles and the turn right onto Queen Street. Ascend Queen for one block and then turn left on South Pinecrest Drive. Ascend Pinecrest Drive for 0.4 miles to the Oak Creek/Twin Peaks Trailhead.

Note: There is very limited parking at the trailhead. You are better off parking in town and walking to the trailhead.

15. Ice Lake Trail ★★★★★

Distance: 7.0 - 8.2 miles (RT)

This wonderful hike visits two gorgeous lake basins, traverses wildflower-filled meadows and passes numerous waterfalls. Dramatic peaks punctuate the ridge forming the backdrop for upper Ice Lake, nestled in an alpine wonderland. Opportunities for exploration include side trips to Island and Fuller lakes.

Distance: 7.0 miles (RT) to Ice Lake
8.2 miles (RT) to Island Lake
Elevation: 9,840-ft. - Trailhead
12,270-ft. - Ice Lake
12,392-ft. - Island Lake
Elevation Gain: 2,430-ft. to Ice Lake
2,552-ft. to Island Lake
Difficulty: moderately strenuous

Basecamp: Silverton, Ouray
Area: Part of the San Miguel Roadless Area, San Juan NF
Best Season: July - September
USGS Map(s): Ophir

Why Hike Ice Lake

The Silverton area boasts a number of great day hikes but none can compete with the sheer scenic beauty of Ice Lake.

The trail wastes no time gaining elevation, climbing 1,600-ft. in 2-miles through forests and wildflower-filled meadows to the beautiful Lower Ice Lakes basin. Upon reaching the lower basin great views open to Fuller, Vermillion Peak, Golden Horn and Pilot Knob rising above the ridge at the head of the basin.

As you wander up the lower basin waterfalls emanating from unseen alpine lakes and snowfields tumble down clefts in the rocky hillside watering a breathtaking array of wildflowers. A sea of columbine, larkspur, aspen daisies, chiming bells and cow parsnips blankets both sides of the trail.

But the best is yet to come. A steep climb to the upper basin leads to the turquoise blue waters of Ice Lake nestled in a magnificent cirque of sculpted ridges and peaks soaring well above 13,000-ft. The alpine wonderland around the lake invites exploration, with routes heading toward Island Lake, Fuller Lake and beyond.

Note: Ice Lakes is one of the most popular and heavily used trails in southwestern Colorado. Social media postings over the past few years have resulted in an explosion of visitors. Meanwhile recent avalanches have scarred the Clear Creek drainage and a fire in October 2020 burned the lower section of the trail. Please read and follow Leave No Trace (lnt.org) principles when visiting Ice Lakes to preserve and protect this beautiful area.

Trailhead to Lower Ice Lake Basin

Distance from Trailhead: 2.25 miles (one-way), 4.5 miles (RT)
Elevation Lower Ice Lake Basin: 11,510-ft.
Elevation Gain: 1,670-ft.

The head of the South Mineral Valley is the starting point for Ice Lake, one of the premier hikes in the San Juan Mountains. The signed trail departs from the west end of the trailhead parking lot, located across from the South Mineral Campground (see driving directions below).

The trail crosses a meadow and starts climbing through a burn area on moderately steep switchbacks. At 0.4 miles the path crosses Clear Creek and ascends the slope to the west of the creek on well graded switchbacks with intermittent views of Twin Sisters rising across the valley to the south.

After 30 minutes a detour to the right (east) leads to a scenic waterfall tumbling down the rocky hillside scarred by avalanche activity. Beyond the waterfall the trail heads west, climbing steeply up a grassy slope filled with wildflowers. Keep a lookout for the ruins of an abandoned mining building and equipment on your left. The grade abates as the trail crosses a meadow and then enters the trees. The trail now climbs steep switchbacks up a headwall to Lower Ice Lake basin.

After gaining 1,600-ft. in 2 miles the trail crests the ridge into the beautiful Lower Ice Lake basin. Rock outcroppings provide a nice place to rest and enjoy the view of Fuller (13,761-ft.), Vermillion Peak (13,894-ft.), Golden Horn (13,780-ft.) and Pilot Knob (13,738-ft.) rising above the ridge at the head of the lower basin.

Lower Ice Lake to Ice Lake

Segment Stat: 1.25 miles (one-way) from Lower to Upper Ice Lakes with **760-ft. elevation gain**
Distance - Trailhead to Ice Lake: 7.0 miles (RT)
Elevation at Ice Lake: 12,270-ft.
Elevation Gain - Trailhead to Ice Lake: 2,430-ft.

The trail now traverses lovely meadows on gentle grades, passing Lower Ice Lake nestled in trees to the left (south). Waterfalls, emanating from unseen alpine lakes and snowfields tumble down clefts in the rocky hillside to the north of the trail. During late July to early August the well-watered meadows around the falls host spectacular wildflower displays. Masses of columbines, larkspur, aspen daisies, chiming bells and cow parsnips blanket both sides of the trail.

At the head of the lower basin the trail curves left (south) and starts a steep ascent up the basin's headwall. Ahead you will see a waterfall on the outlet stream for Fuller Lake cascading down a rocky crevasse. Just before reaching the waterfall the trail swings to the right (west), climbs a few switchbacks and then swings right (north) for the final stiff climb to the upper basin. Reach the top of the headwall in 0.6 miles after gaining 700-ft. in elevation.

The grade now abates as the trail traverse alpine tundra for the final quarter mile to Ice Lake (12,270-ft.). As you walk toward the lake note the faint trail climbing the grassy slope on your right (north). This trail leads to Island Lake.

Turquoise blue Ice Lake sits in a magnificent cirque amid subalpine tundra dotted with wildflowers. U.S. Grant Peak (13,767-ft.) rises to the north. In a clockwise direction the sculpted peaks and ridges of Fuller Peak (13,761-ft.), Vermillion Peak (13,894-ft.), Golden Horn (13,780-ft.) and Pilot Knob (13,738-ft.) form the southwestern wall of the upper lake basin.

Return to the trailhead by reversing your route or, if you have time, take a side trip to Island or Fuller Lakes. (See descriptions below.)

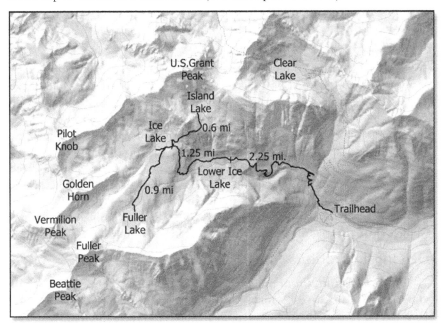

Optional Side Trip: Ice Lake to Island Lake

Segment Stats: 0.7 miles (one-way) from Ice Lake to Island Lake with a 130-ft. elevation gain
Distance from Trailhead to Island Lake: 8.4 miles (RT)
Elevation Island Lake: 12,392-ft.
Elevation Gain from Trailhead: 2,552-ft.

A side trip to Island Lake (12,392-ft.) is well worth the effort. To reach the lake cross Ice Lake's outlet stream (to find the best place to cross wander downstream a bit) and then follow the faint trail climbing the grassy slope to the northeast. The trail is initially hard to see but becomes better defined further up the slope. As you climb, enjoy stunning views of the upper and lower Ice Lake basins.

The trail crosses the base of a tailings pile and then ascends above a rock outcropping before swinging left (north). The grade now abates as the trail traverses a hillside above the lake. The aquamarine lake is nestled in an intimate cirque at the base of U.S. Grant Peak. If you look carefully, you will see a faint trail climbing the talus ridge to the north of the lake. This route leads to the Ophir Valley. Total distance to Island Lake from Ice Lake is just over 0.7 miles with a 130-ft elevation gain.

Optional Side Trip: Island Lake to Fuller Lake

Segment Stats: 0.9 miles (one-way) from Ice Lake to Fuller Lake with a 335-ft. elevation gain.
Distance from Trailhead to Fuller Lake: 8.9 miles (RT)
Elevation Fuller Lake: 12,605-ft.
Elevation Gain from Trailhead: 2,765-ft.

The gentle rolling hillsides beyond Ice Lake invite exploration. One popular side trip is the short hike to Fuller Lake. To reach Fuller Lake (12,605-ft.) head up the hill to the south/southwest of Ice Lake to a pond. (There is now a use trail, which fades in places, to help keep you on track.) Go around the left (east) side of the pond and then climb up the open hillside to the south/southwest of the pond. At the top of the hill is a broad shelf. The way to Fuller Lake should now be obvious. Cross a small creek and then travel along the west side of the creek to Fuller Lake. The lake is 0.9 miles from Ice Lake with a 335-ft. elevation gain.

From the lake enjoy fine views of Fuller Peak, Vermillion Peak and Golden Horn. An old metal-sided mining cabin still stands beside the lake.

Driving Directions

From Silverton: From the intersection of Highway 550 and the turnoff to Silverton (110), drive 1.9 miles north on Highway 550 to County Road 7. Turn left on County Road 7 (signed for the South Mineral Campground) and follow this good gravel road for 4.4 miles to the trailhead parking area on the north (right) side of the road across from the South Mineral Campground.

From Ouray: Follow Highway 550 south from Ouray for 19.6 miles to CR 7. (The distance from Ouray is measured from the bottom of the switchback exiting the south end of town.) Make a sharp right onto County Road 7 (signed for the South Mineral Campground) and follow this good gravel road for 4.4 miles to the trailhead parking area on the north (right) side of the road across from the South Mineral Campground. If you reach Silverton you missed the turn.

16. Columbine Lake and Pass ★★★★☆

Distance: 7.0 - 8.9 miles (RT)

This little known hike climbs steeply through forest and beautiful alpine meadows to a stunning glacial lake set amid rugged 13,000-ft. peaks. Panoramic views from nearby Columbine Pass encompass Bridal Veil Basin and the Sneffels Range.

Distance: 7.0 miles (RT) to
Columbine Lake
8.9 miles (RT) to Columbine Pass
Elevation: 10,346-ft. at Trailhead
12,693-ft. at Columbine Lake
13,094-ft. at Columbine Pass
Elevation Gain: 2,347-ft. to
Columbine Lake
2,748-ft. to Columbine Pass

Difficulty: strenuous
Basecamp: Silverton, Ouray
Area: San Juan NF
Best Season: July - September
USGS Map(s): Ophir, Silverton

Why Hike Columbine Lake

Getting to Columbine Lake involves a steep climb and the trail to Columbine Pass some route finding skills, but it is well worth the effort. The trail is truly off the beaten path, providing a degree of solitude not often found in such a beautiful location just 3.5 miles from a trailhead.

The strenuous hike to the lake traverses dense forest and gorgeous alpine meadows with see forever views. Columbine Lake, a turquoise jewel, is tucked in a stunning glacial bowl ringed by rugged ridges and peaks over 13,000-ft.

A side trip to Columbine Pass is highly recommended for hikers with the time and energy. The pass is located on the ridge to the northwest of the lake. Views from the pass extend west to Bridal Veil Basin, Mt Sneffels (14,150-ft.) and the Sneffels Range.

Trailhead to Columbine Lake

Distance from Trailhead to Columbine Lake: 7.0 miles (RT)
Elevation Columbine Lake: 12,693-ft.
Elevation Gain from Trailhead: 2,347-ft.

The Columbine Lake hike wastes no time gaining elevation. From the trailhead, marked by a blaze on a tree (see driving directions), the path ascends steep switchbacks through spruce-fir forest. After climbing 1.3 miles and gaining over 1,100-ft. the grade abates a bit and the trees thin. Views open to a narrow alpine basin carpeted in meadows sprinkled with wildflowers.

After leaving the last of the trees behind the steep climb resumes up the middle of the basin. Be sure to turn around and enjoy ever improving views of the high peaks rise above the east side of Highway 550.

At the head of the basin the curves to the left (southwest) and then right (north), climbing through rocky meadows and scree to reach a saddle on a ridge at 12,541-ft., about 2.0 miles from the trailhead. Turn around just before reaching the saddle and check out the nice views to the east/southeast of Ohio Peak (12,673), Anvil Mountain (12,537-ft.) and Storm Peak (13,487-ft.).

The worst of the climbing is now over. The trail drops off the saddle and curves to the left (west), entering the Mill Creek drainage. Looking northeast on a clear day you will see the tips of the fourteeners in the Uncompahgre Wilderness. Below is the Chattanooga Loop on Highway 550.

The trail now traverses a meadow and passes a few small tarns as it contours beneath the ridge defining the basin's southern wall. Views extend across the basin to the peaks and ridges to the north and west.

At 2.4 miles (about 0.2 miles from the saddle), the trail reaches a "Y" intersection at a small rock cairn. Here a faint trail branching right (northwest) toward Columbine Pass drops down into the drainage, crosses a stream (Mill Creek) and then climbs the hillside above Mill Creek, heading for the obvious saddle (Columbine Pass) on the ridge. We bear left (west) on the trail to Columbine Lake. Ahead you will see two trails cutting across a scree slope. Both trails lead to the lake. Assuming the lower trail is snow free, follow that path as it contours around the scree pile and heads southwest, staying to left (east) of Columbine Lake's outlet stream.

The trail now climbs steeply up the hillside beside the outlet stream. At the head of the outlet stream is a stone dam. As you climb around the dam and crest the hill Columbine Lake springs into view at 3.5 miles.

Columbine Lake is a turquoise jewel set in a stunning glacial bowl ringed by rugged 13,000-ft. ridges and peaks. Lookout Peak (13,661-ft.) rises above the southwestern end of the lake. The lake's shoreline invites exploration, providing multiple perspectives on the surrounding peaks. After taking a break, return the way you came or hike to the pass.

Columbine Lake to Columbine Pass

Segment Stats: 0.9 miles (one-way) from Columbine Lake to Columbine Pass with 401-ft. elevation gain
Distance from Trailhead to Columbine Lake: 8.9 miles (RT)
Elevation at Columbine Pass: 13,054-ft.
Elevation Gain from Trailhead: 2,749-ft.

Columbine Pass is a recommended side trip for hikers with the time and energy. There is no established trail from the lake to the obvious pass, located on the ridge to the northwest of the lake, but route finding is fairly easy across the open country.

To reach the pass climb about 25-ft. to the top of the hillside running along the lake's north shore and walk northwest, paralleling the lake. Near the end of the lake turn right (north), making a wide arc around a small tarn in a depression. Continue heading north, ascending through rocky meadows and aiming for the obvious saddle (pass) on the ridge.

Along the way you may find a few faint trails but they do not last very long. Continue your ascent until you hit a trail coming down from the pass. (The trail is not very obvious and you may not hit it at all depending on the route you take to the saddle.) If you hit the trail turn left (northwest) and follow the path to the saddle at 13,080-ft. The total distance to the pass is just under 1 mile with a 400-ft. elevation gain.

From the top of the pass enjoy a bird's eye view into Bridal Veil basin on the west side of the pass. (A trail from the pass leads down to the basin and Lewis Lake (12,720-ft.). Mt. Sneffels (14,150-ft.) and the Sneffels Range dominate the view to the north/northwest. To the southeast are distant views of the high peaks of the Grenadier Range.

After taking in the panoramic views, retrace your steps back to the lake and then follow the trail back to the trailhead.

Lewis Lake
Columbine Pass
0.95 mi. to Pass
Lookout Peak
Columbine Lake
Hwy 550
3.5 mi.
Trailhead

Driving Directions

From Silverton: Drive 4.8 miles north from Silverton on Highway 550 to the Ophir Pass Road (County Road 8) on the left. Turn left on the Ophir Pass road and follow it across a bridge. Shortly after crossing the bridge turn right on to Forest Road 820. Drive 0.7 miles to the trailhead located just beyond a wide part of the road. Park on your right at the wide spot and walk up the road (north) a brief distance to the trailhead marked by a blaze on a tree. Here an an obvious trail heads west uphill.

From Ouray: Drive 16 miles south of Ouray on Highway 550 (4.3 miles beyond Red Mountain Pass) and make a sharp right on (Forest Road 820),a gravel road. After the sharp right (essentially a hairpin curve off the highway) you will be on a gravel road heading north, paralleling the highway. Follow the road for a brief distance as it drops down to and cross a bridge over a creek. Beyond the bridge the road curves to the left (northwest) and climbs switchbacks up the hillside. Soon the road turns left (south) and levels out. Just pass a very narrow section of the road watch for a blaze on a tree to your right and a trail heading uphill (west) through the trees. Drive about 150-feet beyond the trailhead and park on the left at a wide spot in the road.

Note: Avalanches and mud slides have created a narrow section on the road, a short distance before the trailhead. There are also good parking spots along the left side of the road before you reach the narrow spot.

17. Porphyry Basin ★★★★⯪

Distance: 5.0 - 7.0 miles (RT)

This scenic hike climbs to two pretty lakes in gorgeous Porphyry Basin. Along the way the trail travels through wildflower-filled meadows and passes waterfalls, interesting rock formations and mining ruins. The lovely alpine meadows of the upper basin offer several options for off-trail exploration.

Distance: 5.0 miles (RT) to Bullion King Lake
6.4 miles (RT) to Porphyry Lake
7.0 miles (RT) to South Ridge Overlook
Elevation: 11,230-ft. at Trailhead
12,570-ft. at Bullion King Lake
12,800-ft. at Porphyry Lake
12,890-ft. at South Ridge Overlook
Elevation Gain: 1,340-ft. to Bullion King Lake
1,570-ft. to Porphyry Lake
1,660-ft. to South Ridge Overlook

Difficulty: moderate
Basecamp: Silverton, Ouray
Area: Uncompahgre NF
Best Season: July - September
USGS Map(s): Telluride, Ironton

Why Hike Porphyry Basin

Typically I am not a big fan of walking jeep roads, but I make an exception when it comes to Porphyry Basin. This scenic, off-the-beaten path hike ascends to Bullion King Lake nestled in the stunningly beautiful Porphyry Basin. The initial segment follows a lightly trafficked dirt road and then a trail. Beautiful, wildflower-filled meadows, pretty waterfalls, interesting rock formations and remnant of old mines accompany the walk.

Beyond the lake faint trails and some route finding leads to the upper basin where lovely Porphyry Lake lies cradled beneath Three Needles Peak (13,481-ft.). The upper basin's open alpine meadows invite exploration. Off-trail routes climbing to saddles on the ridges to the north and west of Porphyry Lake offer terrific views into Bridal Veil Basin. Hikers ascending the route to the ridge crest rimming the south side of the basin are rewarded with a panorama of peaks extending from the Needles in the Grenadier Range in the southeast to the high peaks of the Uncompahgre Wilderness to the northeast.

Trailhead to Bullion King Lake

Distance from Trailhead: 5.0 miles (RT)
Elevation at Bullion King Lake: 12,570-ft.
Elevation Gain: 1,340-ft.

Note: This hiking description starts at the first parking area (see driving directions below) since it allows for a longer walk. If you prefer to continue driving up the dirt road to the second parking area, subtract one mile from the one way distances listed in the description below.

From the first parking area follow the jeep road as it climbs on moderately-easy grades up the hillside along the north side of Porphyry Gulch. Along the way enjoy views that extend south toward Bear (12,987-ft.), Sultan (13,368-ft.) and Anvil (12,537-ft.) mountains. McMillian Peak (12,804-ft.) and Red Mountain massif (12,890-ft.) rise above the Mineral Creek valley to the east. As you gain height, the summits of the high peaks in the Uncompahgre Wilderness appear above the sea of peaks and ridges to the northeast.

Pass two jeep roads branching to the right at 0.6 miles and 1.0 mile. Both roads lead to the Bear Basin road to the north. You will now see a few places to park off the road. This is the second parking area described in the "Driving Directions" below.

At 1.1 miles the road turns sharply to the left (west/southwest) and passes a sign warning of the rough and dangerous road ahead. Here the road narrows and starts climbing along a narrow, rocky shelf with steep drop-offs.

Soon the road rounds a bend and gorgeous Porphyry Basin springs into view. Three Needles (13,481-ft.) and Peak 13375 form the backdrop for basin to the west. Meadows sprinkled with wildflowers grow amid rock outcroppings and walls that define the basin's three levels. Waterfalls cascade down crevasses and over rock walls into Porphyry Gulch below the trail. The high peaks of the Grenadier Range rise in the distance to the southeast.

The grade abates briefly as the road crosses a slide area and then continues climbing the scenic basin. In season the slopes along both sides of the road are clad in wildflower-filled meadows.

At 1.8 miles the wood remains of an old mining structure appear to the left (south) of the road. Soon the road crosses a creek and curves to the left (south) near a very large tailings pile. Walk through a parking area used by high clearance, 4WD vehicles. Past this point the road is closed to vehicular traffic. At the south end of the parking area a hillside covered in dirt now blocks the road. This is the site of mine waste repository constructed as part of a 2015 mine reclamation project.

Walk straight ahead (south) across the dirt hillside to the continuation of the old mining road, marked by a row of boulders, and follow the road as it ascends south on easy grades. At 2.1 miles the road curves to the left (east) and crosses a stream.

Beyond the stream the road/trail climbs a series of switchbacks on moderate grades. At the top of the switchbacks is a large boulder with an old sign indicating where vehicles had to stop prior to the reclamation project. Skirt the boulder and follow the old road, which is faint in spots, as it swings right (west) and ascends to the middle basin, passing a small tarn along the way.

Reach Bullion King Lake (12,570-ft.) at 2.5 miles. The west side of this pretty lake is ringed by rugged cliffs. A waterfall, which can't be seen from the southeast end of the lake, tumbles down a crevasse in the cliff face. Three Needles, Peak 13,375 and the rugged ridge between the two peaks tower above the lake to the west.

The lake is a great spot to take a break and laze in the sun. When you are done enjoying the lake either return to the trailhead for a 5.0 mile round trip hike or continue to Porphyry Lake. If time and energy permit, I strongly suggest hiking to the Porphyry Lake and exploring the upper basin.

To Porphyry Lake

Segment Stat: 0.7 miles (one-way) with a 230-ft. elevation gain
Distance from Trailhead: 6.4 miles (RT)
Elevation at Porphyry Lake: 12,800-ft.
Elevation Gain: 1,570-ft.

To find the trail to Porphyry Lake, cross Bullion King's outlet stream (the South Fork of Porphyry Creek) and then walk east along the north side of the stream for about 130-ft. A wide point on the outlet stream marks where the old mining road crosses the creek. Look left (north) across the meadows. You should be able to see faint vehicle tracks climbing the right (northeast) side of the bench rising to the north of the lake. Walk north across the meadows to where you can see the tracks and then climb on moderately steep grades up the vehicle track to the top of the bench. As you crest the bench (2.7 miles) the grade abates and the trail curves to the left (west/northwest).

Snow cover may make seeing/finding the old road difficult. If snow is covering the trail, walk north across the meadows and then climb up the northeast end of the bench. At the top of the bench you should be able to see vestiges of the old track.

Continue following the old vehicle tracks across the bench on easy grades. At 2.8 mile the tracks curves to the left (south/southwest) and crosses a stream. The vehicle tracks are faint just before the crossing. This area is often covered in snow early in the season, which complicates route finding. On the other side of the creek the tracks, which head south/southwest are easier to follow.

Soon the old road curves to the right (west/northwest) and soon arrives at a small tailings pile and the ruins of a wooden structure at 3.0 miles. This is the site of the Porphyry Mine. Here the old road ends. After exploring the area around the mine walk west/southwest to a pretty, unnamed lake (12,760-ft.) located a short distance from the mine.

To reach Porphyry Lake walk to inlet stream at the north end of the unnamed lake and follow the stream uphill (northwest), staying on the right (east) side of the stream. Note: there may not be any water in the stream but the stream course is evident, a small gully running between two low hills. As the stream bed peters out continue climbing northwest. You will soon crest a hill and see beautiful Porphyry Lake (12,800-ft.) nestled in a bowl beneath Three Needles. The distance from the mine to Porphyry Lake is just under 0.2 miles.

From the lake you can either retrace your steps to Bullion King Lake (11,230-ft.) and the trailhead for a 6.4 miles round trip hike or extend the hike by trying one of the off trail options listed below.

Side Trip to South Ridge Overlook

Distance from Porphyry Lake to the South Ridge: 0.6 miles (one-way) with a 135-ft. elevation gain
Distance from Trailhead: 7.0 miles (RT)
Elevation at the Overlook: 12,890-ft.
Elevation Gain: 1,660-ft.

The easiest option for extending your hike is to climb the ridge rimming the south side of Porphyry Basin. To reach the ridge from Porphyry Lake, retrace your steps to the unnamed lake and then walk south along the lake's east shore. At the south end of the unnamed lake rock hop across a stream and then start climbing up a rocky slope, heading for the grassy slopes leading to the top of the ridge. You will pass a small lake on your left (east) as you start the climb.

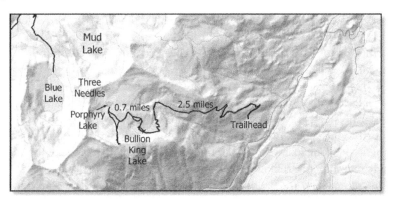

The climb from the south end of the unnamed lake to the top of the ridge will gain about 135-ft. in less than 0.2 miles. From the top of the ridge enjoy terrific views of the sea of peaks extending from the Needles in the Grenadier Range to the southeast to the high peaks of the Uncompahgre wilderness to the northeast.

Side Trips to Mud and Blue Lake Overlooks

Mud Lake Overlook

Distance from Porphyry Lake to Mud Lake Overlook: 0.35 miles (one-way) with a 160-ft. elevation gain
Distance from Trailhead: 7.1 miles (RT)
Elevation at Mud Lake Overlook: 12,960-ft.
Elevation Gain from Trailhead: 1,730-ft.

Looking north from Porphyry Lake you will see a saddle on the low point of the ridge extending northeast from Three Needles to Peak 13477. This is what I call the Mud Lake Overlook. A snow cornice often last well into the season atop the saddle.

To reach the saddle walk around the east side of Porphyry Lake and then pick the route of least resistance to climb the talus slopes up to the saddle. Skirt the snow cornice, if present, to the left. The scenic saddle (12,960-ft.) is about 0.75 miles from the lake and overlooks Mud Lake and the Mud Lake Basin. In the distance to the northwest are nice views of the peaks rising above the north side of the Telluride Valley. La Junta peaks towers above the west side of Bridal Veil Basin.

Blue Lake Overlook

Distance from Porphyry Lake to Blue Lake Overlook: 0.4 mile (one-way) with a 460-ft. elevation gain
Distance from Trailhead: 7.2 miles (RT)
Elevation at Blue Lake Overlook: 13,260-ft.
Elevation Gain from Trailhead: 2,030-ft.

To the west of Porphyry Lake is a small saddle on the ridge running south from Three Needles. This is a much steeper and more difficult climb than the Mud Lake Overlook. I only recommend this option for experienced, well acclimated hikers who are comfortable climbing steep talus slopes. It is not a good option is snow covers the route.

To reach the saddle, skirt the south side of Porphyry Lake and the start climbing the steep grassy slopes beneath the saddle. About two-thirds of the way up the grass gives way to talus. This is a hard climb for most people. Members of your party may be uncomfortable with the steep pitch. I strongly recommend trekking poles on the descent.

Hikers reaching the saddle (13,260-ft.) are rewarded with great views of Blue Lake in Bridal Veil's East Basin. La Junta Peak rises beyond the basin to the west while the peaks towering above Telluride fill the skyline to the northwest

Driving Directions

From Silverton: From the intersection of Main Street and US 550 in Silverton, head north on US 550 N for 9.1 miles and turn left (west) on Forest Service Road 822. You can't see the road number from the highway but you will pass a marker a short distance up the road. (Passenger cars should find a pull off along the highway for parking.)

The beginning of the road is narrow and steep to the first parking area. Some of the switchbacks are rocky and rugged. You will need an AWD SUV/4WD with good clearance. Beyond that point the road gets rougher to the second recommended parking area. Past this point there was a sign warning of a rough and dangerous road ahead. The sign is now gone. This section of the road travels along a very narrow shelf with steep drop-offs and a few rock outcroppings to climb. Passing another car along this road segment is not an option.

To reach the first parking area drive 0.7 miles up the road. Before coming to the end of the first switchback a road branches left (south) to a house. Ignore this road and continue up a series of switchbacks, passing a second road branching left (south) to a second house at the top of the fifth switchback. Beyond this point you will soon see a parking area on the left (south) side of the road below a cluster of spruce trees. This is the first parking area, recommended for people looking for a longer walk or drivers that don't feel comfortable proceeding further up the road.

To reach the second parking area, continue up the road another mile, passing two roads branching right. Between the second road and a cluster of spruce trees you will find several places to park. This is the second parking area, located 1.7 miles from US 550.

High clearance, 4WD vehicle can continue beyond this point for another 0.9 miles to a parking area at the end of the road area near mining debris and a huge mound of mine tailings.

High clearance AWD or 4WD is recommended to the first two parking areas but a passenger vehicle, if driven carefully, can typically make it to the first parking area under good conditions. If driving a 2WD passenger vehicle, I strongly recommend checking on the current road conditions at the tourist offices in Ouray or Silverton.

From Ouray: From Main Street and 6th Avenue in Ouray, drive 13 miles south on US 550 to Red Mountain Pass. Proceed down the south side of the pass for 0.7 miles and turn right (west) on Forest Service Road 822. This will be the first right turn after you pass the road to Black Bear Pass (FSR 823) on the right. You can't see the road number from the highway but you will pass a marker a short distance up the road to verify you are in the right track. (Passenger cars should find a pull off along the highway for parking.)

The beginning of the road is narrow and steep to the first parking area. Some of the switchbacks are rocky and rugged. You will need an AWD SUV/4WD with good clearance. Beyond that point the road gets rougher to the second recommended parking area. Past this point there was a sign warning of a rough and dangerous road ahead. The sign is now gone. This section of the road travels along a very narrow shelf with steep drop-offs and a few rock outcroppings to climb. Passing another car along this road segment is not an option.

To reach the first parking area drive up the road for 0.7 miles. Before coming to the end of the first switchback a road branching left (south) to a house. Ignore this road and continue up a series of switchbacks, passing a second road branching left (south) to a second house at the top of the fifth switchback. Beyond this point you will soon see a good parking area on the left (south) side of the road below a cluster of spruce trees. This is the first parking area, recommended for people looking for a longer walk or drivers that don't feel comfortable proceeding further up the road.

To reach the second parking area, continue up the road another mile, passing two roads branching right. Between the second road and a cluster of spruce trees you will find several places to park. This is the second parking area located 1.7 miles from US 550.

High clearance, 4WD vehicle can continue beyond this point for another 0.9 miles to a parking area at the end of the road near mining debris and a huge mound of mine tailings.

High clearance AWD or 4WD is recommended to the first two parking areas but a passenger vehicle, if driven carefully, can typically make it to the first parking area under good conditions. If driving a 2WD passenger vehicle, I strongly recommend checking on the current road conditions at the tourist offices in Ouray or Silverton.

18. Highland Mary Lakes ★★★★★

Distance: 6.0 - 7.7 miles (RT)

This trail ascends to gorgeous lakes set amid scenic meadows with terrific views. An optional extension follows a segment of the Continental Divide, turning the hike into a loop with extended views of the surrounding peaks.

Distance: 6.0 miles (RT) to Highland Mary Lakes 7.7 miles (loop) with Continental Divide extension
Elevation: 10,790-ft. at Trailhead 12,320-ft. at Highland Mary Lakes 12,580-ft. with Continental Divide extension
Elevation Gain: 1,530-ft. to Highland Mary Lakes 1,790-ft. with Continental Divide extension

Difficulty: moderately strenuous
Basecamp: Silverton, Ouray
Area: Weminuche Wilderness, San Juan NF
Best Season: July - September
USGS Map(s): Howardsville

Why Hike Highland Mary Lakes

Reaching the spectacular alpine tundra of the Weminuche Wilderness usually requires a multi-day backpacking trip. The Highland Mary Lakes trail is an exception, providing day hikers quick access to this alpine wonderland.

The hike visits three of the seven Highland Mary Lakes as well as the Verde Lakes, all above 12,000-ft. Getting to the lakes basin requires a bit of effort. The trail climbs through a diverse landscape of forest and meadows interspersed with picturesque waterfalls to reach the high lakes plateau, gaining over 1,300-ft. in 1.7 miles.

Atop the plateau hikers are greeted with breathtaking views of the glistening lakes set amid a broad expanse of rolling alpine tundra. A gentle climb through the tundra leads to Verde Lakes and wonderful views of the

Grenadier Range where the distinctive pyramid-shaped West Trinity, Vestal and Arrow Peaks are the stars of the show.

The hike can be done as an out-and-back or turned into a loop by following a segment of the Continental Divide Trail that features more great views of the Grenadiers along with fine views of the high peaks rising above the Deep Creek Valley. The final return leg of the loop heads down the Cunningham Gulch trail accompanied by great views of the summits ringing Spencer Basin and the Cunningham Creek valley.

Trailhead to Verde Lakes

Distance from Trailhead: 6.0 miles (RT)
Elevation Verde Lake: 12,320-ft.
Elevation Gain: 1,530-ft.

The Highland Mary Lakes trails starts just beyond the 4WD parking lot at a sign with a large map of the Weminuche Wilderness. (See driving directions below.) Before this sign there is an old wood sign pointing left (east) to the Continental Divide Trail (CDT) -- aka the Cunningham Gulch trail -- and right (south) for the Highland Mary Lakes trail.

The Highland Mary Lake trail wastes no time gaining elevation, ascending on moderately-steep grades through forest interspersed with meadows, staying to the left (east) of Cunningham Creek. Just beyond a waterfall reach a junction (0.2 miles) pointing left to the CDT and straight ahead for the Highland Mary Lakes trail. The trail to the left provides alternative access to the Cunningham Gulch trail and is the return leg of the loop hike.

The trail becomes more rugged as it ascends, occasionally crossing minor creeks with pretty waterfalls. An open area by one of the falls provides nice views to the north.

After climbing for about 30 minutes (1.0 mile) and gaining 860-ft., the trail cross to the right (west) side of the creek and ascends steeply up a rock outcropping. Soon the forest gives way to a picturesque basin with diverse ground cover and small copses of trees set amid rocky knobs. Follow the trail as it curves to the right (west) through the basin and climbs a minor drainage, staying to the right (north) of the creek.

Soon the route turns south again, ascending a steep slope beside the stream. At the base of the talus field the trail forks. Either trail will get you to your destination. I prefer the trail to the left unless the drainage is covered in snow.

The trail to the left climbs steeply up the drainage, hugging the right (west) side of the creek. About halfway up the hill rock cairns mark a crossing to the left (east) side of the creek for the remainder of the climb. The trail to the right climbs up the talus field and then swings to the left, climbing above the talus before swinging left again and crossing a boulder field, a small meadow and the creek to meet the first trail.

A short distance beyond where the two trails meet the first Highland Mary Lake (12,080-ft.) pops into view at 1.7 miles (1,330-ft. ascent from the trailhead). The second lake is soon seen on the right (south) as the trail crosses the narrow strip of land separating the two lakes. This is a great spot to take a break and enjoy the beautiful views to the north of the peaks lining the Cunningham Creek Valley and Spencer Basin to the northwest.

Continue the hike by following the trail as it swings around to the right and travels along the eastern side of the second lake. Views soon open to the left (east) to the third and largest of the Highland Mary lakes (12,090-ft.).

At the top of the third lake the path drops into a marshy area and becomes a little hard to follow as it crosses one of the lake's inlet streams at 2.3 miles. To stay on track, look for wooden post on the hillside above the marsh. As you head toward the post the continuation of the trail, a boot beaten path through the meadows, becomes evident to the left of the post.

A second wooden post in the distance will help keep you on track as the trail climbs gently south across the beautiful alpine meadows. The open landscape offers terrific views of the surrounding peaks and ridges. To the north views extend to Sugarloaf (12,754-ft.), Little Giant Peak (13,416-ft.), Green Mountain (13,049-ft.) and beyond. To the northwest Mount Rhoda (13,402-ft.) and Peak 13,434-ft. dominate the view.

As you crest the hill views open south to the Grenadier Range, with the distinctive pyramid-shaped West Trinity (13,765-ft.), Vestal (13,864-ft.) and Arrow (13,803-ft.) peaks (from left to right). The large massif on the horizon is Peak 2 (13,475-ft.).

The trail now traverses rolling alpine meadows. At 2.9 miles reach an overlook above the Verde Lakes (12,186-ft.). White Dome (13,627-ft.), Peak 1 (13,589-ft.), Storm King Peak (13,752-ft.) and Peak 2 dominate the view to the south while two unnamed 13,000-ft. peaks rise to the east. Follow the trail as it descends on easy grades to the lakeshore at 3.0 miles and continues along the east side of the lake. A short distance beyond the lake the trail fades.

Although Verde Lakes are the turnaround point for the out-and-back hike, the open alpine tundra invites exploration. A quick look at the map will show a number of smaller lakes within the vicinity worth visiting. Be sure to keep an eye on the weather while you explore the basin. The open alpine tundra is exposed and not a good place to be caught in a thunderstorm

Loop Option with Continental Divide Extension

Segment Stat: Loop with the Continental Divide extension adds 1.7 miles with a 530-ft. elevation gain
Distance: 7.7 miles (loop)
Maximum Elevation: 12,580-ft.
Elevation Gain on the Loop: 1,790-ft.

If you wish to do the loop hike, return to the overlook above Verde Lakes. Facing the lake, look up the hillside to the left (east) to locate a wooden post marking the trail to the Continental Divide. Climb the hill toward the posts. Soon an obvious trail appears. On the ascent be sure to turn around and enjoy terrific views of the Grenadiers with West Trinity, Vestal and Arrow Peaks easy to pick out on the skyline. Below you Verde Lakes, set against a backdrop of the high peaks to the north/northwest, lies nestle in alpine meadows. The views continue to improve as you climb.

Reach the high point on this segment of the trail at 3.5 miles. Here the trail briefly levels out. At 3.9 miles the trail curves to the left (northeast) and starts a short steep descent along the north side of a deep gully carrying a stream draining the western slopes of the Continental Divide.

Soon the descent ends and the trail begins ascending on moderate grades through alpine meadows along the west side of the creek. Posts help mark this section of the trail.

Hop across the stream at 4.2 miles and continue climbing toward the Continental Divide along the east side of the stream. Be sure to turn around for more fine views of Vestal and Arrow Peaks.

At 4.6 miles the grade abates as the trail curves to the left (north). To our right (east) another boot beaten path is seen paralleling our trail. This is the Continental Divide Trail (CDT). At 4.8 miles the two trails meet. Just beyond we reach the high point of the loop along the CDT.

The trail now descends on moderate grades through rolling meadows, passing a large tarn along the way. Ahead views open to Canby Mountain (13,478-ft.), Sheep Mountain (13,292-ft.) and the other peaks rising to the north of Deep Creek.

Beyond the tarn the descent steepens and the landscape becomes more rugged with rock outcroppings and rocky knolls. Small clusters of stunted evergreens and low shrubs appear as we lose altitude. At 5.4 miles the trail passes to the west of a tarn.

The trail swings to the left (northwest) at 5.7 miles. Here we have nice views of the Deep Creek Valley with Sheep Mountain and Greenhalgh Mountain (13,220-ft.) rising to the northeast. The grade levels briefly as we travel through meadows across a broad saddle separating the Deep Creek and Cunningham Gulch drainages. To the west/northwest views open to Mount Rhoda, Whitehead Peak (13,269-ft.), Little Giant Peak and the high summits surrounding Spencer Basin.

A signed junction at 6.0 miles points right (east/northeast) to the northbound CDT and southwest to the trail we have just traveled, the southbound CDT. We leave the CDT, walking straight ahead (northwest) on the unmarked trail toward Cunningham Gulch.

The path now descends on moderate to moderately-steep grades. Ahead are great panoramas of the high peaks lining the west side of the Cunningham Creek Valley including Little Giant Peak, the summit with a light colored rock slide. Mount Rhoda, Peak 13,434-ft., Sugarloaf and Peak 13,409-ft. rise to the west above Spencer Basin.

At 6.3 the trail crosses a creek and then starts the steep descent down Cunningham Gulch. Ahead are fine views of Spencer Basin.

Cross a second creek at 6.8 miles. A short distance beyond the trail enters the trees and soon turns left (east), dropping down a series of very steep switchbacks. Turn left at the signed junction at 7.2 miles, continuing the steep descent toward the Highland Mary Trail. (The trail to the right, signed for Cunningham Gulch, is longer and not as steep but ends in the valley to the north of the parking area.)

Reach the junction with the Highland Mary Trail at 7.5 miles. Turn right (north) on the Highland Mary trail and return to the parking area at 7.7 miles.

Driving Directions

From Silverton: Drive northeast through Silverton on Greene Street, the town's main street, pass the courthouse (on the left) and bear right on County Road 2 toward Howardsville. The road is paved for the first 2.0-miles and then turns to a good gravel surface. Just before reaching Howardsville, turn right on County Road 4 (marked with a sign for the Old One Hundred Mine Tour). Follow CR 4, a good dirt road, for 3.7 miles up Cunningham Gulch to the ruins of a mine.

Note: County Road 4 splits part-way up Cunningham Gulch. Either road will get you to the trailhead. The road to the right (lower road) is easier.

Hikers in low clearance vehicles should park off the road near the mine and walk up the road about 0.8 miles, gaining about 380-ft., to the trailhead. If walking the road, add 1.6 miles to the round-trip to the trail distance.

The road crosses a bridge and then starts climbing up the right (west) side of the creek with the aid a long switchback. (The road gets rougher and steeper as it climbs. Vehicles with AWD/4WD with good clearance are recommended.) Follow the road for a little over 0.8 miles to an intersection with a road splitting off to the left. Those with good clearance and 4WD can turn left, following the road downhill and across the creek. The trailhead parking lot is just beyond the crossing. Use care during periods of high water.

If you are concerned about the creek crossing or clearance, continue past this intersection to an obvious parking area on your left. It is always best to check on current road conditions at the Silverton Visitor Center before setting out.

From Ouray: Follow U.S. Highway 550 South from Ouray for 29 miles to the turnoff to Silverton and then follow the Silverton directions to the trailhead.

19. Crater Lake ★★★★

Distance: 11.0 - 11.8 miles (RT)

A scenic hike to a pretty lake nestled beneath North Twilight Peak (13,075). The hike can be extended by hiking to the saddle beyond the lake and/or scrambling to the top of North Twilight.

Distance: 11.0 miles (RT)
11.8 miles (RT) to Saddle
Elevation: 10,770-ft. at Trailhead
11,640-ft. at Crater Lake
11,770-ft. at Saddle Lake
Elevation Gain: 870-ft. to Crater Lake
1,000-ft. to Saddle
Difficulty: moderate

Basecamp: Silverton, Ouray
Area: Weminuche Wilderness, San Juan NF
Best Season: July - September
USGS Map(s): Snowden Peak

Why Hike Crater Lake

The hike to Crater Lake does not require a big expenditure of energy for its scenic rewards. Starting at 10,770-ft. the trail traverses a rolling terrain of meadows and forests with great views of the surrounding peaks, gaining a net 1,300-ft. in 5.5 miles.

The lake, cradled in a pretty timber-lined bowl, is a photographer's delight with North Twilight Peak (13,075), rising to the south, reflected in its still waters.

Any easy side trip takes hikers to a panoramic saddle above the lake. From the saddle, a class 3 scramble up the east ridge of North Twilight Peak provides bird's eye views of the Needle Mountains and the Grenadier Range to the east.

Crater Lake is located in the rugged West Needle Mountains, an area added to the Weminuche Wilderness Area in 1993. This is the only trail penetrating this segment of the wilderness.

Trailhead to Crater Lake

Distance from Trailhead: 11.0 miles (RT)
Elevation at Crater Lake: 11,640-ft.
Elevation Gain: 870-ft.

In 1993 Congress expanded the Weminuche Wilderness to include the rugged West Needle Mountains, wedged between a deep gorge of the Animas River and Lime Creek to the south of Molas Pass. Only one trail, Crater Lake, penetrates this segment of the wilderness.

The hike to Crater Lake starts at pretty Andrews Lake, a popular fishing spot just south of Molas Pass (see driving directions below). Starting at the southwest end of the parking area the trail skirts the west shore of the lake, crosses a meadow and ascends a tree covered hillside on switchbacks, gaining 450-ft. in 1.1 miles. This is the steepest climb of the hike.

Views from the meadows around Andrews, along with intermittent views from openings in the trees while climbing the hillside, include West Turkshead (12,849-ft.) and Grand Turk (13,180-ft.) to the north, Twin Sisters (13,432 and 13,372) and Jura Knob (12,594) rising on the ridge to the west and Snowdon Peak to the southeast.

From the top of the hill the trail drops 240-feet into a drainage traversing pretty meadows with pockets of Engelmann spruce and firs. A second climb gains 370-ft. reaching the top of a hill at 2.4 miles.

Beyond the second climb the trail descends on moderate grades for 0.4 miles and then ascends on easy to moderate grades through meadows and forests for 1.6 miles, gaining 400-ft. Openings offer great views of Engineer Mountain (12,968-ft.), Jura Knob and Twin Sisters to the west. As the trail swings east views open to North Twilight Peak (13,075) to the south.

At 4.0 miles the path enters heavy timber and stays in the woods for the next 1.1 miles. At 5.1 miles the trail drops into a small depression, skirts a

marshy area to your left (east), and then climbs over a hill to the basin holding Crater Lake (11,640-ft.) at 5.5 miles. North Twilight Peak, rising to the southwest, forms the perfect backdrop for this pretty lake ringed by a forest.

Photographers will snap plenty of pictures of North Twilight Peak reflected in the lake's still waters. Fishermen may want to try their luck at catching some of the lake's cutthroat trout. Numerous camping areas are evident in the trees to the north and west of the lake.

Crater Lake to the Saddle

Segment Stat: 0.4 miles (one-way) from Crater Lake to the Saddle with a 130-ft. elevation gain
Distance: 11.8 miles (RT)
Elevation at Saddle: 11,770-ft.
Elevation Gain - Trailhead to the Saddle: 1,000-ft.

For panoramic views of the peaks to the west and south of Molas Pass along with a restricted view of the Needles, hike to the obvious saddle (11,770-ft.) southwest of the lake. The faint trail swings around the east side of the lake and proceeds up a grassy slope, skirting rock piles and a small pond. Round trip to the saddle is 0.4 miles with a 130-ft. elevation gain.

When you are done enjoying the views, retrace your steps to return to the trailhead.

To climb North Twilight Peak (13,075-ft) proceeds west from the saddle, climbing the mountain's northeast shoulder and east ridge. The class 2-3 scramble requires a head for heights when crossing a narrow exposed ridge. Panoramic views from the top provide a bird's eye view of the Needles and the Grenadier Range to the east. Total elevation gain from the trailhead is 2,305-ft. Note: The climb to North Twilight Peak is recommended for experienced parties only.

Driving Directions

From Silverton: From the intersection of Main Street in Silverton (State Highway 110) and U.S. 550, drive south on U.S. 550 for 7.3 miles to the

Andrews Lake Road. It is 6.4 miles to the top of Molas Pass. Andrews Lake Road is 0.94 miles beyond the pass. Turn left and drive a little over 0.5 mile on the narrow paved road to the parking area at Andrews Lake. The trailhead is located on the southwest end of the parking area.

Driving Directions from Ouray: Drive south on U.S. 550 for 30.7 miles and turn left on the Andrews Lake Road. Andrews Lake Road is 0.94 miles beyond Molas Pass. Drive a little over 0.5 mile on the narrow paved road to the parking area at Andrews Lake. The trailhead is located on the southwest end of the parking area.

Driving directions from Durango: Drive 45-miles north of Durango on US 550 and turn right on the Andrews Lake turn off. The turn off is 6.6 miles beyond Coal Bank Pass and about 0.5 miles from the Lime Creek rest area. Turn right and drive a little over 0.5 mile on the narrow paved road to the parking area at the lake. The trailhead is located on the southwest end of the parking area.

20. Colorado Trail: Little Molas Lake to Lime Creek ★★★⭒

Distance: 7.4 - 10.1 miles (RT)

This relatively easy out-and-back hike on a segment of the Colorado Trail provides panoramic views from the high meadows above the West Lime Creek drainage.

Distance: 10.1 miles (RT) to Lime Creek Drainage
Elevation: 10,895-ft. at Trailhead 11,650-ft. at high point
Elevation Gain: 755-ft. at high point
Difficulty: moderate

Basecamp: Silverton, Ouray
Area: San Juan NF
Best Season: July - September
USGS Map(s): Snowden Peak, Engineer Mountain

Why Hike from Little Molas Lake to Lime Creek

This relatively easy walk gives day hikers a scenic taste of the Colorado Trail, an epic 471-mile route stretching between Denver and Durango. The out-and-back hike follows a 5.0-mile segment of the trail, traversing pretty meadows with panoramic views high above the Lime Creek Drainage.

The hike is located just north of Molas Pass (10,910-ft.) in the area of the 1879 Lime Creek Burn that incinerated 26,000-acres of forest. The fire burned with such intensity that the forest has still not recovered.

Vast meadows, sprinkled with replanted lodgepole pines, now cover the area once blanketed with thick forest, offering far reaching vistas of the Grenadier Range to the east, the West Needle Mountains and Engineer Peak to the south and Twin Sisters to the west. West Turkshead Peak dominates the skyline to the north.

Trailhead to Lime Creek Drainage

From the trailhead at the western end of Little Molas Lake (see driving directions below), follow the Colorado Trail as it heads northwest climbing limestone terraces on switchbacks with moderately easy grades. Along the way pass through pockets of trees and open meadows with views south to Engineer Peak (12,698-ft.) and North Twilight Peak (13,075-ft.).

After gaining 390-ft. in 1.3 miles the trail turns right (northeast) and joins a wide dirt track near the top of a ridge. The eroded track ascends to and traverses the ridge towards West Turkshead Peak (12,849-ft.). Here views open west to the Twin Sisters (13,432 and 13,374-ft.) and Jura Knob (12,592-ft.). Snowden Peak and the Grenadier Range fill the skyline to the east.

Follow the track uphill for 0.7 miles. The trail narrows and turns left (northwest) as it nears West Turkshead Peak, two miles from the start of the hike.

The trail now traverses the east side of the North Lime Creek drainage. Toward the head of the drainage the path descends to and crosses a saddle at

3.1 miles, located between the Bear Creek valley (to the north) and the North Lime Creek valley (to the south). Views at the saddle extend north to Bear Mountain (12,987-ft.) and Sultan Mountain (13,368-ft.).

From the saddle the trail heads west, ascending to the high point of the hike (11,650-ft.) at 3.6-miles and then loses 100-ft. over 0.4 miles as it crosses and curves around the ridge separating the North Lime Creek and Lime Creek drainages. Below the trail two tarns lie nestled on the ridge's broad shoulder.

Continue walking until the trail starts to drop towards the head of Lime Creek on switchbacks at 5.0 miles. This is a good place to turn around.

From this vantage point panoramic views encompass Twin Sisters, Jura Knob, Engineer Mountain, North Twilight Peak, the Snowden Mountains and the Grenadier Range. After taking a break and soaking in the scenery, retrace your steps enjoying the views on the return leg.

Note: Mountain bikes are permitted on this trail.

Driving Directions

From Silverton and Ouray: Go 5.5 miles south of Silverton (27 miles south of Ouray, 44.5 miles north of Durango) on US 550 and turn west on Little Molas Lake Road. The Molas Lake Road is 0.4 miles north of Molas Pass. Follow the road for 0.8 miles to the parking area beyond the lake. The Colorado Trail trailhead is located at the northwest end of the parking area.

21. Spencer Basin ★★★★★

Distance: 4.4-7.7 miles (RT)

An old mining road leads to the heart of Spencer Basin, a beautiful, unspoiled and seldom visited valley surrounded by 13,000-ft. peaks. Here use trails and routes lead to two scenic passes.

Distance: 4.2 miles (RT) to Mine
5.4 miles (RT) to Sugarloaf Pass
5.6 miles (RT) to Arrastra Pass
Elevation: 10,830-ft. at Trailhead
12,420-ft. at Mine
12,690-ft. at Sugarloaf Pass
12,940-ft. at Arrastra Pass
Elevation Gain: 1,590-ft. to Mine
1,860-ft. to Sugarloaf Pass
2,110-ft. to Arrastra Pass
Difficulty: moderately strenuous

Basecamp: Silverton, Ouray
Area: Gunnison BLM
Best Season: July - September
USGS Map(s): Howardsville

Why Hike Spencer Basin

Beautiful Spencer Basin is a little known gem to the northwest of the Highland Mary Lakes. An old mining road climbs into the heart of the basin where trails and routes lead to the remnants of a mine and two passes. The solitude and untrammeled condition of the basin adds to the allure.

There are actually three destinations in this large basin that can be combined to create hikes of varying lengths and difficulties. Experienced hikers adept at scrambling will find additional areas to explore.

The trailhead is best reached by a high clearance vehicle. Low clearance passenger vehicles will need to park at the mine ruins near the end of County Road 4 and walk to the trailhead, adding 1.6 miles round-trip to the total distance.

Trailhead to Sugarloaf Pass Junction

Distance from Trailhead: 1.8 miles (one-way)
Elevation to Sugarloaf Junction: 12,220-ft.
Elevation Gain: 1,400-ft.

Note: Hikers in low clearance vehicles should park at the mine ruins near the end of County Road 4 and walk 0.8 miles up the road to the trailhead. (See driving directions below.) Walking the road will add 1.6 miles round-trip to the distance and 380-ft. to the elevation gain.

From the Spencer Basin trailhead parking area (see driving directions below), walk uphill on the dirt road, climbing moderately-steep switchbacks. You will cross Mountaineer Creek twice in the first 0.25 miles. At 0.4 miles keep left, the road branching right ends at a tram tower, visible above the trail to the north. A few more switchbacks bring you to a huge tailings pile blocking the road near a small parking area (2-3 cars).

Climb over/around the tailings on a boot beaten path leading to the continuation of the road. The road now heads southwest, ascending steeply for a short distance before crossing a gully. Beyond the gully the grade moderates as the path climbs through meadows and low shrubs. Turn around for nice views of Cunningham Gulch and Green Mountain (13,049-ft.).

After a mile the road curves to the right (west) and views open up to Peak 13,434-ft. at the head of the valley. Soon the road swings to the left and then the right. Ahead is a large rock formation. A tributary of Mountaineer Creek flows around the left (south) side of the formation and joins the main branch of Mountaineer Creek below the trail. The road now climbs steeply through white-colored rock along the right (north) side of a gully channeling the main branch of Mountaineer Creek. Ahead are views of Peak 13,409-ft. at the head of the valley.

The grade abates as the road reaches the top of a hill, crosses Mountaineer Creek and then swings to the left (southwest), ascending through meadows and scattered clusters of willows. To the south views open to Surgarloaf (12,754-ft.) and an unnamed peak to the west.

At 1.7 miles the road swings left (south) around a large rock outcropping. This feature is important in finding the trail/route climbing to the pass west of Sugarloaf. Soon the road starts curving to the right and widens. Now watch for an unmarked trail branching left (south) through a clump of willows at 1.8 miles. This is the trail to the pass.

Here you will have great views of the gray-colored ridge rimming the south side of Spencer Basin. The high peak with a squarish top anchoring the southwest end of the ridge is Mount Rhoda (13,402-ft.). Peak 13,434 rises to the north of Rhoda. Surgarloaf is the roundish peak anchoring the southeast end of the ridge. The pass, which I refer to as Sugarloaf Pass, is the saddle to the right (west) of Sugerloaf.

You now have a choice of walking to Sugarloaf Pass or continuing up the valley. With an early start, fit hikers can accomplish both options in one day.

Here is the mileage and elevation gains for the various options:

4.4 mile to the Mine (12,420-ft.): +1,590-ft.

5.4 miles (RT) to Sugarloaf Pass (12,690-ft.): +1,860-ft.

5.6 miles to Arrasta Pass (12,940-ft.): +2,110-ft.

6.2 miles combining trips to the Mine and Sugarloaf Pass:+2,050-ft.

7.7 miles to both passes:+2,580-ft.

Junction to Sugarloaf Pass

Segment Stat: 0.9 miles (one-way) from Junction to Sugarloaf Pass with a 470-ft. elevation gain

Distance – Trailhead to Sugarloaf Pass: 5.4 miles (RT)

Elevation at Pass: 12,690-ft.

Elevation Gain - Trailhead to Pass: 1,860-ft.

To reach Sugarloaf Pass, turn left and follow the trail as it head south through pretty meadows with fine views of the ridge to the south and the peaks at the head of Spencer Basin. At 1.9 miles the trail curves to the left (southeast) and crosses creek set amid marshy meadows at 2.1 miles.

Beyond the creek the trail fades as it traverses the meadows. To the left you will see some stakes. Don't walk toward the stakes. Instead head across the marshy meadows, aiming for a low point between two hills.

At the far end of the marshy-meadows the trail becomes evident as it ascends a low rise, staying to the left (north) of the creek. After topping the rise the grade steepens as trail climbs towards the pass, passing a small pond along the way. The ascent is accompanied by great views of the cirque at the head of Spencer Basin and the ridge rimming the north side of the valley.

Reach Sugarloaf Pass (12,690-ft.), a saddle on the ridge, at 2.7 miles. From the pass enjoy fine views of the Highland Mary Lakes Basin to the south/southeast. The Needles rise to the south beyond the basin. To the north/west the high peaks towering above Spencer Basin dominate the view while the peaks looming above the Cunningham Creek Valley and beyond fill the skyline to the northeast.

A trail of sorts climbs along the ridge to the top of Sugarloaf. There is also a trail that continues heading southwest from the pass. This path traverses the basin beyond the pass and then becomes faint as it drops down to intersect a route along the east facing slopes of Mount Rhoda. I have met hikers who use this route to form a loop with the Highland Mary Lakes but have never done so myself. This route involves off-trail hiking and requires parties to carry good maps of the area. Large herds of sheep graze these meadows so expect a lot of animal tracks to lead you astray.

I advise turning around at the pass and either returning to your vehicle via the Spencer Basin trail or continuing further up Spencer Basin. Leave the Highland Mary Lakes hike, including the loop option with the Continental Divide Trail, for another day.

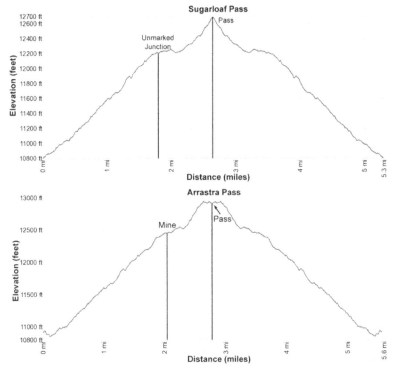

To the Mine and Arrastra Pass

Segment Stat: 0.3 miles (one-way) from Junction to the Mine with a 200-ft. elevation gain

0.75 miles (one-way) from Junc. to Arrastra Pass with a 520-ft. elevation gain

Distance – Trailhead to the Mine: 4.2 miles (RT)

Trailhead to Arrastra Pass: 5.6 miles (RT)

Elevation - At the Mine: 12,420-ft. and at Arrastra Pass: 12,940-ft.

Elevation Gain - Trailhead to the Mine: 1,590-ft.

Trailhead to Arrastra Pass: 2,110-ft.

A short distance past the unmarked trail to Sugarloaf Pass the road again curves to the right and climbs steeply up a rocky hillside. The short climb ends atop a bench where the path turns to the left and ascends on easy to moderate grades.

At 2.1 miles reach a "Y" intersection with the remnants of a two-track road branching left. To the right is the mine (12,420-ft.), set amid a flattened gravel area. The hillside above is littered with tailings and a mine shaft. Straight ahead is a moist meadow with a stream and small pond. Scattered around the area are evidence of mining. Turn right and walk across the gravel toward the tailings, passing the ruins of a rock building.

Beyond the tailings a faint trail heads northwest up a grassy hill, staying to the right of a seasonal creek. Talus spills down the hill along the left side of the creek. At the top of the hill, at 2.2 miles, the trail disappears. To the left (west) is the cirque ringing the head of Spencer Basin. Straight ahead to the north is an obvious saddle on the ridge rimming the north side of the basin. The unnamed saddle, which I call Arrastra Pass, is to the right (east) of Peak 13409. Below is a marshy meadow.

Here again hikers have a choice, find a place to enjoy the views at the head of the valley before retracing your steps to the trailhead or climb the saddle to the north. There is no trail to the saddle so blaze your own route. I recommend initially curving around the left side of the marshy meadows and then keeping to the grass, as much as possible, as you climb the steep slopes to Arrastra Pass (12,940-ft.). Its about 0.75 miles to the pass and will take a half hour or more (depending on your conditioning).

From the pass enjoy fine views of Silver Lake and the Arrastra Basin to the north. Little Giant Peak (13,416-ft.) towers above the east side of the lake while Kendall Peak (13,451-ft.) rises to the west. When you are done enjoying the views, retrace your steps to the trailhead.

Driving Directions

From Silverton: Drive northeast through Silverton on Greene Street, the town's main street, pass the courthouse (on the left) and bear right on County Road 2 toward Howardsville. The road is paved for the first 2.0-miles and then turns to a good gravel surface. Just before reaching Howardsville, turn right on County Road 4 (marked with a sign for the Old One Hundred Mine Tour). Follow CR 4, a good dirt road, for 3.7 miles up Cunningham Gulch to the ruins of a mine.

Note: County Road 4 splits part-way up Cunningham Gulch. Either road will get you to the trailhead. The road to the right (lower road) is easier.

Hikers in low clearance vehicles should park off the road near the mine and walk up the road about 0.8 miles, gaining about 380-ft., to the trailhead. If walking the road, add 1.6 miles to the round-trip to the trail distance.

The road crosses a bridge and then starts climbing up the right (west) side of the creek with the aid a long switchback. (The road gets rougher and steeper as it climbs. Vehicles with AWD/4WD with good clearance are recommended.) Follow the road for a little over 0.8 miles to an intersection with a road splitting off to the left. Continue past this intersection to an obvious parking area on your left.

It is possible to continue up the road another 0.5 miles to a small parking area that holds 2-3 cars. You will need to ford two streams, potentially problematic during high water. It is a nice walk and a short enough hike that I advise walking.

From Ouray: Follow U.S. Highway 550 South from Ouray for 29 miles to the turnoff to Silverton and then follow the Silverton directions (above) to the trailhead.

22. Pass Creek–Engineer Mountain ★★★★
Distance: 4.8-12.8 miles (RT)

This scenic hike, traveling through the high meadows to northwest of Coal Bank Pass, features terrific views of Engineer Mountain, Twin Sisters, the high peaks ringing the Cascade Valley and the summits rising to the south of Silverton.

Distance: 4.8 miles (RT) to Junction Engineer Mtn Trail
12.8 miles (RT) to Trail End
Elevation: 10,670-ft. at Trailhead
11,670-ft. at Junction
12,210-ft. at Trail End
Elevation Gain: 1,020-ft. to Junction
2,425-ft. to Trail End
Difficulty: strenuous

Basecamp: Silverton
Area: San Juan
Best Season: July - September
USGS Map(s): Engineer Mountain

Why Hike Pass Creek & Engineer Mtn. Trails

Combine the Pass Creek and Engineer Mountain trails to create a long, scenic hike through beautiful meadows with fine views of Engineer Mountain, Jura Knob, the high peaks along the Cascade Valley and the summits to the south of Silverton.

The hike ends near a pretty tarn high above the West Lime Creek Valley. Here Twin Sisters, Rolling Mountain, Beattie Peak (13,342-ft.), Fuller Peak (13,761-ft) and Vermillion Peak (13,894-ft.) grace the skyline to the north/northwest. Jura Knob, Sultan and Grand Turk dominate the view to the east/southeast.

Over the course of this long hike the trail gains almost 2,500-ft. and loses over 900-ft. as it dips in and out of drainages and crossing the rolling terrain. The elevation gains along with the distance make this a strenuous hike.

Pick a beautiful day and get an early start so you can take you time traveling through this scenic area, enjoying the views both near and far. The initial Pass Creek trail segment will be busy with hikers seeking to climb Engineer Mountain. After 2.4 mile you will leave the crowds behind and encounter few hikers along the remainder of the trail.

Note: The Pass Creek and Engineer Mountain trails are open to bikes. Hike the trail on a weekday to avoid most of the bike traffic. Typically you will see few bikes on the Engineer Mountain section of the hike.

Trailhead to Junction with Engineer Mountain Trail

Distance from Trailhead: 4.8 miles (round-trip)
Elevation at Junction: 11,690-ft.
Elevation Gain: 1,020-ft.

The Pass Creek Trailhead is located near Coal Bank Pass, south of Silverton, Colorado (see driving directions below). The trail, which starts from the northeast end of the trailhead parking area, ascends through meadows on moderate grades and soon enters viewless spruce-fir forest. After a half mile the path crosses a ridge and then turns west/northwest, climbing moderate switchbacks. The grade briefly abates after a mile as the path dips into a basin with a small pond.

Beyond the pond the ascent continues through trees and small intermittent meadows. Openings in the trees at 1.75 miles offer views of Grizzly Peak (13,738-ft.) rising to the northwest.

At 1.9 miles the grade briefly abates and trees thin. Ahead great views open to Engineer Mountain (12,968-ft.) towering above the meadows to the west. A short climb soon delivers you to the Engineer Plateau, a beautiful expanse of meadows below the iconic peak, at 2.25 miles.

From the plateau enjoy stunning views of Engineer Mountain. Jura Knob (12,614-ft.) and the Twin Sisters (13,432-ft., 13,374-ft.) rise to the north. Sultan Mountain (13,368-ft.), Grand Turk (13,148-ft.) and the summit of Bear Mountain (12,987-ft.), along with Kendall Peak (13,451-ft.) and a sea of 13,000-ft. peaks around Silverton fill the skyline to the west.

The trail now ascends west across the plateau on easy grades, reaching the junction at 2.4 miles with the Engineer Mountain trail. This is a good turn around point for hikers looking for a short day. The open meadows invite exploration and are a lovely place to hang out on a sunny day.

Junction to the End of the Engineer Mountain Trail

Segment Stat: 4.0 miles (one-way) from Junction to Trail End with a 1,405-ft. elevation gain
Distance from Trailhead: 12.8 miles (RT)
Maximum Elevation: 12,210-ft.
Elevation Gain from Trailhead: 2,425-ft.

Hikers looking for a longer day should turn right (north) on the unmarked Engineer Mountain trail. Almost immediately the social trail used to climb Engineer Mountain branches to the left (west). (Note: This popular climb is difficult due to loose talus, a narrow ridge and exposure on the most difficult part of the climb.) We continue straight ahead (north) traversing pretty meadows on the Engineer Mountain trail.

The open meadows feature fine views of the peaks to the east/northeast. As you walk north Snowdon Peak (13,077-ft.) appears across the valley to the east. Soon North Twilight Peak (13,075-ft) and the Grenadier Range join the scene. Behind you the sheer north face of Engineer Mountain, eroded into deep fins, comes into view.

At 2.9 miles the trail passes through some scattered trees as it dips in and out of the bowl at the head of the Coal Creek drainage. A short distance beyond we reach a junction at 3.4 miles with the Coal Creek trail, which heads right (east). The sign at the junction indicates that the trail straight ahead (north) (the Engineer Mountain trail) leads to the White Creek and Colorado Trail while the Deer Creek Trail breaks from the Coal Creek trail to the east. We continue straight ahead (north) on the Engineer Mountain trail, which curiously is not listed on the sign.

Note: You may see references to a Pass Creek – Coal Creek Loop, which turns right (east) at this intersection and drops down to Highway 550, 3.0 miles north of the Pass Creek Trailhead. Completing the loop without a car shuttle requires a 3.0 mile walk along Highway 550. Highway 550 is a very narrow road with little or no shoulder and no guard rails. Walking along the road is not safe and not recommended.

Beyond the Coal Creek junction the trail ascends rolling meadows scattered with trees along the southern slopes of Jura Knob's south ridge. To the west Sliderock Ridge (12,460-ft.) rims the north side of the Cascade Valley. Hermosa Peak (12,579-ft.) rises in the distance. Soon Grizzly Peak and San Miguel Peak (13,752-ft.), along the ridge to the north, come into view. To the southwest Grayrock Peak (12,504-ft.) anchors the south end of the ridge. On a clear day the La Plata Mountains, 15 miles northwest of Durango, are seen on the horizon.

Views of Engineer Mountain continue to change. The full north-face is soon in view. Massive talus fields, etched by meltwater, cover the lower slopes of the massif.

At 3.9 miles the ascent ends as the trail starts a traverse along the western slopes of Jura Knob's south ridge. Ahead great views open to the multi-colored south face of Jura Knob and Peak 12,766-ft. at the head of the Engine Creek Valley. The Rolling Mountain massif (13,693-ft.) dominates the view in the distance.

At 4.7 miles the trail curves to the left (west) and descends a few steep switchbacks before crossing a gully along the south face of Jura Knob. Beyond the gully the trail descends through meadow with scattered trees on more moderate grades.

After losing about 240-ft. the path levels and reaches an unmarked junction at 5.2 miles with two trails. Here the Engine Creek trail makes a sharp left (south), descending toward the valley floor. The White Creek trail branches left (west/southwest) and traverses the slopes beneath the south face of Peak 12,703-ft. We continue straight ahead (north/northwest) on the Engineer Mountain trail that climbs steeply toward the head of the valley.

The grade abates briefly at 5.7 miles as we reach the upper basin ringed by Peak 12,703-ft. to the west, Peak 12,766-ft. to the north and Jura Knob to the east. The path now swings right (east) and then left (north) as it climbs through meadows and willow patches beneath Jura Knob's western slopes.

At 6.0 miles the grade moderates as we reach a high, tundra-clad plateau. Ahead Twin Sisters dominates the view. The summit of Grizzly Peak appears above the ridge to the west.

Stunning views open as we crest a low rise at 6.3 miles. Rolling Mountain, Beattie Peak (13,342-ft.), Fuller Peak (13,761-ft) and Vermillion Peak (13,894-ft.) grace the skyline to the north and form the backdrop for a small pond nestled in the meadows below the trail. Twin Sisters rise to the north/northeast while Jura Knob dominates the views to the southeast. Sultan and Grand Turk, along the peaks to the south of Silverton, rise to the east.

The Engineer Mountain trail ends at 6.4 miles at the junction with the Colorado Trail. To the right (northeast) the Colorado Trail descends along the West Lime Creek drainage and ultimately drops to Little Molas Lake and Highway 550 at Molas Pass. To the left (northwest) the Colorado Trail ascends to meet the Rico Silverton Trail and then climbs to Rolling Pass at 7.4 miles.

The junction with the Colorado Trail is the turnaround point for our hike. Find a nice spot with panoramic views overlooking the creek to take a break and have lunch before returning to the trailhead.

Driving Directions

From Silverton: From the intersection of Highway 550 and the turnoff to Silverton (Green Street/CO Highway 110), drive 13.5 miles south on Highway 550 and turn right (west) on an unmarked dirt spur road. This is the trailhead for the Pass Creek Trail and Engineer Mountain. The turn is between mile posts 57 and 56, right before you reach Coal Bank Pass. Slow down when you see mile marker 57 so you don't miss the turn. At the pass there is a parking lot with bathrooms on the left (east) side of the road. If you reach the pass, turn around and head back a short distance, looking for the dirt road on the left (west).

23. Rico-Silverton ★★★★

Distance: 5.2 miles (RT)

This nice half-day hike climbs on moderate to moderately-steep grades to Rolling Pass (12,450-ft.) with panoramic views of the surrounding valleys and high peaks.

Distance: 5.2 miles (RT)
Elevation: 10,640-ft. at Trailhead
12,468-ft. at Rolling Pass
Elevation Gain: 1,828-ft.
Difficulty: moderately strenuous

Basecamp: Silverton, Ouray
Area: San Juan NF
Best Season: July - September
USGS Map(s): Ophir, Engineer
Mountain

Why Hike the Rico-Silverton Trail

This pleasant half-day hike ascends through forest and meadows to Rolling Pass (12,450-ft.) with fine views of the high peaks lining the South Fork and Cascade Valleys. In late July and August the high meadows are awash with wildflowers.

Extend the hike by climbing Peak 12,766, walking east along the Colorado Trail to an overlook above the West Lime Creek Valley or climbing nearby Jura Knob.

This trail is open to mountain bikers. Hike the trail on a weekday and you will probably see few if any people or bikes.

Note: The last 2.6 miles to the trailhead requires a high clearance vehicle. 4WD is needed during wet conditions.

Trailhead to Rolling Pass

From the Rico-Silverton trailhead parking area (see driving directions below) walk south and almost immediately wade or rock-hop across the South Fork of Mineral Creek. The wide crossing will require getting your feet wet early in the season or during periods of high water.

Past the creek the trail wanders through meadows and soon enters the forest. From the meadows the summits of Fuller Peak (13,761-ft.) and Beattie Peak (13,342-ft.) are seen above the tree tops.

Cross a small stream draining the western flanks of Twin Sisters at 0.4 miles. Reach a second crossing of the South Fork after walking a little over a half mile. Beyond the second crossing the trail climbs steeply for a quarter mile and then breaks out of the trees at South Park, a large, scenic meadow. Twin Sisters (13,432-ft., 13,374-ft.) tower above the trail to the east while Rolling Mountain (13,693-ft.) rises to the west. Look for wildlife around a series of small ponds at the north end of the meadows.

The trail now ascends on easy grades up the meadow accompanied by terrific views of the Twin Sisters massif. Behind you, to the north, the high peaks to the north of the South Mineral Campground dominate the view. Look carefully and you will see the Clear Lake 4WD road snaking up the steep slopes of Peak 13,156-ft. The multi-hued summits of Beattie and Fuller Peaks, along with Fuller Peak's eastern ridge, fill the skyline to the northeast.

At 1.1 miles the trail crosses a small rockslide at the base of Rolling Mountain's eastern ridge. Soon the trail starts ascending on moderate to moderately-steep grades through meadows scattered with clusters of willows and stunted spruce trees. Ahead views open to Peak 12,766-ft. at the head of the valley.

Enjoy ever improving views as the trail climbs. At 1.5 miles the trail rounds the eastern ridge of Rolling Mountain. Views now open to colorful Peak 13,050-ft., along the ridge to the south of Rolling Mountain. A short distance beyond pass a pretty falls set again a backdrop of Peak 13,050. Across the valley the southern end of Twin Sister is now in view. Behind you are fine views down the valley.

Past the waterfall the trail climbs steeply until you reach a small creek at 2.0 miles. The grade now abates a bit as the trail continues the stiff climb through alpine tundra to the pass. You are now over 12,000-ft. and above the timberline.

At 2.25 miles views open east to the Grenadier Range and the high peaks to the south of Silverton. A few large rock cairns help mark the trail, now a boot beaten path, as it climbs through alpine tundra toward the pass.

At 2.4 miles reach an unmarked junction with the Colorado Trail. Turn right (west) onto the Colorado Trail and climb two moderately-steep switchbacks to wind-swept Rolling Pass (12,450-ft.) at 2.6 miles. Here Grizzly Peak (13,738-ft.) and Sliderock Ridge tower above the Cascade Valley to the west/southwest. In the distance are the summits rising to the east of Rico. Closer at hand rugged Peak 13,050-ft rises above the northwest side of the ridge.

Turn around to the north for fine views the Twin Sisters and the high peaks rising above the head of the South Fork Valley. To the northeast views extend to Sultan Mountain (13,368-ft.) and Grand Turk (12,148-ft.).

For even better views, climb Peak 12,766-ft. to the east of the pass. This should add a little over a half mile (round-trip) and 30-45 minutes to the hike. From the summit Engineer Mountain (12,968-ft.) dominates the view to the south while Jura Knob (12,614-ft.) rises to the southeast. To the east/northeast are the high peaks of the Grenadier range and the summits soaring above the Silverton and the Animas Valley. To the west are more fine views of Grizzly Peak.

Hikers with the time and energy can return to the Colorado Trail junction and head southeast, following the trail for 0.3 miles to overlook above the West Lime Creek Valley. A tarn lies to the west of the trail. To climb Jura Knob, continue along the trail past the pond. Now leave the trail and plot your own course to the top of Jura Knob (12,614-ft.) in about 0.75 miles, with more panoramic views of the surrounding area.

Driving Directions

From Silverton: From the intersection of Highway 550 and the turnoff to Silverton (Greene Street/CO Highway 110), drive north on Highway 550 for 2.0 miles to County Road 7/South Mineral Road. Turn left on County Road 7 (signed for the South Mineral Campground) and follow this good gravel road for 4.4 miles to the South Mineral Campground. Beyond the campground the road changes names to Forest Service Road 585 and gets rougher. Continue along the road for 2.2 miles to the Bandora Mine. Bear left at the mine to stay on FS 585, which descends and then crosses a creek. The trailhead is a short distance beyond the creek, 7.0 miles from the turnoff from Highway 550.

From Ouray: Follow Highway 550 south from Ouray for 19.6 miles to CR 7. (The distance from Ouray is measured from the bottom of the switchback exiting the south end of town.) Make a sharp right onto County Road 7/ South Mineral Road. Follow this good gravel road for 4.4 miles to the South Mineral Campground. Beyond the campground the road changes names to Forest Service Road 585 and gets rougher. Continue along the road for 2.2 miles to the Bandora Mine. Bear left at the mine to stay on FS 585, which descends to and then crosses a creek. The trailhead is a short distance beyond the creek, 7.0 miles from the turnoff from Highway 550.

24. Sneffels Highline ★★★★★

Distance: 8.0 - 12.7 miles (loop)

This is my favorite hike in Telluride. The trail crosses a high saddle separating two gorgeous alpine basins, traverses meadows filled with thigh-high wildflowers and serves up spectacular views of the high peaks surrounding the Telluride Valley and the San Miguel Mountains in the Lizard Head Wilderness.

Distance: 12.7 miles (loop)
Elevation: 8,900-ft. at Trailhead
Maximum elevation: 12,280-ft.
Elevation Gain: 3,380-ft.
Difficulty: strenuous

Basecamp: Telluride
Area: Mt. Sneffels Wilderness, Uncompahgre NF
Best Season: July - September
USGS Map(s): Mt. Sneffels, Telluride

Why Hike the Sneffels Highline Trail

If I only had time for one hike in the Telluride area, I'd choose the Sneffels Highline. This classic loop hike, leaving right from town, features spectacular views, two beautiful alpine basins and pretty meadows with thigh-high fields of wildflowers.

Be forewarned the trail is strenuous, covering 12.7 miles and climbing 3,380-ft. to its high point on a saddle below Mt. Emma (12,280-ft.). Don't let the challenge deter you. Pick a beautiful day and get an early start so you can enjoy this premier hike at a leisurely pace.

Trailhead to Saddle

Distance from Trailhead: 8.0 miles (RT)
Elevation at Saddle: 12,280-ft.
Elevation Gain: 3,380-ft.

The Sneffels Highline loop starts and ends at the Jud Wiebe trail at the north end of Aspen Street in Telluride (see directions to the trailhead below). Completed in 1990, the trail combines existing routes with new trails to create one of the classic hikes in the San Juan Mountains.

Follow the Jud Wiebe uphill as it crosses a bridge and swings west, ascending on a broad track. As you climb views open to downtown Telluride and the ski area across the valley. Reach a trail junction at 0.8 miles after gaining 670-ft. and turn left on the Deep Creek (#418) trail. (The Jud Wiebe trail branches right at the junction.) Cross Butcher creek and, in about 300-ft., arrive at a second junction signed for the Sneffels Highline (#434) and Deep Creek.

I recommend hiking counter-clockwise, turning right (north) on the Highline Trail and returning via the Deep Creek Trail (to the left). While initially steeper, you will get over the high point in the trail early in the day before the onset of afternoon thunder storms, a frequent occurrence in the Rockies.

Follow the Highline as it climbs along the west side (left) of the Butcher creek drainage, passing through stands of aspen, spruce-fir forest and small meadows. Switchbacks ease the moderately steep climb up the drainage.

About 40 minutes from the junction the trail breaks out of the trees and continues its ascent on switchbacks, climbing through grassy meadows to a ridge. From the meadows enjoy views of the ski area and the rugged peaks defining the Bear Creek drainage across the valley. To the southwest the peaks of the San Miguel Mountains in the Lizard Head Wilderness, including Wilson Peak (14,017), Mount Wilson (14,246), El Diente Peak (14,159) and the distinctive profile of Lizard Head Peak (13,113), grace the skyline.

Beyond the meadows the trail continues climbing, passing through a notch to gain the west side of the ridge. Openings in the spruce-fir forest provide views of the steep, eroded hillside of the Pack Basin drainage to the west. A final set of switchbacks through a nice stand of spruce brings you to lower end of Pack Basin (11,750-ft.), a pretty alpine bowl carpeted with an emerald green meadow sprinkled with wildflowers.

The basin is cradled beneath the steep, jagged walls of Mt. Emma (13,581-ft.), rising above the head of the basin, and Greenback Mountain (12,976-ft.) to the south. Behind you are distant views of the San Miguel Range.

A narrow trail, marked by rock cairns, leads through the meadow to the head of the basin where a series of steep switchbacks climb the north wall of the bowl to a saddle (12,280-ft.) on the ridge extending west from Mt. Emma. The saddle, separating Pack and Mill Basins, is reached in just under 4-miles from the start of the hike.

The saddle offers panoramic views of the San Miguel Mountains and Lizard Head Wilderness to the southwest and the peaks rising above the Telluride Ski area to the south. Looking north beautiful Mill Creek Basin is nestled beneath a rugged ridge running between Gilpin Peak (13,694-ft.) and Dallas Peak (13,809-ft.).

Completing the Loop

Segment Stat: 8.7 miles (one-way) from the top of the saddle back to the trailhead
Total Distance for the Loop: 12.7 miles (loop)
Maximum Elevation: 12,280-ft.
Elevation Gain/Loss for the Loop: 3,380-ft. / -3,380-ft.

From the saddle the trail descends on rocky switchbacks to the head of the Mill Creek basin and then winds its way past a waterfall and down through meadows, staying to the right (north) of Mill Creek. During the height of wildflower season the trail travels through fields of waist-deep wildflowers at the lower end of the basin.

At the end of the basin the path descends a series of short, tight switchbacks near a waterfall on Mill Creek and then contours along grassy slopes beneath Dallas Peak. After crossing a minor ridge the route climbs 200-ft. through intermittent pockets of trees to the ridge dividing the Mill and Eider Creek drainages. Along the way enjoy beautiful views of Mill Basin, the steep, colorful cliffs lining the east side of the Mill Creek drainage and ever expanding views of the high peaks to the south and east of Telluride.

From the top of the ridge the trail descends on steep switchbacks through pretty stands of aspen to the Deep Creek Trail, losing 900-ft. in 1.3 miles. Turn left (east) on the Deep Creek trail and descend through meadows and trees to another set of steep switchbacks dropping to Mill Creek at 9,900-ft. At this point the trail meets a dirt road. A Deep Creek trail sign points left toward the Jud Wiebe trail and right (south) toward Mill Creek Road. Head left to complete the loop.

The trail soon crosses a bridge over Mill Creek and then heads south following a section of the Deep Creek trail locally referred to as the Waterline Trail because it follows an old water pipe. (Note mountain bikes are permitted on this section of the trail.) A little over a mile after the bridge the route crosses a ridge and turns left (east), heading back to the intersection with the Highline trail. From the intersection turn right to reach the Jud Wiebe trail leading back to town.

Total hiking time, including stops, is between 7.5 to 8 hours.

Driving Directions

Walking Directions in Telluride: From Telluride's main street (Colorado Avenue) turn north onto Aspen Street and proceed uphill past the last of the houses to the Jud Wiebe trailhead.

Parking in Telluride: Parking is by permit only at the trailhead and limited to two-hour parking along Colorado Avenue. Permits are required to park on most of the side streets around town.

Free day-use parking is available in Carhenge Lot, just off West Pacific Avenue at the west end of town near the base of Lift 7, or at the south end of Mahoney Drive, near the west entrance to town. A free shuttle bus, called the Galloping Goose, runs between the parking lots and various stops in downtown Telluride.

There is also free parking in the mountain village. From there you can take the free gondola into town and easily walk to the trailhead.

25. Lewis Lake and Mine ★★★★★

Distance: 8.0 - 8.8 miles (RT)

This scenic hike winds up Bridal Veil Basin past the historic Lewis Mill to Lewis Lake, nestled in a stark glacial basin at 12,700-ft. Along the way pass remnants of the area's rich mining history, numerous waterfalls and hillsides filled with spectacular wildflowers displays.

Distance: 8.0 miles (RT) to Mine
8.8 miles (RT) to Lewis Lake
Elevation: 10,400-ft. at Trailhead
12,448-ft. at Lewis Mine
12,700-ft. at Lewis Lake
Elevation Gain: 2,048-ft. to Mine
2,300-ft. to Lewis Lake

Difficulty: moderately strenuous
Basecamp: Telluride
Area: Uncompahgre NF
Best Season: July - September
USGS Map(s): Telluride

Why Hike Lewis Lake and Mine

Pretty Bridal Veil Basin begins atop the headwall at the eastern end of the Telluride Valley. A seldom used mining road traverses the length of this hanging valley, leading to scenic glacial lake basins nestled in alpine meadows. Along the way the route passes remnants of the area's rich mining history, numerous waterfalls on Bridal Veil Creek and hillsides filled with spectacular wildflowers displays.

Lewis Lake and Mine, one of the best hikes in the area, leads past the largely intact 5-story historic Lewis Mill (12,448-ft.) to Lewis Lake (12,700-ft.), set amid a magnificent alpine amphitheater in the upper basin. Beyond the lake a trail climbs to an unnamed pass with views of the Columbine Lake basin near Silverton and a panorama of peaks around the Telluride.

Along the way to Lewis Lake you will pass the turn off to the Blue Lake trail, a great destination for hikers looking for a shorter day. The trail to Blue Lake, nestled in a stark glacial cirque scattered with mining debris, leads past the remains of an old tram, mining cabins and a bunkhouse. (See the Blue Lake hiking description for more information.)

Whatever your destination getting to the beginning of Bridal Veil basin is its own adventure. The 4WD road to the trailhead switchbacks up the headwall of Telluride's box canyon, providing terrific view of the town, Bridal Veil Falls and the historic power plant at the top of the falls.

Trailhead to the Lewis Lake Junction

Distance to Lewis Lake Junction: 6.2 miles (RT)
Elevation at Junction: 12,360-ft.
Elevation Gain: 1,960-ft.

A hiking trip to Bridal Veil Basin starts with a walk or a drive up the 4WD jeep road just past the Pandora Mill at the east end of Telluride. The road features stunning views of Bridal Veil Falls, Telluride and the restored historic power plant atop the falls.

Bridal Veil Falls, the tallest freefalling waterfall in Colorado, plunges 365-ft. from just beneath the power plant to headwaters of the San Miguel River. An excellent viewpoint at the base of the falls is located 1.2 miles up the jeep road at a hairpin curve on one of the switchbacks. The viewpoint is often enveloped in mist from the water thundering over the rock face and hitting a small pool at the base of the falls.

The walk or drive up the remaining 0.8 miles of the road to the trailhead enjoys great views of the steep cliffs forming the head of the Telluride valley and the town in the distance. Along the way dramatic views open to the power plant perched on a ledge just above the falls. The building, restored in the 1990's, is listed on the National Register of Historic Places.

The power plant, the second oldest AC generation facility in the country, was built in 1907 to supply the Smuggler's Union Mine. Water driving the generators is piped from Blue Lake (see Blue Lake trail description).

If you plan to walk up the road add 4.0-miles to the round trip hiking distances and get an early start. Walking the road turns this into a 12.8-mile round trip hike to Lewis Lake gaining 3,680-ft. in elevation. For more details on walking the road see the Bridal Veil Falls trail description.

The trail into Bridal Veil Basin starts at a gate blocking vehicle access to the power plant. Duck through the opening in the gate and stay on the seldom used mining road as it swings to the left (south) and enters the basin. In a few minutes pass above the power plant building (on the right). The building and the area around the plant is private property.

Follow the rocky road as it ascends on moderate grades along the left (east) side of the creek, past picturesque cascades and waterfalls. Switchbacks ease the way up a few steep sections.

During mid-July to early-August the hillsides along the trail are awash in wildflowers. As you climb the trees thin and views open to the north (behind you) to the mountains forming the northern wall of the Telluride Valley.

An unmarked intersection at 11,470-ft. is reached after walking 1.7 miles and gaining 1,072-ft. Continue straight ahead (the road on the right) toward

Lewis Lake. The road to the left leads to Blue Lake. (See the Blue Lake description for more information.)

Stay on the road as it climbs through meadows and then crosses the stream. Reach an unmarked "Y" intersection at 2.4 miles, a short distance beyond a stream crossing. The road to the right has a pipeline running along the right (west) side of the path. Bear right on the road with the pipeline and continue ascending through pretty meadows, passing a few small tarns along the way. Near the head of the basin two paths are seen in the distance climbing toward the ridge. The path on the left ascends to Columbine Pass above Lewis Lake while the road on the right heads to Ophir.

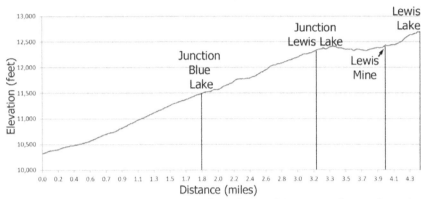

Reach a third junction at 3.1 miles after walking 1.4 miles and gaining about 900-ft. from the junction with the Blue Lake trail. Turn left to reach the Lewis Mill/Mine and Lewis Lake. (There is no trail sign at the intersection, just a post.) The trail to the right continues toward the head of the basin.

To the Lewis Mill

Segment Stats: 0.9 miles (one-way) with an 88-ft. elevation gain
Distance - Trailhead to Lewis Mill: 8.0 miles (RT)
Elevation Lewis Mill: 12,448-ft.
Elevation Gain - Trailhead to Lewis Mill: 2,048-ft.

Follow the trail as it heads southeast, traversing a rolling landscape of meadows and rock outcrops on easy grades. Upon reaching a creek (the outlet stream for Lewis Lake) the trail swings south, climbing along the right (west) side of the creek.

The Lewis Mill (12,448-ft.) is situated about 0.9-miles from the junction on the left (east) side of the trail. A small cabin is located near the Mill and mining debris is scattered around the site.

The 5-story Mill, built in 1907, served as a 60-ton capacity ore-concentration facility in the early 1900's. Work in 2001 stabilized the structure and a new roof was added in 2006. The building, owned by San Miguel County, is listed the National Register of Historic Places.

To Lewis Lake

Segment Stats: 0.4 miles (one-way) with a 252-ft. elevation gain
Distance - Trailhead to Lewis Lake: 8.8 miles (RT)
Elevation Lewis Lake: 12,700-ft.
Elevation Gain - Trailhead to Lewis Lake: 2,300-ft.

Beyond the Mill the trail climbs a steep rocky drainage gaining 250-ft. in 0.4-miles to reach the dam at the end of Lewis Lake (12,700-ft) at 8.8 miles. The lake is set amid a large rocky basin surrounded on three sides with peaks towering above 13,000-ft.

Hikers with the time and energy can follow the very rocky route climbing to Columbine Pass on the ridge to the southeast of the lake. The pass is about 0.5-miles from the lake and entails a climb of 380-ft. From the top of the pass you have a bird's-eye view of Columbine Lake to the south and the vast panorama of peaks surrounding Telluride.

After taking a break return the way you came, enjoying the wildflowers, waterfalls and scenic views of the mountains rising above Telluride.

Wasatch Trail Junction: The trail up Bridal Veil Basin links to the Wasatch trail. At the junction with the Lewis Lake and Mine trail stay right (Lewis Lake and Mine are to the left) and follow the trail as it climbs in a southwest direction toward a scree covered hillside. The trail will cross the edge of the scree and ascend toward the head of the basin.

A junction is reached just before the head of the basin. The trail straight ahead leads to Ophir and the Blixt trail. Take the faint trail heading right (west), ascending to an obvious saddle. At the top of the saddle a trail is seen descending into the Bear Creek drainage. This is the Wasatch Trail that eventually meets with the Bear Creek trail that descends steeply to Telluride. (This is a VERY long loop and only recommended for experienced hikers!)

Driving Directions

From Telluride: Drive east through Telluride on Colorado Avenue for a little over 2.0 miles past the Pandora Mill to a large unmarked parking area.

Park here if you are driving a 2WD vehicle. High clearance AWD or 4WD is recommended beyond this point.

If you are in a high clearance AWD / 4WD follow the dirt road, marked as Forest Road #636 on maps, for 2.0-miles up a series of switchbacks to the Bridal Veil Power plant. The road gets rougher and rockier as you climb.

Parking is VERY limited at the top and fills up early in the morning. Be sure not to block the gate. If there is no available parking, turn around and go back down the road until you find a safe, wide spot to park out of the flow of traffic (and not on private property.) A good place to park is at the base of the waterfall. From the waterfall walk 0.8-miles up the road.

Note: Two-way traffic is permitted between the Pandora Mine and the power plant. The road above the power plant, the notorious Black Bear Road, is one-way downhill toward Telluride. [The Black Bear road, starting south of Red Mountain Pass on Highway 550, goes over Black Bear Pass (12,840-ft.) and descends Ingram Basin on dangerous and difficult switchbacks to meet the 4WD road coming up from Telluride.]

26. Blue Lake (in Telluride) ★★★★

Distance: 6.0 miles (RT)

This nice hike up pretty Bridal Veil Basin leads past waterfalls and wildflowers to Blue Lake (12,220-ft.) nestled in a glacial cirque littered with mining relics.

Distance: 6.0 miles (RT)
Elevation: 10,400-ft. at Trailhead
12,220-ft. at Blue Lake
Elevation Gain: 1,820-ft. to Blue Lake
Difficulty: moderately strenuous

Basecamp: Telluride
Area: Uncompahgre NF
Best Season: July - September
USGS Map(s): Telluride
See Page 114 for Map

Why Hike Blue Lake Trail

Wildflowers and waterfalls abound on this pretty walk up Bridal Veil Basin to a large alpine lake set in a stark glacial cirque at 12,220-ft. Along the way the trail passes historic mining structures including the remains of an old tram, mining cabins and a bunkhouse. More mining debris is scattered around the lake.

Getting to the start of this hike is its own adventure. The 4WD road leading to the trailhead switchbacks up the headwall of Telluride's box canyon, providing terrific views of Telluride, Bridal Veil Falls -- Colorado's longest freefalling waterfall, and the historic power plant atop the falls.

Trailhead to Blue Lake Junction

Distance from Trailhead: 3.4 miles (RT)
Elevation at Junction: 11,472-ft.
Elevation Gain: 1,072-ft.

A hike to Bridal Veil Basin starts with a walk or a drive up the 4WD jeep road that begins just past the Pandora Mill at the east end of Telluride (see driving directions below). The road features stunning views of Bridal Veil Falls, Telluride and the restored historic power plant at the top of the falls.

Bridal Veil Falls, the tallest freefalling waterfall in Colorado, plunges 365-ft. from just beneath the power plant to a stream feeding the San Miguel River running through Telluride. An excellent viewpoint at the base of the falls is located 1.2 miles up the jeep road at a hairpin curve on one of the switchbacks. The viewpoint is often enveloped in mist from the water thundering over the rock face and hitting a small pool at the base of the falls.

Beyond the viewpoint it is a 0.8-mile walk or drive to the gate blocking further vehicle access and the start of the hike. This section of the road enjoys wonderful views of the steep cliffs forming the head of the Telluride valley and the town in the distance. Along the way dramatic views open to the power plant perched on a ledge just above the falls. The building, restored in the 1990's, is listed on the National Register of Historic places.

The power plant, the second oldest AC generation facility in the country, was built in 1907 to supply the Smuggler's Union Mine. Water driving the generators is piped from Blue Lake, our destination.

If you plan to walk up the road add 4.0-miles to the round trip hiking distances and get an early start. Walking the road turns this into a 10-mile round trip hike to Blue Lake gaining 3,200-ft. in elevation. For more details on walking the road see the Bridal Veil Falls trail description.

The trail into Bridal Veil Basin starts at the gate blocking vehicle access to the power plant. Duck through the gate and stay on the seldom used mining road as it swings to the left (south) and enters the basin. In a few minutes you will pass above the power plant building (on the right). The building and the area around the plant is private property.

Follow the rocky road as it ascends on moderate grades along the left (east) side of the creek, past picturesque cascades and waterfalls. Switchbacks help ease the way up a few steep sections.

During mid-July to early-August the hillsides along the trail are awash in wildflowers. As you climb the trees thin and views open to the north (behind you) to the mountains forming the northern wall of the Telluride valley.

An unmarked intersection is reached after walking 1.7 miles and gaining 1,072-ft. Ahead you will see the top of a distinctive pyramid shaped mountain peeking over the steep hillside. Turn left at the junction to reach Blue Lake. The road continuing straight ahead (the road on the right) leads to upper Bridal Veil basin and the turn off to the Lewis Mill and Lake. (See the Lewis Mill and Lake trail description for more information.)

Junction to Blue Lake

Segment Stat: 1.3 miles (one-way) with a 748-ft. elevation gain
Distance - Trailhead to Blue Lake: 6.0 miles (RT)
Elevation Blue Lake: 12,220-ft.
Elevation Gain - Trailhead to Blue Lake: 1,820-ft.

Beyond the turnoff the trail gets rougher as it ascends a few steep pitches. When you hit a second intersection go right. (Turning left leads to Mud Lake.)

Old tram towers and other evidence of past mining activity is evident along the trail. At 2.6-miles the trail reaches the top of a hill and passes an old wood building with a metal roof.

The grade abates and the trail now climbs gently towards the lake. Several wood mining buildings with metal siding and roofs are seen to the right (west) in the flower-filled meadow below the trail. (Stay on the road. The area around Blue Lake is private property.)

Straight ahead the craggy ridge forming the head of East Basin fills the skyline while to the west you will see La Junta Peak (13,472-ft.) and Wasatch Mountain (13,555-ft.).

Follow the road for another 0.4 miles as it winds through meadows to a rocky overlook above the lake. Blue Lake (12,220-ft.) lies nestled in the rocky East Basin surrounded by peaks towering over 13,000-ft. From this vantage point you can see pipes and other mining debris strewn around the lake.

After taking a break return the way you came, enjoying the wildflowers, waterfalls and views to the north of the peaks rising above the Telluride valley.

Driving Directions

From Telluride: Drive east through Telluride on Colorado Avenue for a little over 2.0 miles past the Pandora Mill to a large unmarked parking area. Park here if you are driving a 2WD vehicle. High clearance AWD / 4WD is recommended beyond this point.

If you are in a high clearance AWD/4WD follow the dirt road, marked as Forest Road #636 on maps, for 2.0-miles up a series of switchbacks to the Bridal Veil Power plant. The road gets rougher and rockier as you climb.

Parking is VERY limited at the top and fills up early in the morning. Be sure not to block the gate. If there is no available parking, turn around and go back down the road until you find a safe, wide spot to park out of the flow of traffic and not on private property. A good place to park is at the base of the waterfall. From the waterfall walk 0.8-miles up the road.

Note: Two-way traffic is permitted between the Pandora Mine and the power plant. The road above the power plant, the notorious Black Bear Road, is one-way downhill toward Telluride. [The Black Bear road, starting south of Red Mountain Pass on Highway 550, goes over Black Bear Pass (12,840-ft.) and descends Ingram Basin on dangerous and difficult switchbacks to meet the 4WD road coming up from Telluride.]

27. Bridal Veil Falls ★★★

Distance: 4.0 miles (RT)

This hike ascends a jeep road and offers stunning views of Bridal Veil Falls, the tallest freefalling waterfall in Colorado, the historic power plant at the top of the falls and the Telluride valley. The views are an added bonus for hikers who walk or drive up the road to reach the Bridal Veil trailhead leading to Blue Lake, Lewis Lake and other destinations in the Bridal Veil basin.

Distance: 4.0 miles (RT)　　　　**Basecamp:** Telluride
Elevation: 9,020-ft. - Trailhead　　**Area:** Uncompahgre NF
10,400-ft. at Bridal Veil Falls　　**Best Season:** July - September
Elevation Gain: 1,380-ft.　　　**USGS Map(s):** Telluride
Difficulty: moderate

Trailhead to Bridal Veil Falls

The hike to the top of Bridal Veil Falls starts at a large parking area just past the Pandora Mill at the east end of Telluride (see the driving directions below). From the parking area follow the dirt and gravel jeep road as it switchbacks up the northeast wall of the dramatic box canyon at the head of the Telluride valley. Colorful eroded canyon walls loom overhead while in the distance Bridal Veil Falls, Colorado's tallest free falling waterfall, plunges 365-ft. from just beneath the Bridal Veil power plant.

After negotiating a few switchbacks the road straightens out for about 0.5 miles, continuing its steady ascent to the canyon's headwall. At the headwall the road climbs a series of long sweeping switchbacks to a dramatic viewpoint at the base of the falls at 1.2 miles. The viewpoint, located at a hairpin curve on one of the switchbacks, is often enveloped in mist from the water thundering over the rock face and hitting a small pool at the base of the falls.

The remaining 0.8 miles of the hike to the top of the falls enjoys wonderful views of Telluride Valley. Along the way great views open to the power plant perched on a ledge just above the falls. The building, restored in the 1990's, is listed on the National Register of Historic places.

The power plant, the second oldest AC generation facility in the country, was built in 1907 to supply the Smuggler's Union Mine. Water driving the generators is piped from Blue Lake (see Blue Lake trail description).

At the top of the fourth switchback from the base of the falls you will see a gate blocking vehicle access to the power plant. This is the beginning of the hiking trail up Bridal Veil basin. (The jeep road takes a sharp left before the gate, continuing its climb to Ingram Basin on the notorious Black Bear 4WD road.)

Duck through the large openings in the gate and follow the old mining road for a short distance to a overlook just above the power plant (on your right). Please stay on the road. The building and the area around the plant is private property.

While this is the turnaround point for many people, the pretty basin encourages further exploration. For more information on walks in the basin see the Blue Lake and Lewis Lake and Mine trail descriptions.

Note that two-way traffic is permitted on the jeep road between the Pandora Mine and the Power plant. The Black Bear Road above the power plant is one way – heading downhill toward Telluride. (The Black Bear Road starts south of Red Mountain Pass on Highway 550, goes over Black Bear Pass (12,840-ft.) and descends Ingram Basin on dangerous and difficult switchbacks to meet the jeep road coming up from Telluride.)

My advice is to get an early start if you plan to do this walk. Jeep traffic is much lighter in the morning due to the one-way restrictions on the Black Bear road. The road is also a favorite of mountain bikers. Keep a watch at all times for mountain bikes flying down the road.

Driving Directions

From Telluride: Drive east through Telluride on Colorado Avenue for a little over 2.0 miles past the Pandora Mill to a large unmarked parking area and park.

28. See Forever / Bear Creek Loop ★★★★

Distance: 5.5 - 8.4 miles (loop)

This interesting loop hike features panoramic views of Telluride, Bear Creek Canyon and the distant peaks of the Lizard Head Wilderness.

Distance: 5.5 miles (RT) to See Forever
1.5 miles (one-way) See Forever to Wasatch via Connector Trail
8.4 miles (loop) to Telluride via the Wasatch and Bear Creek Trails
Elevation: 10,540-ft. at Trailhead
12,100-ft. at See Forever
11,530-ft. at end of the Wasatch Connector Trail
8,820 at Telluride (end of the Wasatch/Bear Creek Trail
Elevation Gain: 1,560-ft. to See Forever
-570-ft. at the end of the Wasatch Connector Trail
-2,710-ft. (loss) to Telluride via the Wasatch/Bear Creek Trails

Difficulty: strenuous
Basecamp: Telluride
Area: Uncompahgre NF
Best Season: July - September
USGS Map(s): Telluride

Why Hike the See Forever / Bear Creek Loop

This interesting loop hike, starting at the St. Sophia gondola station in the Telluride Ski Area, is actually a combination of four trails, the See Forever, the Wasatch Connector, a segment of the Wasatch Trail and the Bear Creek Trail, each with its own distinct personality.

Be forewarned that the See Forever portion of the hike traverses ski slopes and follows gravel ski service roads. I am typically not a big fan of road walking or hiking in ski areas, but the panoramic views of peaks towering above the Telluride Valley and the Lizard Head Wilderness more than compensate for the less than desirable trail conditions for the first 2.75 miles of the hike.

Just 0.4 miles down the Wasatch Connector trail you leave the ski area behind and head for the beautiful upper basin of the Bear Creek drainage and dramatic Bear Creek Canyon. This portion of the trail enjoys wonderful views of the Wasatch basin, the incredible peaks defining the north wall of the Telluride Valley and the sculpted cliffs of the Bear Creek canyon.

Note that the 8.4-mile loop is best done in a counter-clockwise direction and involves sections of steep switchbacks gaining 1,540-ft. and dropping 3,280-ft. (Reverse the gains and losses if you hike in a clockwise direction.)

Trailhead to Junction with Wasatch Connector Trail

Distance from Trailhead: 5.5 miles (RT)
Elevation at Junction with the Connector Trail: 12,100-ft.
Elevation Gain: 1,560-ft.

While the trail can be hiked in either direction, I recommend starting at the St. Sophia gondola station at 10,540-ft. and hiking in a counter-clockwise direction (see driving directions below). This starting point limits the elevation gain to 1,540-ft. versus the alternative start at Bear Creek that involves a 3,280-ft gain.

Telluride's free gondola links the town of Telluride with the Mountain Village, located south of town behind the San Sophia ridge. The St. Sophia station is an intermediate stop on the gondola, providing access to hiking, biking and ski trails.

Exit the gondola station and walk south for 0.4-miles, following a gravel ski access road uphill to a snowmaking pond. The start of the See Forever trail is marked by a Forest Service sign on the left side of the road just past the south end of the pond.

The trail traverses a tree covered hillside to the See Forever ski run, where a series of steep steps climb the western side of the run to a junction with the Lookout ski trail that heads downhill to Telluride. While climbing the steps enjoy wonderful views of the peaks and ridges rising to the north and northeast of Telluride. To the west are distance views of the San Miguel Mountains and the Lizard Head Wilderness.

At the junction the hiking trail crosses to the eastern side of the ski slope where a sign with a photograph identifies the peaks to the north/northeast. After taking in the views follow the trail, now on the eastern side of the See Forever run, as it continues its steep ascent.

At 1.2 miles signs for the See Forever hiking trail direct you to follow a gravel ski road, which switchbacks steeply up the ridge. The views of Lizard Head and the peaks to the north of Telluride help you ignore that you are walking through a ski area on a road.

At 1.8 miles the grade abates a bit. Be sure to watch for the trail signs directing you to stay right at the intersection of two ski roads. (The road to the left heads to the top of a ski lift). A short distance beyond the intersection views open to the east (your left) to the cliffs lining the eastern wall of Bear Creek canyon.

Continue following the road as it climbs the ridge to meet the Wasatch Connector trail, which branches left from the road at 2.75 miles. At this point it is worth following the ski road for a short distance to a crest on the ridge. This section of the trail enjoys wonderful 360-degree views of the surrounding area. The 14,000-ft. peaks of the Lizard Head Wilderness dominate the skyline to the west. To the north the peaks and ridges of the Sneffels range tower above Telluride. To the east are the sculpted and highly eroded walls of the Bear Creek drainage while to the southeast Wasatch Mountain and the San Joaquin Ridge rise above the East Fork of the Bear Creek basin. Directly to the south a steep road climbs over 300-ft in 0.3-miles to the top of Gold Hill.

Wasatch Connector to Junction with the Wasatch Trail

Segment Distance: 1.5 miles (one-way)
Elevation at Junction with the Wasatch Trail: 11,530-ft.
Elevation Gain/Loss: -570-ft.

If you wish to do the loop hike after soaking in the scenery, head back to the Wasatch Connector and follow the trail as it traverses the Revelation ski bowl below Gold Hill. At 3.1 miles the trail crosses a minor ridge, leaving the ski area behind, and starts a steep descent on a rocky trail that loses 570 feet in a little over a mile. Views of Bear Creek canyon, the East Fork/Wasatch basin and the Telluride valley make it hard to keep your eyes on the narrow trail.

The connector trail ends at Bear Creek and the Wasatch Trail at 4.2 miles. Here a sign points back to the ski area and across the basin to the upper portion of the Wasatch trail, which crosses the creek and ascends a grassy hillside on the other side of the drainage.

Wasatch and Bear Creek Trails back to Telluride

Segment Stats: 4.2 miles (one-way) with a 2,710-ft. elevation loss
Loop Distance: 8.4 miles (loop)
Elevation: 11,530-ft. at Wasatch Trail Junction to 8,820-ft. at the trailhead
Elevation Gain/Loss for the Loop: 1,560-ft. / -3,280-ft.

Look for a sign that simply says "trail" pointing north (downhill) on the west side of Bear Creek. This is the section of the Wasatch trail we will descend to meet the Bear Creek trail, which will take us back to Telluride.

At the trail junction Bear Creek drops steeply down a rocky gorge. To circumvent the gorge, the narrow Wasatch trail contours north along the hillside, staying high above the creek for 0.75 miles, then drops steeply down to the creek on switchbacks, losing 500-ft. in about 0.5 miles. The trail meets the creek just above the junction with the East Fork Bear Creek trail. (The East Fork Bear Creek trail climbs the eastern side of the East Fork to meet the Wasatch trail in 0.9 miles in the upper East Fork/Wasatch basin.)

Continue following the Wasatch trail downhill. In a short distance you will pass the remnants of the Nellie mine on your left. Beyond the mine the trail descends a steep gully, then traverses the western canyon wall high above the creek. This scenic section of the trail offers great views of the cliffs towering above the canyon.

The final leg of the Wasatch trail drops steeply on switchbacks through groves of aspen and mixed conifers to the junction with the Bear Creek trail at 6.4 miles. While descending the final set of switchbacks look up canyon for nice views of beautiful Bear Creek Falls. (A 0.6 miles round-trip detour leads from the trail junction to a viewpoint near the base of the falls.)

The rest of the 2.0-mile walk is a breeze, following a wide dirt track descending the western side of the Bear Creek drainage back to Telluride at 8.4 miles. See the Bear Creek trail description for more information.

Note: The loop hike loses 3,280-ft. in elevation from the start of the Wasatch Connector trail at 12,100-ft. to the beginning of the Bear Creek trail at 8,820-ft.

Driving Directions

To the St. Sophia Gondola Station in Telluride: In Telluride, CO, walk to the gondola located on San Juan Avenue between S. Aspen and S. Oak Street, 3 blocks south of Colorado Avenue (main street). Take the free gondola to the St. Sophia station. From the gondola station, walk south on the Nature Trail for about 200 yards to the log cabin. Continue on the adjacent road (Basin Road/Trail) for approximately 300 yards as it proceeds south past the Village Trailhead sign to the snowmaking pond and See Forever Trailhead sign on the left.

To the Bear Creek Trailhead in Telluride: From Telluride's main street (Colorado Avenue), turn south onto Pine Street and walk 4 blocks. After crossing the river the street turns into a dirt road that becomes the Bear Creek Trail.

Note: Parking in Telluride can be difficult. Parking is by permit only on many of the streets in the residential section of town and is limited to two-hour parking along Colorado Avenue and its adjacent side streets. Free day-use parking is available in Carhenge Lot, just off West Pacific Avenue at the west end of town near the base of Lift 7, or at the south end of Mahoney Drive near the west entrance to town. A free shuttle bus, called the Galloping Goose, runs between the parking lots and various stops in downtown Telluride.

There is also free parking in the mountain village. From there you can take the free gondola to/from the St. Sophia Gondola Station and town.

29. Wasatch Trail ★★★★
Distance: 12.3 miles (RT)

Dramatic views of Bear Creek Canyon, beautiful alpine basins, wildflowers and waterfalls are a few of the delights on this steep trail to visit the saddle (13,050-ft.) on the divide between Bear Creek and Bridal Veil basins. The hike includes an initial 2.0-mile segment of the popular Bear Creek Falls trail.

Distance: 12.3 miles (RT)   **Basecamp:** Telluride
Elevation: 8,800-ft. at Trailhead   **Area:** Uncompahgre NF
 13,050-ft. at Wasatch Saddle   **Best Season:** July - September
Elevation Gain: 4,250-ft.   **USGS Map(s):** Telluride
Difficulty: strenuous   **See Page 124 for Map**

Why Hike the Wasatch Trail

Many people hike beautiful Bear Creek Canyon to the waterfall. Fewer continue beyond, up the canyon on the Wasatch trail.

The steep hike to the upper canyon and into the Wasatch Basin is well worth the effort. In the upper canyon hikers are rewarded with dramatic views of the sculpted and highly eroded walls of the Bear Creek drainage. Beyond the canyon the Wasatch trail traverses beautiful flower-filled alpine meadows nestled in a narrow cirque beneath Wasatch Mountain and the San Joaquin Ridge before climbing to a 13,050-ft. divide separating the Bear Creek and Bridal Veil Basins.

It is possible to make a long loop out of the hike by crossing the saddle and returning via Bridal Veil Basin. Walking the entire loop, including the road down from the Bridal Veil Power Plant and back to downtown Telluride, is about 14.3 miles. The better option is to get dropped at the Bridal Veil Power plant and do the hike in reverse, up Bridal Veil basin and down the Wasatch. This reduces the elevation gain to 2,650-ft. from 4,250-ft. and cuts 4.0-miles off the trip. (See the hike to Lewis Lake and Mine for more information on the hike up Bridal Veil basin.)

Trailhead to Junction with the Wasatch Connector

Distance from Trailhead: 8.2 miles (RT)
Elevation at Junction: 11,530-ft.
Elevation Gain: 2,730-ft.

Follow the Bear Creek trail, a wide dirt track shared with bikers and horseback riders, as it climbs at a steady pace through a forest of aspen and mixed conifers. As you ascend the trees thin and intermittent meadows provide fine views of the dramatic cliffs defining the canyon's eastern wall.

Reach the junction with the Wasatch trail after walking 2.0-miles and gaining 1,380-ft. Turn right (west) at the junction on the Wasatch Trail and follow the narrow path as it climbs steep switchbacks through groves of aspen and evergreens, gaining 575-ft. in over 0.5 miles. At the top of the switchbacks the grade abates and the trail traverses high above the canyon floor for about a mile, eventually meeting Bear Creek at the base of a gully.

Ascend the gully on a steep track. Bear Creek cascades over rocks and wood debris in the stream bed next to the trail. Near the top of the gully pass the remnants of the Nellie mine on the right (west) side of the trail.

Beyond the mine cross a debris pile caused by a rock slide and come to junction with the East Fork Bear Creek trail. The East Fork Bear Creek trail, going left at the junction, climbs the eastern side of the East Fork of Bear Creek for 0.9 miles to meet the Wasatch trail in the upper East Fork basin. This section is much shorter but also considerably steeper than the alternative route up the Wasatch trail. Some hikers make a loop out of the Wasatch and East Fork or simply use it as an alternate means of descending from the Wasatch Basin on the return hike.

My advice is to go right at the trail junction and stay on the Wasatch. To circumvent the basin's rocky headwall, the trail climbs a series of steep switchbacks, gaining 500-ft. in 0.5 miles, and then traverses the canyon's western wall on a gentle grade to meet Bear Creek at the top of the headwall. A short distance from the top of the headwall the Wasatch meets the Wasatch Connector trail descending from the ski area to the west (right).

Wasatch Connector Junction to the Saddle

Segment Stat: 2.1 miles (one-way) with a 1,520-ft. elevation gain
Distance - Trailhead to the Saddle: 12.3 miles (RT)
Elevation at the Saddle: 13,050-ft.
Elevation Gain - Trailhead to the Saddle: 4,250-ft.

At the signed junction turn left (east) and follow the Wasatch Trail as it crossed Bear Creek and then climbs steeply through meadows to a shelf atop a rocky knoll. As you climb enjoy the fine views extending north/northwest across the Telluride Valley and west to the Gold Hill ski area.

At the top of the knoll the trail drops gently to and crosses the East Fork of Bear Creek, arriving at a junction where the East Fork of Bear Creek Trail rejoins the Wasatch Trail. Go right (east) at the junction, continuing on Wasatch Trail as it ascends 600-ft. over a mile through wildflower-filled meadows toward the base of the saddle at the head of the cirque anchored by the San Joaquin Ridge to the south and Wasatch Mountain (13,555-ft.) to the north.

The final ascent to the saddle is quite steep, climbing almost 500-ft in just under 0.5 miles. From the saddle views extend west toward the San Joaquin Ridge and Silver Mountain. To the east are the peaks and ridge rising above upper Bridal Veil Basin.

Once you are done soaking in the scenery, turn around and retrace your steps. For variety you can take the East Fork trail on the return leg, but be forewarned that it is quite steep.

With planning it is possible to extend the hike into a long loop by crossing the saddle and returning via Bridal Veil Basin. Walking the entire loop, including the road down from the Bridal Veil Power Plant to the Pandora Mine and back to downtown Telluride, is close to 14.3 miles. The better option is to get dropped at the Bridal Veil Power plant and do the hike in reverse, up Bridal Veil basin and down the Wasatch. This reduces the elevation gain to 2,650-ft. from 4,250-ft. and cuts 4.0-miles off the trip.

To do the loop, descend the east side of the saddle to a unmarked junction. Turn left (northeast) and descend through Bridal Veil Basin. (The trail to the right climbs to saddle and ends up in Ophir.) At the first intersection, marked by a post, head left (northeast). The trail to the right climbs to Lewis Lake and Mine.

Follow the trail, which starts as a double track and then becomes a gravel road, down the basin to the Bridal Veil Power Plant, where hopefully a car awaits to take you back to Telluride. If not, walk down the Bridal Veil 4WD road to the Pandora Mine and then follow the Idarado Legacy Trail and the San Miguel River Trail back to town. Note the walk from the power plant to town is 4.0-miles.

See the Lewis Lake and Mine trail description for more information on hiking Bridal Veil basin.

Driving Directions

From Telluride: From Telluride's main street (Colorado Avenue), turn south onto Pine Street and walk 4 blocks. After crossing the river the street turns into a dirt road that becomes the Bear Creek Trail. Proceed south on the trail for 2.0 miles to the Wasatch Trail.

Note: Parking in Telluride can be difficult. Parking is by permit only on many of the streets in the residential section of town and is limited to two-hour parking along Colorado Avenue and its adjacent side streets. Free day-use parking is available in Carhenge Lot, just off West Pacific Avenue at the west end of town near the base of Lift 7, or at the south end of Mahoney Drive near the west entrance to town. A free shuttle bus, called the Galloping Goose, runs between the parking lots and various stops in downtown Telluride.

30. Bear Creek Falls ★★★★

Distance: 4.6 miles (RT)

This half day hike up Bear Creek Canyon offers scenic views of the rugged cliffs lining the canyon and ends at a pretty waterfall. It's a nice option if you have limited time or just want an easy day.

Distance: 4.6 miles (RT)
Elevation: 8,800-ft. at Trailhead
9,940-ft. at Bear Creek Falls
Elevation Gain: 1,140-ft.
Difficulty: easy-moderate

Basecamp: Telluride
Area: Uncompahgre NF
Best Season: July - September
USGS Map(s): Telluride
See Page 124 for Map

Why Hike to Bear Creek Falls

A pretty waterfall and scenic views of the rugged cliffs lining Bear Creek canyon is your reward for hiking 2.3 miles up the Bear Creek trail from Telluride. The popular path, which is shared with bikers and horseback riders, is a good workout and great way to acclimate. The trail connects with the Wasatch trail that heads further up the canyon and provides options for longer loop hikes to Telluride's ski area and Bridal Veil basin.

Trailhead to Bear Creek Falls

The Bear Creek trail starts on the end of South Pine Street (see driving directions) on a wide dirt track shared with bikers and horseback riders. Follow the trail as it heads up hill to a sign marking the beginning of the Bear Creek Preserve. The San Miguel Conservation Foundation, in partnership with the town of Telluride, acquired and donated a 320-acre parcel of land in the Bear Creek Canyon to the citizens of Telluride in 1995 to preserve Bear Creek as public open space.

Beyond the sign the trail heads southeast toward Bear Creek Canyon, climbing through a forest of aspen and mixed conifers. Openings in the trees offer nice views to the north of the cliffs and peaks towering above Telluride.

At 0.6 miles the trail swings to the south and enters the canyon, continuing its ascent along the west side of Bear Creek, which can't be seen from the trail. After hiking about 1.2 miles the trees start to thin and meadows appear along the trail. The openings offer great views of the dramatic cliffs defining the canyon's eastern wall.

The scenery continues to improve as you climb. At just under 1.7 miles the creek comes into view at a pretty spot with a small waterfall. Rock cairns of all shapes and sizes decorate the meadow by the creek.

Reach a junction with the Wasatch trail in a large open meadow at 2.0 miles. Beautiful Bear Creek Falls is seen through the trees cascading down a rocky cliff at the head of a small basin. Continue straight ahead on the trail for 0.3 miles, following the path as it wandering beside the creek through meadows to the base of the falls. (The Wasatch trail branches to the right (west) and climbs the hillside above the trail.)

After exploring the falls, retrace your steps to the trailhead, enjoying nice views of the peaks and ridges rising to the north of Telluride.

Hikers with the time and energy will want to explore further up the canyon on the Wasatch trail. The Bear Creek trail is also used as part of a loop that connects with the See Forever trail. (See the Wasatch trail and See Forever trail descriptions for more information.)

Driving Directions

From Telluride: From Telluride's main street (Colorado Avenue), turn south onto Pine Street and walk 4 blocks. After crossing the river the street turns into a dirt road that becomes the Bear Creek Trail.

Note: Parking in Telluride can be difficult. Parking is by permit only on many of the streets in the residential section of town and is limited to two-hour parking along Colorado Avenue and its adjacent side streets. Free day-use parking is available in the Carhenge Lot, just off West Pacific Avenue at the west end of town near the base of Lift 7, or at the south end of Mahoney Drive near the west entrance to town. A free shuttle bus, called the Galloping Goose, runs between the parking lots and various stops in downtown Telluride.

31. Lake Hope ★★★★

Distance: 4.5 - 5.9 miles (RT)

This popular hike to a high alpine lake surround by 13,000-ft. peaks offers panoramic views of the Wilson Range and the high peaks in the Lizard Head Wilderness.

Distance: 4.5 miles (RT) to Lake
5.9 miles (RT) to Unnamed Pass
Elevation: 10,750-ft. at Trailhead
11,880-ft. at Lake Hope
12,445-ft. at Unnamed Pass
Elevation Gain: 1,130-ft. to Lake
1,695-ft. to Unnamed Pass

Difficulty: moderate
Basecamp: Telluride
Area: Uncompahgre NF
Best Season: July - September
USGS Map(s): Ophir

Why Hike to Lake Hope

The red, rust and purplish-gray colors of Vermilion Peak form the backdrop for brilliant green meadows filled with spectacular displays of wildflowers. In the distance to the west the fourteeners of the Wilson Range and the distinctive spire of Lizard Head Peak fill the skyline. Views, both near and far, are the reason to hike to Lake Hope and the unnamed pass above this pretty glacial lake.

This moderately-easy hike is deservedly popular, so you won't be alone. Get an early start and pick a weekday to avoid the crowds. You won't be sorry.

Trailhead to Lake Hope

Distance from Trailhead: 4.5 miles (RT)
Elevation at Lake Hope: 11,880-ft.
Elevation Gain: 1,130-ft.

The Lake Hope trail, which starts at a sharp curve on a switchback on FS Road #627 (see driving directions below), ascends through spruce-fir forest on gentle grades up the east side of the Lake Fork Valley. A stream crossing at Poverty Gulch (0.3 miles) provides the first views of Sheep Mountain and San Miguel Peak (13,752-ft.) across the valley.

Continuing up the valley the path crosses rock slides and traverses small, wildflower-filled meadows that offer sweeping views of the fourteeners of the Wilson Range and the distinctive spire of Lizard Head Peak to the northwest. As you climb enjoy ever improving views of the peaks lining the south and west walls of the valley. To the east above to the trail a large rust-colored scree field spills off the shoulder of Vermilion Peak.

At the head of the valley the trail swings southwest through meadows filled with waist-high wildflowers. After crossing the third stream, about 45 minutes from the start of the hike, the trail begins a moderate-steep climb, aided by switchbacks, through woods up the headwall of the lake basin. Openings in the trees provide nice views of Trout Lake and nearby peaks.

After gaining 800-ft. in 0.6 miles the trees give way to beautiful meadows sprinkled with wildflowers. To your left (east) the skyline is dominated by Vermilion Peak, clad in red, rust and purple-gray rock, rising above the emerald green alpine basin.

Lake Hope (11,880-ft.), at 2.25 miles, comes as somewhat of a surprise, springing into view as you crest a grassy slope between two rocky hills. The man-made lake, storing water for the Ames Power Plant, sits in a pretty cirque surrounded on three sides by 13,000-ft. peaks. Use trails extend along the lake's eastern shore to a dam at the north end of the lake.

Lake Hope to Unnamed Pass

Segment Stat: 0.7 miles (one-way) with a 565-ft. elevation gain
Distance - Trailhead to the Pass: 5.9 miles (RT)
Elevation at the Pass: 12,445-ft.
Elevation Gain - Trailhead to the Pass: 1,695-ft.

The trail to the pass above Lake Hope heads south around the left (east) side of the lake and soon starts climbing a moderately steep slope through meadows dotted with wildflowers. At 2.6 miles the trail swings east and switchbacks up a rocky hillside, reaching the unnamed pass in 0.7 miles after gaining 545-ft.

From the pass enjoy views of Rolling Mountain (13,693) to the south and the Twin Sisters (13,374 and 13,432) to the east. San Miguel Peak dominates the scenic ridge rising above Lake Hope to the west.

After taking a break return the way you came, enjoying the great views as you descend. Allow 4 to 4.5 hours for the round trip hike to the pass, including a lunch break.

Driving Directions

From Telluride: From downtown Telluride drive 3 miles west on West Colorado Avenue (the main street) to the intersection with State Hwy 145 and turn left (south). Follow Hwy 145 for approximately 10.1 miles and take a left at the road signed for Trout Lake (Forest Road #626/ North Trout Lake Road). Follow the road around the northwest shore of Trout lake for approximately one mile to Forest Road #627. Turn left on #627. Proceed up this rough road for 2.5 miles to the Hope Lake Trailhead. The trailhead is located on the sharp curve of a switchback. (Note: High clearance vehicles are recommended for FS627. Passenger cars, if driven carefully, have successfully negotiated the road. It is best to check with the Forest Service to learn about current road conditions.)

32. Lizard Head ★★★★✦
Distance: 7.6 - 11.7 miles (loop)

One of the top hikes in the Telluride area, this scenic loop traverses the panoramic spine of Blackface Mountain on its way to the base of Lizard Head Peak (13,113-ft.), an eroded 400-ft. tall spire shaped like the gaping maw of a lizard with its face to the sky.

Distance: 7.6 miles (RT) to Black Face Peak
11.7 miles on Loop
Elevation: 10,250-ft. at Trailhead
12,147-ft. at Black Face Peak
Elevation Gain: 1,897-ft. to Black Face Peak
2,900-ft. on Loop

Basecamp: Telluride
Area: Lizard Head Wilderness, San Juan and Uncompahgre NF
Best Season: July - September
USGS Map(s): Mt. Wilson

Why Hike Lizard Head

The Lizard Head trail traversing Black Face Mountain's broad, panoramic ridge is not the shortest route to the base of Lizard Head peak but it is certainly the most scenic. From the ridge leading to the top of Black Face Mountain, the San Miguel Range, including Mount Wilson (14,245-ft.), Gladstone Mountain (13,913-ft.) and Wilson Peak (14,017-ft.), forms a dramatic backdrop for Lizard Head's lone spire soaring 400-ft. above its rock pedestal.

To the east spectacular views encompass Trout Lake and the peaks surrounding the Lake Hope basin, including Sheep Mountain, Pilot Knob, Golden Horn and Vermillion Peak. To the north Sunshine Mountain rises above picturesque Wilson Meadows. In the distance, to the northeast, is the jagged profile of the Mt. Sneffels range.

The trail can be done as an out-and-back hike or a loop using the Cross Mountain trail and the old Railroad Grade route on the return leg. The loop covers 11.7 miles of diverse terrain with a net elevation gain over 2,900-ft.

Be aware the loop hike follows ridges and crosses high alpine meadows for over 4 miles. These areas are dangerous places to be in the event of a thunderstorm. Pick a nice day and get an early start so that you are down from the high country before the onset of afternoon thunder storms, a frequent occurrence on summer afternoons in the Rockies.

Trailhead to Black Face Peak

Distance from Trailhead: 7.6 miles (RT)
Elevation at Black Face Peak: 12,147-ft.
Elevation Gain: 1,897-ft.

The Lizard Head trail heads northeast from the parking area (see driving directions below) on easy grades through pretty meadows and forests of aspen and mixed conifers beneath the steep south face of Black Face Mountain (12,147-ft.). Openings in the trees provide views of Trout Lake and the jagged ridge of 13,000-ft. peaks rising to the east.

After 1.5 miles the trail swings left (west) and starts a moderately steep ascent on switchbacks through spruce-fir forest and meadows, at times skirting the edge of talus slopes, to a junction with the Wilson Meadows trail (heading straight ahead). Keep left, staying on the Lizard Head trail as it climbs steeply up switchbacks on a forested slope. As you climb, the trees gives way to rocky slopes. Reach the ridge leading to the summit of Black Face at 3.0 miles after gaining 1,400-ft.

As the trail attains the ridge crest the rocky slopes give way to alpine meadows dotted with wildflowers. Watch for posts to help guide you through areas where the trail is indistinct.

The path now ascends on gentle to moderate grades along the ridge to the summit of Black Face (12,147-ft.) at 3.8 miles. Along the way enjoy spectacular views to the east of Trout Lake and the peaks surrounding the Lake Hope basin, including Sheep Mountain, Pilot Knob, Golden Horn and Vermillion Peak. To the west the skyline is dominated by Lizard Head's distinctive profile set against a backdrop of the high peaks of the San Miguel Range, including Mount Wilson (14,245-ft.), Gladstone Mountain (13,913-ft.) and Wilson Peak (14,017-ft.). Sunshine Mountain (12,930-ft.) towers above the beautiful emerald green expanse of Wilson Meadows to the north. In the distance to the northeast is the jagged profile of the Sneffels range.

The summit of Black Face Mountain is a good turn around point for hikers looking for a shorter day or if the weather is taking a turn for the worse.

Black Face to Junction with the Cross Mountain Trail

Segment Stat: 2.3 miles with a 600-ft. / -780-ft. elevation gain/loss
Distance - Trailhead to the Cross Mountain: 6.3 miles (one-way)
Elevation at Cross Mtn. Trail Junction: 12,080-ft.
Elevation Gain/Loss - Trailhead to Cross Mountain: 2,497-ft. / -780-ft.

To continue the loop follow the trail down the west side of the ridge to a saddle between the Wilson Creek and Lizard Head drainages, losing about 630-ft. From the saddle the trail ascends a rocky slope on moderate grades and then swings southwest, traversing high meadows to cross a ridge (12,080-ft.) jutting from Lizard Head's southern flank at 5.9 miles. From the saddle to the ridge the trail gains about 600-ft.

Hikers continuing along this segment of the trail are rewarded with amazing views of Lizard Head towering above the trail. The 13,113-ft. eroded volcanic plug was called, "one of the most difficult of Colorado's summits to reach," by Robert Ormes in his 1979 Guide to Colorado Mountains.

Anyone except the most experienced parties thinking about scaling the peak should heed Ormes' warning, "our advice when you reach the base, take [a] picture and go home."

Take a break at the top of the ridge to enjoy the spectacular views of the high peaks of the San Miguel Range. From the ridge top the trail loses about 150-ft. as it contours beneath Lizard Head to the junction with the Cross Mountain trail at 6.25-miles.

Optional Bilk Basin Overlook Extension

Distance from the Cross Mountain junction: 0.6 miles (RT)
Elevation of the Bilk Basin Overlook: 12,114-ft.
Elevation Gain to the Bilk Basin Overlook from the Junction: 180-ft.

A quick side trip to the Bilk Basin overlook is highly recommended if you have the time and energy. To reach the overlook from the Cross

Mountain junction, continue along the Lizard Head trail as it ascends northwest through rocky meadows to a saddle, 0.3 miles from the junction. This wonderful vantage point features panoramic views of Bilk Basin and the jagged peaks and ridges of the San Miguel Range, including Mount Wilson, Gladstone Peak and Wilson Peak, towering above the west side of the basin. After soaking in the views, return to the Cross Mountain trail junction (11,940-ft.).

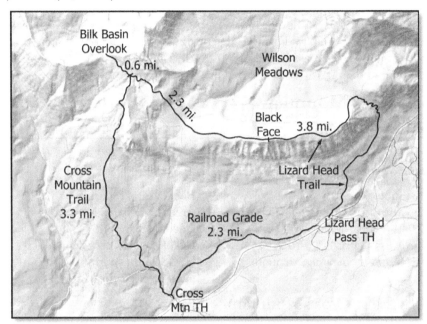

Cross Mountain and the Old Railroad Grade back to the Lizard Head Trailhead

Segment Stat: 5.6 miles from the junction of the Cross Mountain trail back to the Lizard Head trailhead using the Cross Mountain and old Railroad Grade trails.
Total Distance for the Loop Hike: 11.7 miles (loop)
Maximum Elevation: 11,940-ft.
Elevation Gain/Loss for the Loop: 2,900-ft. / -2,900-ft.

To complete the 11.7-mile loop, using the Cross Mountain trail and the old Railroad Grade route back to the Lizard Head Parking lot, head downhill on the Cross Mountain trail. The trail descends through meadows and spruce/fir forest, losing 1,900-ft in 3.25 miles as it drops to a parking area just off Highway 145. (For more information see the Cross Mountain trail description.)

Just before reaching the highway you will see a wide, unmarked trail/dirt road heading left (northeast) through open meadows. The wide path ascends on easy grades along an old railroad grade that essentially parallels Highway 145 for 2.25 miles back to the Lizard Head Pass parking area. (See the Railroad Grade route description for more information.)

Driving Directions

From Telluride: Drive south from Telluride on Colorado 145 for 12.3 miles to Lizard Head Pass. On the right (west) side of the highway is a rest area and interpretive site. Turn right into the rest area and park. The trailhead is located at the northeast end of the parking area. You can also park in a separate trailhead parking area by driving through the rest area (past the restroom) for approximately 1000-ft., then turn right onto a spur road that ends at the Lizard Head trailhead parking area.

33. Cross Mountain ★★★

Distance: 6.6 miles (RT)

A nice hike to the base of Lizard Head Peak, a distinctive 13,113-ft. rock spire towering above Highway 145 just south of Lizard Head Pass.

Distance: 6.6 miles (RT)	**Basecamp:** Telluride
Elevation: 10,040-ft. at Trailhead	**Area:** Lizard Head Wilderness,
11,940-ft. at Cross Mountain	Uncompahgre NF
Elevation Gain: 1,900-ft.	**Best Season:** July - September
Difficulty: moderately strenuous	**USGS Map(s):** Mt. Wilson
	See Page 137 for Map

Why Hike Cross Mountain

There are two main routes to the base of Lizard Head Peak (13,113-ft.), the landmark 400-ft. tall pinnacle in the Lizard Head Wilderness. Cross Mountain is the shorter and more direct, albeit less scenic, route when compared to the Lizard Head Trail.

The trail can either be done as an out-and-back hike or a loop combining the Lizard Head and the Railroad Grade trails on the return leg. The loop covers 11.7 miles of diverse terrain with a net elevation gain of over 2,700-ft.

Be aware the loop hike follows ridges and crosses high alpine meadows for over 4 miles. These areas are dangerous places to be in the event of a thunderstorm. Pick and nice day and get an early start so that you are down from the high country before the onset of afternoon thunder storms, a frequent occurrence on summer afternoons in the Rockies.

Trailhead to Junction with the Lizard Head Trail

Distance from Trailhead: 6.6 miles (RT)
Elevation at Junction: 11,940-ft.
Elevation Gain: 1,900-ft.

From the parking area the trail crosses a creek on a bridge and heads northwest, crossing a dirt track along the way. For the first half mile the Cross Mountain trail ascends through meadows with views to the east of the peaks and ridges around the Trout Lake area, including Sheep Mountain, Vermilion Peak, Golden Horn and Pilot Knob. At 0.4-miles pass the junction with the Groundhog Stock trail (heading left). Shortly after the junction the trail enters a spruce-fir forest with restricted views.

After 1.9 miles and an elevation gain of 1,200-ft., the trees give way to open meadows with ever improving views. Soon Lizard Head Peak comes into view along with the high peaks of the San Miguel Range, including Cross Mountain, Mt. Wilson and Gladstone Peak.

After climbing 1,900-ft. in 3.25 miles the trail arrives at the junction with the Lizard Head trail at the base of Lizard Head Peak, a distinctive 400-ft. rock spire. The 13,113-ft. peak, an old, eroded volcanic plug looming above the trail, is said to look like the gaping maw of a lizard with its face to the sky. From this vantage point it is hard to see the likeness.

Resist any temptation to climb the spire. Robert Ormes, publisher of one of the first guidebooks to the Colorado Mountains, issued the following warning about climbing the peak in his 1979 edition of the Guide to the Colorado Mountains:

"Lizard Head is the most difficult of Colorado summits to reach. In fact the rottenness of its 400-ft. tower makes safety too much a matter of luck for comfort. Returning visitors have formed the opinion that the peak has become noticeably rottener and more dangerous. Our advice when you reach the base, take [a] picture and go home."

After admiring the pinnacle many people will turn around and return to the trailhead.

Optional Bilk Basin Overlook Extension

Distance from Junction to Bilk Basin Overlook: 0.6 miles (RT)
Elevation at Bilk Basin Overlook: 12,114-ft.
Elevation Gain from Junction to Bilk Basin Overlook: 180-ft.

A quick side trip to the Bilk Basin overlook is highly recommended if you have the time and energy. To reach the overlook, turn left at the junction and follow the Lizard Head trail as it ascends northwest through rocky meadows to a saddle, 0.3 miles from the junction. This wonderful vantage point features panoramic views of Bilk Basin and the jagged peaks and ridges of the San Miguel Range, including Mount Wilson, Gladstone Peak and Wilson Peak, towering above the west side of the basin. After soaking in the views, return to the Cross Mountain trail junction.

Lizard Head and old Railroad Grade to Cross Mountain Trailhead

Segment Stats: 8.4 miles (one-way) with a 780-ft. elevation gain and 2,700-ft. elevation loss
Distance: 11.7 miles (loop)
Maximum Elevation: 12,147-ft.
Elevation Gain/Loss for the Loop: 2,900-ft. / -2,900-ft.

The hike can be turned into an 11.7-mile loop by taking a right at the Cross Mountain junction and following the Lizard Head trail to the top of Blackface Mountain in 2.4 miles. From here the trail descends to Lizard Head Pass on Highway 145 in 3.8 miles.

Complete the loop by walking west through the parking area to the road leading downhill toward the highway. Follow the road for a short distance. Just before the road reaches the highway you will see an unmarked trail heading right (southwest). Take this unsigned trail, which follows an old railroad grade paralleling the highway for 2.25 miles back to the Cross Mountain trailhead parking area. The total walking distance for the loop is 11.7 miles

Note: the views are better when the loop is done in reverse, starting at the Lizard Head Trail.

For more information see the Lizard Head and Railroad Grade route descriptions.

Driving Directions

From Telluride: Drive south from Telluride on Colorado 145 over Lizard Head Pass (12.5-miles). Continue south for 2.2 miles and turn right onto a dirt road signed for the Cross Mountain trailhead.

34. Old Railroad Grade ★★★

Distance: 2.25 miles (one-way)

The 2.25-mile unmarked Railroad Grade route, linking the Cross Mountain trailhead to the Lizard Head trailhead, enables hikers to complete a great 11.7 mile loop over Black Face Mountain to the base of the Lizard Head spire in the Lizard Head Wilderness. The walk may also be of interest to people looking for a nice easy stroll from the Lizard Head Pass parking area or the Cross Mountain trailhead.

Distance: 2.25 miles (one-way)
Elevation: 10,040-ft. at the trailhead
Maximum Elevation: 10,280-ft.
Elevation Gain: 240-ft.
Difficulty: easy

Basecamp: Telluride
Area: San Juan NF
Best Season: July - September
USGS Map(s): Mt. Wilson
See Page 137 for Map

Description of Old Railroad Grade Trail

One of the great hikes in the Telluride area is the 11.7-mile Lizard Head loop. The trail, which starts just off of Highway 145 at Lizard Head Pass, traverses the panoramic spine of Blackface Mountain on its way to the base of Lizard Head peak (13,113-ft.), an eroded 400-ft tall spire shaped like the gaping maw of a lizard with its face to the sky. At the base of Lizard Head the trail meets the Cross Mountain trail, which drops down to Highway 145 just over 2-miles southwest of the pass.

Hikers complete the loop by walking 2.25 miles back to the Lizard Head trailhead on the unmarked former railroad bed of the Rio Grande Southern Railroad. In its heyday the narrow gauge railroad linked Durango, Colorado to Ridgway, Colorado, crossing 10,222-ft Lizard Head Pass en route to Placerville and ultimately Ridgway over Dallas Divide. The railroad ceased operation in 1951.

Hikers descending the Cross Mountain trail seeking to return to the Lizard Head trailhead should look for a wide, dirt path leading left (northeast) about 0.1 miles before the Cross Mountain trailhead parking area. Follow the unmarked path through meadows as it swings away from the highway to avoid a small drainage. Red metal markers, warning people not to dig in the area due to buried high voltage power lines, appear at intervals along the first half of the route.

The trail ascends gently, essentially paralleling the highway and offering nice views of Black Face Mountain and the peaks around Trout Lake, including Sheep Mountain, Vermilion Peak, Golden Horn and Pilot Knob. As you progress the dirt route turns to grass, but the way is always clear. At 0.9 miles skirt a metal barrier across the trail intended to block further vehicle access.

In slightly over a mile from the start the trail levels out and only experiences minor ups and downs for the remainder of the walk. Shortly after this point the trail swings toward the highway and stays about 75-yards from the artery until you reach the access road to the Lizard Head Pass parking area. Walk up the access road to where you left your vehicle.

For more information on the loop trail see the Lizard Head and Cross Mountain trail descriptions.

Driving Directions

From Telluride to the Lizard Head Trailhead: Drive south from Telluride on Colorado 145 for 12.3 miles to Lizard Head Pass. On the right (west) side of the highway is a rest area and interpretive site. Turn right into the rest area and park. To find the unmarked trailhead walk to the southwest end of the parking area and proceed down the access road toward the highway. The trail takes off to the right about 100 yards before the road meets Highway 145.

From Telluride to the Cross Mountain Trailhead: Drive south from Telluride on Colorado 145 over Lizard Head Pass (12.5-miles). Continue south for 2.2 miles and turn right onto a dirt road signed for the Cross Mountain trailhead. Walk up the Cross Mountain trail for about 0.1 miles and look for a wide, unmarked dirt track heading right (northeast). This is the railroad grade route.

35. Navajo Lake Trail ★★★★

Distance: 9.2 miles (RT)

This popular hike climbs through forest and meadows to a stark alpine lake basin surrounded by high peaks in the Lizard Head Wilderness.

Distance: 9.2 miles (RT)
Elevation: 9,320-ft. at Trailhead
11,154-ft. at Navajo Lake
Elevation Gain: 1,834-ft.
Difficulty: moderately strenuous

Basecamp: Telluride
Area: Lizard Head Wilderness,
San Juan NF
Best Season: July - September
USGS Map(s): Dolores Peak

Why Navajo Lake

The West Dolores River originates at the head of Navajo Basin, a stark elongate glacial bowl lined by steep 13,000-ft. peaks and ridges. Gladstone Peak (13,913-ft.) dominates the head of the basin while El Diente (14,159-ft.) and Mount Wilson (14,017) soar above the bowl's south ridge. Wilson Peak (14,246-ft.) serves as the terminus for the basin's northern wall.

Nestled deep in the lower end of the basin is scenic Navajo Lake (11,154-ft.). The trail to the lake climbs the broad valley formed by the West Dolores River before steeply ascending to the lake. En route the trail travels through forests, passes waterfalls and traverses beautiful, wildflower-filled meadows with good views of Dolores Peak (13,290-ft.) and El Diente.

You'll not be alone on the trail. Navajo Lake is a popular destination for day hikers, backpackers and climbers. Peak baggers use the lake as a base camp to summit the nearby fourteeners. If you do not mind company, a hike to the lake is well worth the effort.

Trailhead to Kilpacker Trail Junction

Distance from Trailhead: 2.2 miles (one-way)
Elevation at Junction: 10,190-ft.
Elevation Gain: 870-ft.

There are two access routes to Navajo Lake from the south, the Navajo Lake Trail and the Kilpacker Trail, which meet and share the final 2.4 miles to the lake. The Navajo Lake trail is shorter and the lower portion of the trail is more scenic. The Kilpacker trail starts higher (10,060-ft.) and does not involve as much elevation gain. (See the Kilpacker Trail description in this guide for more information.)

From the Navajo Lake trailhead (see driving directions below) follow the trail up the right (east) side of the West Dolores River past the Groundhog trail, which heads left (west) on a footbridge crossing the River. In less than a mile the Navajo Lake Trail crosses to the west side of the river on a bridge.

The trail now climbs above the river on moderate grades, traveling through wildflower-filled meadows and intermittent groves of mixed conifers. Views from the meadows include Dolores Peak (13,290-ft.) to the northwest and El Diente (14,159-ft.) to the east. After gaining 870-ft. in a little over 2.2 miles the trail meets the Kilpacker trail (coming in from the east) in a large meadow. The junction is marked with a small sign.

Kilpacker Junction to Navajo Lake

Segment Stat: 2.4 miles (one-way) with a 964-ft. elevation gain
Distance - Trailhead to Navajo Lake: 9.2 miles (RT)
Elevation Navajo Lake: 11,154-ft.
Elevation Gain - Trailhead to Navajo Lake: 1,834-ft.

Beyond the junction the trail ascends, steeply at times, through forest and meadows toward the head of the valley. The meadows offer nice views to the northeast of El Diente's rust-colored western ridge and the ridge defining Navajo Basin's northern wall.

At 3.1 miles the trail starts a steep climb up the valley's north wall. The trail breaks from the trees at 3.4 miles and ascends a series of steep switchbacks through meadows sprinkled with wildflowers and dispersed groups of trees to the junction with the Woods Lake trail at 4.0 miles, gaining 870-ft. over 0.9 miles. Turn right (east) at the signed junction toward Navajo Lake.

The trail climbs slightly, then drops 160-ft. and then climbs again to reach the western shore of Navajo Lake (11,154-ft) at 4.6 miles. The lake sits in a stark basin ringed by steep, rugged ridges. Gladstone Peak (13,913) rises above the headwall at the eastern end of the basin. El Diente (14,159-ft.) and Mount Wilson loom above the basin's south rim, hidden from view by steep scree slopes. Wilson Peak (14,017) anchors the head of the basin's northern wall but is also concealed from view.

This is the end of the day hike for most people. Backpackers camping at the lake and day hikers with excess energy (and good weather) can continue on the trail along the north side of the lake. Beyond the lake the trail climbs talus slopes to reach the upper end of the basin where it turns left (northwest) and climbs switchbacks up to the Rock of Ages saddle (13,000-ft.) and the junction with the new Rock of Ages trail, gaining 1,846-ft. in 2.4 miles. Total round trip from the Navajo Lake trailhead to the saddle is 14.0 miles.

Driving Directions

From Telluride: Drive south from Telluride on Colorado 145 for 17.9 miles and turn right onto the Dunton Road (#207). The turnoff is located 5.4 miles south of Lizard Head Pass. The narrow gravel and dirt road ascends the hillside on a switchback and then traverses the northeast side of the Coal Creek drainage, crossing the creek in a little under 4 miles.

Continue on the Dunton Road and turn right (north) at the marked entrance for the Navajo Lake trailhead (7 miles from the intersection with Colorado 145). The turn off is located just beyond a sharp left curve in the road. Drive 0.1 miles to the parking area.

36. Kilpacker Trail to Navajo Lake ★★★
Distance: 11.5 miles (RT)

This alternative route travels through forest and then joins the Navajo Lake trail, a popular hike to a pretty alpine lake basin surrounded by high peaks. The combined route involves less elevation gain then the Navajo Lake trail but is 2.6 miles (RT) longer.

Distance: 11.8 miles (RT) to Navajo Lake
Elevation: 10,060-ft. at Trailhead 11,154-ft. at Navajo Lake
Elevation Gain: 1,094-ft. to Navajo Lake
Difficulty: moderately strenuous

Basecamp: Telluride
Area: Lizard Head Wilderness, San Juan NF
Best Season: July - September
USGS Map(s): Dolores Peak
See Page 145 for Map

Why Hike the Kilpacker Trail to Navajo Lake

There are two access routes to the Navajo Lake basin from the south, the Navajo Lake trail and the Kilpacker trail. The two trails meet and share the final 2.4 miles of the Navajo Lake trail to the lake.

The Kilpacker trail starts higher (10,060-ft. versus 9,320-ft.) and does not involve as much elevation gain, but is longer adding 1.3 miles to the one way distance. (The Kilpacker Trail replaces the initial 2.2 miles of the Navajo Lake trail with a 3.5 mile segment.) It should be noted that the Kilpacker trail loses elevation to reach the Navajo Lake trail junction, making the net elevation difference about 520-ft.

Views on the Navajo Lake trail are better, steadily improving as you climb. The Kilpacker trailhead, located in a large meadow to the west of Morgan Camp, initially features great views of the surrounding peaks as it heads northwest through the meadows. At 0.6 miles the trail enters a mixed conifer forest with only occasional views until it meets the Navajo Lake trail.

Trailhead to Junction with Navajo Lake Trail

Distance from Trailhead: 3.5 miles (one-way)
Elevation at Junction: 10,190-ft.
Elevation Gain/Loss: 404-ft. / -274-ft.

The Kilpacker trail starts at a large sign board in the meadow west of Morgan Camp (see driving directions below). Follow the trail as it gently climbs west/northwest through meadows and enters a mixed conifer forest.

The easy walk through the forest traverses an undulating landscape in and out of minor drainages. At 2.3 miles reach a trail junction and turn left (west) on the Kilpacker trail. (The trail continuing straight ahead leads to Kilpacker Basin and is used by climbers to reach El Diente and Wilson Peaks.)

The trail now drops through trees and intermittent meadows, losing 274-ft. over the 0.9 miles on its way to the West Dolores River. Cross the river on logs and follow the trail uphill for 0.2 miles to the signed junction with the Navajo Lake trail. Turn right (north) toward the lake basin.

Junction to Navajo Lake

Segment Stat: 2.4 miles (one-way) with a 964-ft. elevation gain
Distance - Trailhead to Navajo Lake: 11.8 miles (RT)
Elevation Navajo Lake: 11,154-ft.
Elevation Gain - Trailhead to Navajo Lake: 1,094-ft.

Beyond the junction the trail ascends, steeply at times, through forest and meadows toward the head of the valley. The meadows offer nice views to the northeast of El Diente's rust-colored western ridge and the ridge defining Navajo Basin's northern wall.

At 4.4 miles the trail starts a steep climb up the valley's north wall. The trail breaks from the trees at 4.7 miles and ascends a series of steep switchbacks through meadows sprinkled with wildflowers and dispersed groups of trees to the junction with the Woods Lake trail at 5.3 miles, gaining 870-ft. over 0.9 miles. Turn right (east) at the signed junction toward Navajo Lake.

The trail climbs slightly, then drops 160-ft. and then climbs again to reach the western shore of Navajo Lake (11,154-ft) at 5.9 miles. The lake sits in a stark basin ringed by steep, rugged ridges. Gladstone Peak (13,913) rises above the headwall at the eastern end of the basin. El Diente (14,159-ft.) and Mount Wilson loom above the basin's south rim, hidden from view by steep scree slopes. Wilson Peak (14,017) anchors the head of the basin's northern wall but is also concealed from view.

This is the end of the day hike for most people. Backpackers camping at the lake and day hikers with excess energy (and good weather) can continue on the trail along the north side of the lake. Beyond the lake the trail climbs talus slopes to reach the upper end of the basin where it turns left (northwest) and climbs switchbacks up to the Rock of Ages saddle (13,000-ft.) and the junction with the new Rock of Ages trail, gaining 1,846-ft. in 2.4 miles. Total round trip from the Kilpacker trailhead to the saddle is 16.6 miles.

Driving Directions

From Telluride: Drive south from Telluride on Colorado 145 for 17.9 miles and turn right onto the Dunton Road (#207). The turnoff is located 5.4 miles south of Lizard Head Pass. The gravel and dirt road ascends the hillside on a switchback and then traverses the northeast side of the Coal Creek drainage, crossing the creek in a little under 4 miles.

To reach the Kilpacker Trailhead follow the Dunton Road from the intersection with Colorado 145 for a 5.1 miles. Just past Morgan Camp watch for a dirt road on your right (north side of the road). Turn right and follow the road a short distance past a group of trees to an obvious parking area. The trailhead, designated with a large information board, is located to the west of the parking area.

38. Liberty Bell/Marshall Basin ★★★★

Distance: 6.2 - 10.6 miles (loop)

This lightly traveled trail climbs steeply to Liberty Bell basin and a scenic ridge. Extend the hike by descending through Marshall Basin, scattered with mining ruins, on an off trail route to the Tomboy Mine and ghost town. Complete the loop by walking the Tomboy Road back to town.

Distance: 7.2 miles (RT) to Liberty Basin and Divide
6.0 miles (one way) to Marshall Basin/Tomboy Mine
10.6 miles (loop) to Telluride
Elevation: 8,880-ft. at Trailhead
12,575-ft. at Liberty Basin Divide
11,400-ft. at Marshall Basin/Tomboy Mine
8,800-ft. at Telluride
Elevation Gain: 3,695-ft. to Liberty Basin Divide
-1,175-ft. to Marshall Basin/Tomboy Mine
-2,520-ft. to Telluride

Difficulty: strenuous
Basecamp: Telluride
Area: Uncompahgre NF
Best Season: July - September
USGS Map(s): Telluride
See Page 110 for Map

Why Hike Liberty Bell / Marshall Basins

This varied hike, off the beaten track, offers walkers a good workout, great views and an opportunity to see ruins of the two top producing mining operations in the Upper San Miguel Mining District – the Smuggler-Union and Tomboy mines.

From downtown Telluride a good trail with limited views climbs steeply to Liberty Bell basin. For the first mile the trail travels along the Tomboy Road and the Jud Wiebe Trail. Beyond this point you will see few people until you reach the Tomboy Mine.

At the foot of the basin a steep trail ascends to the ridge separating the Liberty Bell and Marshall basins. As you climb to the ridge enjoy great views of Greenback Mountain (12,997-ft.), Mount Emma (13,581-ft.), the Saint Sophia ridge and, in the distance, the high peaks of the Lizard Head Wilderness. Atop the ridge views extend down the length of the Marshall Basin. Savage Basin and the road snaking to Imogene Pass are visible to the southeast.

Hikers comfortable with off-trail route finding can extend the hike by heading down the east side of the ridge into the Marshall Basin where the discovery of the Smuggler Vein in 1875 led to the formation of the Smuggler-Union mine in 1887-1889. Today remnants of the large mining operation are scatter about the valley.

The off-trail route soon connects with old mining roads that descend the basin and intersect the Tomboy Road just below the Tomboy Mine. A short walk up the Tomboy Road leads to the substantial ruins of the Tomboy Mine at the foot of Savage Basin. About 900 people lived and worked at the mine during the late 1800's to early 1900's. Wander a further half mile up the road to see a ghost town and more mining structures.

The loop trail returns to Telluride along the Tomboy Road. The ruins of interesting mining structures along with great views of the Savage Basin, Bridal Veil Basin and Falls, the Bear Creek Valley and the town of Telluride will help you to forget you are walking along a road back to town.

Be advised that the off-trail section of the loop descends very steep grass and talus slopes. When passing through the basin please view the mine ruins from a distance. Exploring tailings, mine shafts and unstable building is extremely dangerous. The ruins of the Tomboy Townsite are on private property, please do not trespass.

Trailhead to Liberty Basin and Divide

Distance from Trailhead: 3.6 miles (one-way) / 7.2 miles (RT)
Elevation at the Divide: 12,575-ft.
Elevation Gain: 3,695-ft.

From the north end of Oak Street (see driving directions below), turn right (east) on the Tomboy Road and walk up the jeep road for 0.4 miles to the Jud Wiebe Trail (eastern trailhead) on the left (north) side of the road. There is a metal gate and a sign board marking the trail.

Turn left (northwest) on the Jud Wiebe Trail (#432) and follow the broad dirt track as it climbs steep switchbacks up the north side of the Telluride Valley, passing the town's water storage tanks. The trail initially ascends through meadows with nice views of Telluride and the ski area across the valley before entering the forest.

After walking about a mile the grade abates as the trail enters the Cornet Creek Valley and soon reaches a signed junction at Liberty Bell Flats. Here the Jud Wiebe Trail branches left (west). We bear right (northeast) on the Liberty Bell Trail (#870). After a short stint through a pretty glade of aspens the steep climb resumes up the east side of the Cornet Valley.

The trail, actually an old road, travels through trees, crosses a creek and arrives at an unsigned junction at 1.8 miles. Keep right at the intersection to stay on the Liberty Bell trail. The track to the left provides access to the Stillwell Tunnel which channels water to the storage tanks passed earlier.

At 2.0 miles pass the remains of an old cabin and other structures on the left. Beyond the ruins the trail climbs a switchback and then crosses a meadow with views of the peaks towering above the head the Telluride valley. Wilson Peak (14,017-ft.), Mount Wilson (14,246-ft.), El Diente (14,159-ft.), Sunshine Mountain (12,930-ft.) and Lizard Head (13,113-ft.) in the Lizard Head Wilderness fill the skyline to the southwest.

The views are short lived. Soon the trail plunges back into the trees and continues its relentless climb, crossing a minor ridge along the way. Occasional openings in the trees offer glimpses of the peaks rimming the Cornet Valley.

At 2.7 miles the trail turns right (east/southeast) and climbs steeply up a series switchbacks, reaching Liberty Bell basin at 3.1 miles. Here the trees give way to meadows with great views of Greenback Mountain (12,997-ft.) and Mount Emma (13,581-ft.) rising above the head of the Cornet valley. The jagged profile of the St. Sophia Ridge, extending southeast from Mt. Emma, dominates the view to the north.

As you enter the basin the road curves to the right (south). Here you will see a trail heading east (essentially straight ahead) and climbing the basin to the ridge separating Liberty Bell Basin and Marshall Basin. A large rock cairn marks the intersection.

If time and energy allow, I recommend hiking to the ridge. The trail initially ascends along the north side of a line of trees and then curve to the left as it climbs through pretty alpine meadows dotted with wildflowers. At 3.5 miles the trail hits the scree slopes beneath the ridge and arcs to the right. Exercise care where the narrow trail crosses a few small landslides.

Reach the top of the ridge 3.6 miles. Here terrific views extend northwest toward Mt. Emma. Dallas Peak (13,741-ft.) rises to the west. The peaks of the Lizard Head Wilderness dominate the view to the southwest. On the east side of the pass views extend down the length of the Marshall Basin. To the southeast is Savage Basin and the road to Imogene Pass.

At this point parties can turn around and retrace their steps back to Telluride for a 7.2 mile round-trip hike or descend the Marshall Basin to the Tomboy Mine and then walk back to Telluride along the Tomboy Road. If you like old mine sites and mining ruins your will love the Marshall Basin and the Tomboy mine. The walk, which includes an off trail segment with very steep grades, also includes great views of the Marshall and Savage basins and the Telluride box canyon. The final segment travels along the Tomboy Road, which is not heavily traveled, especially if you avoid the weekends.

To Marshall Basin and the Tomboy Mine

Distance from Trailhead: 6.0 miles (one way)
Elevation at Tom Boy Mine: 11,400-ft.
Elevation Gain: -1,175-ft.

In 1875 John Fallon discovered what is now known as the Smuggler Vein in the upper Marshall Basin. The next year J.B. Ingram and two others staked a claimed called the Smuggler in the lower section of the basin. The mines along the Smuggler Vein claim consolidated to form the Smuggler-Union Mining Co. twelve years later. These mines, along with the Tomboy Gold Mine in neighboring Savage Basin, were the top producing companies in the San Miguel Mining district until the claims played out in the 1920's.

The second half of this loop hike descends through the Marshall Basin, passing the ruins of these mining operations. From the ridge follow the boot beaten path heading northeast along scree clad slopes into Marshall Basin. Use care on the short sections of the trail that cross minor slide areas.

Soon the rocky slopes give way to meadows and the walking is easier. As you look ahead you will see the trail climbing the scree slopes to the north as the trail heads for Virginus Pass, a small notch on the ridge. This pass leads to Governor's Basin, accessed from Ouray along the Yankee Boy basin road.

After 0.25 miles the trail crosses two small drainages. Ahead you will see the trail start to climb toward the head of the basin. I typically leave the trail here and descend about 100-ft before crossing to the east side of the Marshall Basin.

(Note: There are vestiges of a trail dropping down the west side of the Marshall Basin. In the past I have found parts of this route obliterated by slides/avalanches. I now prefer the route described below.)

Once on the east side of the drainage descend the basin on very steep grassy slopes, skirting the mine tailings and talus fields in the middle of the basin. The goal is to drop down to the next level of the basin and then cross back to the west side of the valley between the two huge tailings piles scattered with mine debris.

As you descend you will see a white cement drainage ditch built to control runoff from the defunct mines. Cross to the west side of the basin above this ditch, selecting a route that avoids crossing tailings piles and other debris. Now descend the west side of the basin, staying to the right (west) of the cement drainage ditch until you hit an old road.

Follow the road down the basin, past more tailing piles and mine ruins. At 4.6 miles the road crosses the cement ditch. On the other side of the ditch follow a gravel road that curves to the left (east) and soon crosses a stream. On the other side of the sream turn right (southeast) on a gravel road and follow the road as it descending along the east side of the basin to meet the Tomboy Road at 5.8 miles, just below the Tomboy Mine. This section of the hike will pass the remains of interesting mining structures including the ruins of the tramway.

Turn left (east) on the Tomboy road and walk a short distance up the road to the substantial ruins of the Tomboy mine at 6.0 miles, located at the foot of Savage Basin. During the mine's heyday in the late 1800's and early 1900's, about 900 people lived and worked at the mine. When the ore ran out in 1927 the town went bust and was soon abandoned.

Ghost town enthusiasts will want to wander a half mile up the road to see the remains of the ghost town and more mining structures. Beyond the last structures the road climbs to Imogene Pass (13,114-ft.), a total distance of 2.2 miles from the main ruins at the foot of the basin.

Tomboy Mine to Telluride

Distance from Trailhead: 10.6 miles (loop)
Ending Elevation: 8,800-ft.
Elevation Gain: -2,520-ft.

When you are done exploring the mine follow the Tomboy Road back to Telluride. There is some traffic on the road. A few Telluride tour operators run half day tours to the Tomboy Mine and Imogene Pass. Skilled 4WD enthusiasts like to drive the rough road over Imogene Pass, typically starting in Telluride and ending in Ouray. Most like to get over Imogene Pass early in the day to beat any afternoon thunderstorms, which can make the road impassable. As such, traffic tends to be lighter in the afternoon when most hikers will be completing this portion of the loop.

From the mine the road descends to Telluride on moderate to easy grades, traveling above the north side of Savage Creek. At 6.7 miles you will see an old cabin perched above the north side of the road. Beyond the cabin the road crosses a bridge over Marshall Creek and then head southwest high above the north side of Marshall Creek. Ruins and debris of an old tramway are visible below the road. Behind you are nice views up Savage Basin.

At 6.9 miles pass the Bullion Tunnel and the remnants of the Smuggler-Union mine, which includes the ruins of a crusher house and a multistory boarding house, which has now slid down the hill. Nearby are two large boilers, pipes and cables from the tramway that once carried ore to the Pandora Mill, located in the Telluride Valley.

As you continue down the road nice views open to Bridal Veil Falls and the Bridal Veil Basin at the head of Telluride's box canyon.

At 7.6 miles the trail curves to the right (west), leaving the Marshall Creek Valley and now travels high above the north side of the Telluride valley.

Pass through a tunnel on the road at 7.9 miles. This is a popular spot for photographers.

Beyond the tunnel the road curves into and out of Rover Gulch. Near the head of the gulch are some nice waterfalls cascading down the cliffs above the road. As the road exits the gulch it heads down two long switchbacks. Across the valley to the south are nice views of Bear Creek Valley. Behind you views stretch southeast to Bridal Veil Falls and the peaks rising above the head of the Telluride Valley.

The final section of the trail descends along the road above the town, passing the Jud Wiebe trail junction at 10.2 miles and reaching the top of Oak Street at 10.6 miles.

Driving Directions

From Telluride: Note: Free day-use parking in Telluride is available in the Carhenge Lot just off West Pacific Avenue at the west end of town near the base of Lift 7. Day use parking for larger vehicles is available in the parking lot at the south end of Mahoney Drive near the west entrance to town. A free shuttle bus, called the Galloping Goose, runs between the parking lots and various stops in downtown Telluride.

There is also free parking in the mountain village lot. From there you can take the free gondola into town and easily walk to the trailhead.

Walking Directions: From Telluride's main street (Colorado Avenue), turn north onto Aspen Street and proceed one block. Turn right (east) onto Columbia Avenue and proceed one block. Turn left (north) onto Oak Street and walk to the end of the street. Turn right (east) on the Tomboy Road, a good dirt road.

38. Swamp Canyon ★★★★
Distance: 6.0 – 7.6 miles (RT)

Waterfalls, wildflowers and stunning views are the rewards for hikers making the stiff climb up Swamp Canyon to a high bench nestled below Ulysses S. Grant Peak. Extend the hike to Grant-Swamp Pass for breathtaking views of the Ice Lake area.

Distance: 6.0 miles (RT) to Scenic Bench
7.6 miles (RT) to Grant-Swamp Pass
Elevation: 10,130-ft. at Trailhead
11,660-ft. at Scenic Bench
12,910-ft. at Grant-Swamp Pass
Elevation Gain: 1,530-ft. to Scenic Bench
2,780-ft. to Grant-Swamp Pass
Difficulty: moderately strenuous, strenuous to the pass

Basecamp: Telluride
Area: Uncompahgre NF
Best Season: July - September
USGS Map(s): Ophir

Why Hike Swamp Canyon

The town of Ophir Valley to the south of Telluride is off the radar of most hikers yet the area is quite scenic with soaring peaks rising above lovely meadows and crystal clear streams. Trailheads aren't well marked and the paths can be sketchy in places. Determined hikers willing to seek out these elusive trails will be well rewarded for their efforts.

The Swamp Canyon trail is a case in point. Finding the trailhead and keeping on track for the first mile can be challenging if you aren't paying attention. Beyond that point the trail climbs through forest and then scenic meadows high above the west side of Swamp Canyon. Along the way you will see few if any hikers.

As you emerge from the trees views open to V3 (13,528-ft.), Ulysses S. Grant Peak (13,767-ft.) and Peak 13309 towering above the head of the canyon. Soon South Lookout Peak (13,357-ft.) joins the scene. Below the trail along the valley floor, wet meadows and ponds that give the trail its name, come into view.

As the trail curves around the head of the valley is ascends to a bench clad in gorgeous meadows awash in wildflowers. Three waterfalls tumble down the rugged slopes of Ulysses S. Grant Peak. The area is truly breathtaking and will cause you to pause often to soak in the scene.

For many hikers the bench is the perfect destination. Experienced hikers comfortable on shifting talus and looking for a challenge can climb the very steep and rocky trail to the upper basin. The last 0.2 miles involves a scramble up extremely steep and unstable scree slopes to Grant-Swamp Pass. This section of the trail is not for the faint hearted gaining over 1,200-ft in 0.8 miles.

Trailhead to the Scenic Bench

Distance from Trailhead: 6.0 miles (round trip)
Elevation at Bench: 11,660-ft.
Elevation Gain: 1,530-ft.

Note: Hikers without a high clearance or 4WD vehicle should add 1.2 miles to the round trip distance.

The Swamp Canyon trail starts about 0.6 miles past the Ophir Pass sign on the Ophir Road/Forest Road #630, just to the east of a large avalanche chute channeling a stream. (See driving directions below.) Here a two-track on the right (south) side of the Ophir Road heads southeast. Follow the two-track as it descends the hillside. After walking a little over 0.1 miles bear right to stay on the road. Soon you will hit a flooded section of the two-track. Bypass the water by walking above the left (east) side of the road.

Continue the descent to an area that appears to have been cleared by a bull dozer. Ahead a creek cuts across the remnants of the road. Turn right at the creek and follow the creek downhill to where it hits Howard Creek.

Cross Howard Creek by wading or rock-hopping. On the south side of Howard Creek is a well-defined dirt/gravel road. Ascend the forested road up the south side of the valley, initially on moderate grades. At 0.3 miles the road crosses under electrical lines and soon reaches a green gate with a trail marker.

Beyond the gate the road climbs steeply up three switchbacks (making a left, a right and a left). At 0.7 miles, at the end last switchback, the road reaches an intersection. At 0.7 miles come to an intersection of sorts. To the right is the continuation of the road, overgrown and blocked by a branch. Straight ahead is a good boot beaten trail. Continue heading east on the boot beaten trail through viewless forest.

At 0.9 miles come to an unmarked junction. Bear right on the trail climbing the hillside. A short distance beyond is a second junction. Again take the right (southeast/south) branch ascending the hillside. Make note of both of these unmarked intersections so that you turn the correct way on the return to the trailhead.

At 1.3 miles reach an unmarked four-way junction. Turn right (southwest) and climb steep switchbacks up timbered slopes. Soon the trail curves to the left (south) and starts ascending on a diagonal along the western slopes of the Swamp Canyon.

At 1.6 miles the trees begin the thin and the grade moderates a bit. Soon we are passing through intermittent meadows with views of V3 (13,528-ft.), Ulysses S. Grant Peak (13,767-ft.) and Peak 13,309 towering above the head of the valley.

At 1.8 miles we travel through a large meadow scattered with small conifers. Below the trail the valley floor of the appropriately named Swamp Canyon is littered with ponds and wet meadows. Ahead are stunning views of the rugged cirque at the head of the valley, anchored by V3 and Ulysses S. Grant massif to the west and South Lookout Peak (13,357-ft.) to the east. Turn around for fine views of Silver Mountain's multi-hued ridge rimming the north side of the Ophir Valley. Look carefully to see the Blixt Trail, an old mining road, switchbacking up the ridge's very steep slopes to the left of Chapman Gulch.

At 2.1 miles we temporarily lose the views as the path enters clusters of trees interspersed with small meadows littered with skunk cabbage and wildflowers. A short distance beyond we pass a campsite site amid the trees.

Beyond the campsite the trail emerges from the trees and views open to a small valley along the west side of V3. The path soon crosses a creek and curves to the left (southeast), climbing the talus slopes around the end of a ridge extending north from V3. Beautiful cluster of columbines grow amid the rocks. Great views extend north down the length of the Swamp Canyon Valley to the colorful ridge defining the north side of the Ophir valley. Ahead views open to the lovely high basin at the head of the valley.

At 2.7 miles the grade abates as the trail reaches the western end of a stunning bench set beneath the south-facing flanks of V3 and Ulysses S. Grant Peak. During early to mid-July the bench is clad in emerald green meadows filled with wildflowers. Three waterfalls cascade down the rugged slopes above the bench. To the north Silver Mountain forms the backdrop for Swamp Canyon. Progress will be slow as you wander through the breathtaking scene.

The easy walk across the bench ends at 3.0 miles where the trail starts climbing toward the upper basin and the Grant-Swamp Pass. For many hikers the meadows are a perfect destination to eat lunch and take in the incredible views before returning to the trailhead..

To Grant-Swamp Pass

Segment Stat: 0.8 miles (one-way) with a 1,250-ft. elevation gain
Distance - Trailhead to Pass: 7.6 miles (RT)
Elevation at Pass: 12,910-ft.
Elevation Gain - Trailhead to Pass: 2,780-ft.

Experienced hikers who are fit, well acclimated and comfortable on very steep, unstable scree slopes many want to continue to the upper basin and the Grant-Swamp Pass. You should not underestimate the difficulty of the next segment that gains over 1,200-ft in 0.8 miles.

From the end of the bench the trail climbs very steep rocky slopes, marked with cairns. After about 0.5 miles the grade eases for a short distance to reach a point below the base of the pass. From here it is an extremely steep scramble up loose talus slopes to the pass. Cairns and a thin trail mark the way.

As you crest the pass at 3.8 miles gorgeous views open to the Ice Lakes area and beyond. Island Lake, with its distinctive rock island, lies nestled in the basin beneath the pass. Pilot Knob, Golden Horn, Vermillion Peak and Fuller Peak form the dramatic cirque surrounding the upper Ice Lake Basin. Fuller Lake is seen cradled beneath Fuller Peak. Closer at hand Ulysses S. Grant Peak looms above the pass to the west while South Lookout Peak towers above the pass to the northeast.

When you are done taking in the views, carefully descend from the pass and retrace your steps to the trailhead.

Driving Directions

From Telluride: Drive south from Telluride on Colorado 145 S for 7.3 miles and then turn left (east) onto the Ophir Road (Forest Service Road #630). Continue on the Ophir Road for 2.8 miles. At 2.1 miles you will need to bear right to stay on route and at 2.7 miles turn right to stay on the Ophir Road. A short distance beyond (0.1 miles) is a sign for Ophir Pass and a second sign warning that further travel requires a 4WD.

Typically a high clearance vehicle can make it to the trailhead. 4WD is required if the road is wet. Parties without a high clearance or 4WD should park off the road near the Ophir Pass sign and walk to the trailhead. This will add 1.2 miles to the round-trip distance.

Ascend the rough 4WD for 0.6 miles and find a place to park off the road either before or after the large avalanche chute channeling a creek.

There are several pullouts in the area. Just past the avalanche chute (the east side of the chute), look for a two-track road branching right (south/southeast). This road is the starting point for the hike.

Some parties with high clearance 4WD vehicles try to drive a short distance down the two-track. This is not advisable. The road is often flooded and impassable to vehicles.

39. Ajax Peak ★★★★
Distance: 5.6 miles (RT)

Stunning, birds-eye-views of the high peaks of the Telluride area are the reward for hikers making the steep climb to the summit of Ajax Peak.

Distance: 5.6 miles (RT)
Elevation: 10,310-ft. at Trailhead
12,785-ft. at Ajax Peak
Elevation Gain: 2,475-ft.
Difficulty: strenuous

Basecamp: Telluride
Area: Uncompahgre NF
Best Season: July - September
USGS Map(s): Telluride

Why Hike to Ajax Peak

Iconic Ajax Peak towers above the eastern end of Telluride's box canyon. When looking up at the peak from downtown Telluride it is hard to believe that a hikers trail reaches the summit. Fortunately the Bridal Veil Road snakes its way up the canyon's head wall, climbing 1,300-ft. as it ascends to the power plant atop the wall. From here a stiff climb up a section of the Black Bear Road leads to a trail ascending steep switchbacks to the summit of Ajax Peak, gaining almost 2,500-ft. in 2.8 miles.

Hikers are rewarded for their efforts with stunning 360-degree views from atop the peak. Here stunning views extend to the summits and ridges ringing the Marshall Basin, the Savage Creek Valley, Ingram Basin and Bridal Veil Basin. In the distance are the high peaks of the Mount Sneffels and Lizard Head Wildernesses. Telluride lies cradled in the valley to the west while the ruins of the Tom Boy Mine are visible at the base of the peak's north slopes.

This trail is not recommended for anyone with a fear of heights or any discomfort when climbing steep trails to dizzying heights. A 4WD is recommended for reach the trailhead at the top of the Bridal Veil road. Check at the Telluride Visitor Center for current road conditions.

Trailhead to Ajax Peak

The trail mileage in this description assumes you park at the end of the Bridal Veil Road high above the east side of Telluride (see driving directions below). Add 4.0 miles to the round-trip distance and 1,300-ft. in elevation gain for the hike if parking at the 2WD lot near the Pandora Mine.

Near the end of the Bridal Veil Road is an intersection with the Black Bear Road marked with a sign reading, "One Way Only, Do Not Enter." (The Black Bear Road is a very difficult 4WD road that begins off Highway 550, south of Ouray, Colorado.) Ascend the Black Bear Road on a series of steep switchbacks, passing the ruins of the Black Bear Mill and Ingram Falls. Beyond the falls the road curves around a very tight switchback called "Adios Corner" and then climbs a series of rock slabs known as "The Steps" alongside a creek cascading down the gully to the right of the road. This is considered one of the most difficult parts of the road for vehicles.

After 1.1 miles you will see mining cables overhead. The trail to Ajax peak, marked with a rock cairn, starts on the left (north) side of the road between the second and third cable. The narrow, but well-defined trail ascends steeply through meadows on long switchbacks. As you gain elevation enjoy ever improving views to the east/southeast of Peak 13,510-ft. and Trico Peak (13,321-ft.) rising above Ingram Basin. Ballard Mountain (12,804-ft.) towers above Silver Lake to the southwest. Soon Lizard Head (13,113-ft.), Wilson Peak (14,017-ft.) and Mount Wilson (14,246-ft.) in the Lizard Head Wilderness are seen in the distance to the west.

After 2.2 miles the trail crosses scree covered slopes. Ignore any faint trails you see branching to the left. Instead stay on the main trail heading east.

Reach the top of the ridge at 2.6 miles. As you crest the ridge terrific views open to the high peaks rimming the north side of Savage Creek and the Marshall Basin cirque. Deep in the valley below the trail are the ruins of the Tom Boy Mine and the road leading to the mine.

On the ridge the trail turns left (west), crosses a scree-covered saddle and then climbs on moderate grades to the top of Ajax Peak (12,785-ft.) at

2.8 miles. The last section of the trail ascends on stable scree along the south side of the ridge, a bit below the ridge crest.

Atop Ajax Peak enjoy 360-degree views. From this perspective we have a birds-eye-view of Telluride nestled in the valley to the west. Mendoza Peak (13,275-ft.) towers above the head of Marshall Basin to the northeast. Mount Emma (13,581-ft.), Gilpin Peak (13,694-ft.) and Mount Sneffels (14,150-ft.) rise in the distance beyond Mendoza.

To the north, Chicago Peak soars over the Tom Boy Mine complex and the Savage Creek Valley. Further up the valley are fine views of Telluride Peak and the 13,000-ft. summits ringing the head of Savage Basin. The Tom Boy Mine/Imogene Pass road is seen snaking up Savage Basin and crossing the divide at Imogene Pass.

To the south the high summits surrounding the Bridal Veil Basin fill the skyline. Peaks easy to pick out on the horizon include Ballard Mountain, La Junta Peak (13,472-ft.) and Peak 13,614-ft. Telluride Peak and Trico Peak dominate the view to the east. If you look carefully you will be able to see Black Bear Pass on the divide to the south of Trico Peak.

When you are done taking in the views retrace your steps to the trailhead. Use care as you descend the steep trail. Keep an eye out for traffic along the Black Bear Road. Step off the narrow road to let vehicles pass safely.

Driving Directions

From Telluride: Drive east through Telluride on Colorado Avenue for a little over 2.0 miles past the Pandora Mill to a large unmarked parking area. Park here is you are driving a 2WD vehicle. 4WD is recommended beyond this point. (Check with the Telluride Visitor Center on current road conditions before setting out on the hike.) Add 4.0 miles to the round-trip distance and 1,300-ft. in elevation gain for the hike if parking at the 2WD lot near the Pandora Mine.

If you are in a 4WD follow the dirt road, marked as Forest Road #636 on maps, for 2.0-miles up a series of switchback to the Bridal Veil Power plant. The road gets rougher and rockier as you climb. Parking is VERY limited at the top and fills up early in the morning. Be sure not to block the gate. If there is no available parking, turn around and go back down the road until you find a safe, wide spot to park out of the flow of traffic (and not on private property.) A good place to park is at the base of the waterfall. From the waterfall it is 0.8-mile walk to the end of the road.

Note: Two-way traffic is permitted between the Pandora Mine and the power plant. The road above the power plant, the notorious Black Bear Road, is one-way downhill toward Telluride.

(The Black Bear road, starting south of Red Mountain Pass on Highway 550, goes over Black Bear Pass (12,840-ft.) and descends Ingram Basin on dangerous and difficult switchbacks to meet the 4WD road coming up from Telluride.)

40. Hawn Mountain ★★★☆

Distance: 4.9-5.0 miles (Loop)

This scenic hike ascends a hand-laid trail to the summit of Hawn Mountain with terrific views of the Lizard Head Wilderness and the high peaks to the east and southeast of downtown Telluride.

Distance: 4.9-5.0 miles (Loop)   **Basecamp:** Telluride
Elevation: 9,180-ft. at Trailhead   **Area:** Uncompahgre NF
10,922-ft. at Hawn Mountain   **Best Season:** July - September
Elevation Gain: 1,742-ft.   **USGS Map(s):** Telluride
Difficulty: moderately strenuous

Why Hike Hawn Mountain

The 885-acre private community of Gray Head to the west of Telluride offers an unusual amenity, a 16-mile trail system. Happily this trail system is open to the public. The crown jewel of the system is the Hawn Mountain trail that climbs through talus to the summit of its namesake mountain on 13 switchbacks, painstakingly hand-crafted to facilitate hiking. From the summit and adjacent ridge enjoy great views of the peaks in the Lizard Head and Mount Sneffels Wildernesses and the mountains rising above Telluride.

Turn the out-and-back hike (5.0-mile RT) into a loop by combining the hike to the summit, dubbed "The Front of Hawn," with "the Back of Hawn." From the summit, the Back of Hawn trail descends through trees down Hawn's western slopes and then heads down the Willow Creek Valley to return to the trailhead for a 4.9 miles hike. This portion of the hike is on public land.

The loop can be hiked in either direction. I prefer ascending the talus slopes and returning on the Back of Hawn. This option offers great views on the climb and allows you to return the same way should you decide you don't want to do the loop. I also prefer hiking uphill on rocky slopes. Each to his or her own.

Hawn Mountain Loop

The Hawn Mountain trail starts along the Last Dollar Road at the northern entrance to Hawn Lane where a second sign for Hawn Lane is surrounded by a large rock cairn (see driving directions below.) Follow the trail as it begins climbing 13-switchbacks on moderate to moderately-steep grades up talus slopes scattered with trees. One can only imagine the hours of work that went into the hand-laid trail. Flat, platter size pieces of talus are fitted together to form a good, stable path.

On the end of the third switchback reach a signed junction. Here a metal sign points to the left for the "Back of Hawn" trail and right for the "Front of Hawn"/ Hawn Mountain. Make a sharp right turn and continue climbing up the Front of Hawn trail. As you ascend enjoy ever improving views of Wilson Mesa and the high peaks of the Lizard Head Wilderness to the south/southwest.

The good trail ends as you reach the ridge crest at 2.5 miles. Lounge chairs, formed by cleverly arranged flat rocks, offer a welcome respite from the climb. From this high vantage point enjoy wonderful views of Sunshine Mountain (12,930-ft.), Lizard Head (13,113-ft.), Wilson Peak (14,017-ft.), Wilson Mountain (14,246-ft.) and El Diente (14,159-ft.) in the Lizard Head Wilderness.

Beyond the "chairs" rock cairns mark the ascent along the ridge crest through trees to the first summit along the ridge at (10,887-ft.). Past the trees the trail continues along the ridge with fine views of Ruffner Mountain (13,003-ft.), Mears Peak (13,496-ft.) and Iron Mountain (12,7474-ft.) rising above the East Fork of Deep Creek to the northeast. Whipple Mountain (11,922-ft.) rises to the north while a sea of summits soaring above Telluride fill the skyline to the east.

Travel along the rocky ridge to the high point of Hawn Mountain (10,922-ft.) at 2.9 miles. Beyond the high point the trail starts descending through trees down the western slopes of Hawn Mountain. Cairns help keep you on track on this lightly trafficked trail. Some openings in the forest offer limited views. The trail swings to the left (southwest) as it crosses Willow Creek and heads down the west side of the drainage. At 4.3 miles the trail crosses to the east side of the creek and soon reaches a junction with a spur trail connecting to the switchbacks

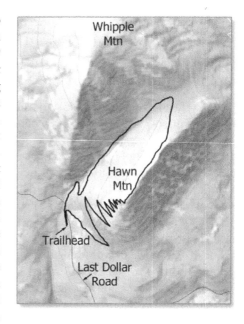

with the Front/Back of Hawn sign. Alternatively, continue down the trail as it zig-zags through trees, ignoring the "Stairway to Heaven" trail branching to the right. A few more twists and turns returns reconnects you with the trail near the road at 4.9 miles.

Driving Directions

From Telluride: From West Colorado Avenue and Aspen Street in downtown Telluride, head west on Colorado Ave for 3.2 miles and turn right onto Airport Road/Last Dollar Road. Drive for 1.9 miles to a "Y" intersection, just before the airport, and bear right on the continuation of Last Dollar Road. Airport Road heads east to the Airport Terminal.

Follow Last Dollar Road for another 4.6 miles to the second intersection with Hawn Lane (the second sign for Hawn Lane surrounded by a large rock cairn). Park off the road so as not to obstruct traffic or block the horse trail. Remember the owners of this private property are allowing everyone to use their trail system. Please be considerate and pack out anything you take on the trail.

41. Iron Mountain ★★★★

Distance: 8.0 miles (RT)

Iron Mountain climbs a steep mining road with fine views of the surrounding mountains along with Wilson Peak and the Lizard Head Wilderness. Aspen groves, waterfalls and an old mine add interest to the hike.

Distance: 8.0 miles (round trip)
Elevation: 9,090-ft. at Trailhead
10,857-ft. at Hawn Mountain
Elevation Gain: 1,767-ft.
Difficulty: moderately strenuous

Basecamp: Telluride
Area: Uncompahgre NF
Best Season: July - September
USGS Map(s): Gray Head, Telluride

Why Hike the Iron Mountain Trail

The scenic Iron Mountain trail climbs an old mining road along the north side of the East Fork of Deep Creek Valley, known locally as Snodgrass Canyon. Ruffner Mountain (13,003-ft.) and Mears Peak (13,496-ft.) tower above the east side of the valley while Iron Mountain (12,747-ft.) and Campbell Peak (13,213-ft.) define the southern wall. At the head of the valley is a rugged cirque of 13,000-ft. peaks. Fine views extend southwest to Wilson Peak and the Lizard Head Wilderness.

The Iron Mountain trail up Snodgrass Canyon is reach after a short stint along the Deep Creek and Whipple Mountain trails. From the foot of the canyon the stiff ascent to the Flower Mountain Mine travels through nice aspen groves and passes high above waterfalls along the creek. After two miles views open to the valley's high peaks. The mine is a good turnaround point for most hikers although it is possible to explore further up the valley.

The hike is a good option if the weather is threatening the high country or for hikers trying to acclimate. This lightly used trail sees few hikers so you are likely to have the valley to yourself.

Trailhead to Mountain Flower Mine

Access to the Iron Mountain Trail is via the Deep Creek Trail. (See driving directions below). From the trailhead, walk north/northeast on the Deep Creek Trail ascending moderate switchbacks through meadows. The high peaks of the Lizard Head Wilderness, including Wilson Peak (14,017-ft.) and Sunshine Mountain (12,930-ft.), dominate the view to the southwest. Whipple Mountain (11,992-ft.) and the unnamed peaks rising along the west side of the Deep Creek fill the skyline to the northwest.

After 0.3 miles reach an unsigned junction on a dirt road and turn left. Make note of this intersection so you don't miss your turn on the way back to your vehicle.

At 0.4 miles the grade levels as the trail reaches a signed junction for the Deep Creek Trail where a road joins from the south. Continue straight ahead (northwest) through trees on the Deep Creek Trail that now runs along an irrigation ditch.

At 1.2 miles reach a signed junction and turn left (west) on the Whipple Trail. Openings in the trees along the trail offer fine views of Wilson Peaks and the Lizard Head Wilderness. A tenth of a mile beyond the turn reach a small sign pointing to the continuation of the trail dropping down a wooded hillside to a crossing of the East Fork of Deep Creek at 1.7 miles. Cross the creek on a wood log and then ascend a hillside to a dirt road at 1.8 miles.

Turn right (northeast) on the road, a two track, signed for the Iron Mountain Trail (#495). To the left is the continuation of the Whipple Mountain Trail.

The road now climbs on moderate to moderately steep grades through aspen groves and scattered evergreens above the north side of the creek. Ignore a trail branching right at 2.1 miles. This trail drops to the creek.

A short distance beyond the road becomes rocky as it crosses talus slopes. Here views open up the valley, known locally as Snodgrass Canyon after a local who died in the area in the 1940's. Ruffner Mountain (13,003-ft.) and Mears Peak (13,496-ft.) tower above the north side of the valley.

Look for a waterfall along the creek at 2.8 miles. Over the next 0.4 miles the valley floor drops steeply down a series of steps, each with a photogenic falls. Some of the falls are difficult to see because of the dense foliage along the valley floor. Early in the morning the valley bottom is in deep shade, making photographing the falls difficult.

At 3.0 miles and 3.1 miles cross seasonal creeks flowing down the steep slopes above the trail. Beyond each of the crossings turn around for more nice views of the Lizard Head Wilderness. If you look closely you should be able to see Lizard Head Peak, a slender spire rising to the left of Sunshine Mountain.

As you continue ascending enjoy ever improving views of Mears Peak. The trail is now gradually curving to the right (east), opening views to the rugged summits forming the cirque at the head of the valley.

At 3.2 miles you will see to a section of burnt timber below the trail. Here is another good place to see a waterfall along the creek. Across the valley Iron Mountain's (12,747-ft. and 12,525-ft.) rugged ridge and summits towers above the falls.

After passing through a pretty meadow a short section of the road becomes overgrown but the way is stil clear. Beyond this point the road turns rocky as it ascends along talus slopes and enters a spruce forest. Watch for a pile of limbs blocking the road at 3.5 miles. Here the road makes a sharp left and climbs a rocky switchback. Rock cairns help mark the turn.

The trees soon give way to rocky slopes as you climb the switchback. Great views open to Iron Mountain across the valley. At 3.6 miles reach a second pile of branches marking a sharp turn to the right. A short overgrown section of the trail impedes progress ahead but beyond the brush the trail is again clear.

The trail now heads northeast again, climbing on moderately-steep to steep grades up rocky slopes through scattered trees. Soon the trees give way to open talus slopes and nice views open to the rugged 13,000-ft. peaks at the head of the valley. Iron Mountain dominates the view across the valley. Multi-hued Ruffner Mountain soars above the trail. The Wilson Peak massif fills the skyline to the southwest.

At 3.9 miles the trail splits, stay left here, taking the high route which reaches the Mountain Flower Mine tunnel (10,857-ft.) at 4.0 miles. Nearby a piece of metal equipment sits atop a large tailings pile that also serves as a great overlook and fine spot for lunch. Below the tailings pile are the collapsed wood ruins of an old cabin and an outhouse. Rusted mining remnants and household items are strewn across the ground around the cabin area. Please don't take any souvenirs. Leave everything where you found it.

From the tailings pile enjoy fine views of Snodgrass Canyon. Iron Mountain rises directly across the valley. Campbell Peak (13,213-ft) anchors the southeast end of the cirque. Ruffner Mountain and Mears Peak rims the valley to the north.

A path in the talus above the cabin site continues up the valley. The trail is faint and easily lost as it climbs along open talus slopes and meadows on the north side of the valley before climbing a series of benches populated with stands of Engelmann spruce. The talus/scree near the head of the canyon is loose and unstable, making for difficult scrambling.

Driving Directions

From Telluride: From West Colorado Avenue and Aspen Street in Telluride, head west on W. Colorado Ave. for 3.2 miles and then bear right onto Airport Road / Last Dollar Road. This turn is right before the traffic circle (Society Turn) where West Colorado Ave reaches CO 145. Follow Airport/Last Dollar Road for 1.9 miles and turn right onto the continuation of Last Dollar Road. This turn is just before you reach the Telluride Airport.

Follow Last Dollar Road for 1.0 mile to the Deep Creek Trailhead on the right (east) side of the road. The marked trailhead is located at the north end of the circular spur road.

42. Handies Peak ☆☆☆☆☆

Distance: 2.3 - 5.4 miles (RT)

This terrific hike wanders through beautiful American Basin, visits scenic Sloan Lake and then ascends to the summit of Handies Peak (14,048-ft.) with spectacular panoramic views of the San Juan Mountains.

Distance: 2.3 miles (RT) to Sloan Lake
5.4 miles (RT) to Handies Peak
Elevation: 11,600-ft. at Trailhead
12,920-ft. at Sloan Lake
14,048-ft. at Handies Peak
Elevation Gain: 1,320-ft. to Sloan Lake
2,448-ft. to Handies Peak

Difficulty: strenuous
Basecamp: Lake City
Area: Gunnison BLM
Best Season: July - September
USGS Map(s): Handies Peak

Why Hike to Handies Peak

The stunning panoramic views from the top of Handies Peak (14,048-ft.) are among the best in the Lake City area. From the summit a large expanse of a the San Juan Mountains are visible including the Needle Mountains, the Grenadier Range, the La Garita Mountains and the peaks of the Uncompahgre and Mt. Sneffel Wilderness Areas.

The hike to the summit is filled with visual delights. The trail wanders through beautiful American Basin, one of the most scenic valleys in the San Juan Mountains. The entire basin, located above timberline, is covered in pretty meadows that are awash in a spectacular display of wildflowers during late July and early August. An impressive chain of craggy peaks towers above the head of the basin while the valley's eastern wall is dominated by the massive bulk of Handies Peak (14,048-ft.). Rising to the west are the steep flanks of 13,000-ft. peaks clad in tundra and scree.

At the head of the valley the route climbs to picturesque Sloan Lake (12,920-ft.), an alpine gem tucked in a rocky bowl beneath the valley's rugged headwall.

While the hike to Handies is steep, gaining almost 2,500-ft. in 2.7 miles, it follows a good trail the entire way and is not difficult. Indeed the peak is considered one of the easiest of the fourteeners to climb in the Lake City Area. Well acclimated and reasonably fit hiker should have no problems reaching to top.

Be sure to select a day full of promise and get an early start so you can take your time enjoying the incredible views from the top and then descend before the onset of afternoon thunder storms, a frequent occurrence in the Rockies.

Trailhead to Sloan Lake

Distance from Trailhead: 2.3 miles (RT)
Elevation at Sloan Lake: 12,920-ft.
Elevation Gain: 1,320-ft.

Few trailheads boast the impressive scenery at the start of the hike to Handies Peak. From the parking area views extend south across the basin's emerald green meadows to the rugged 13,000-ft. ridge towering above the head of the valley. The scenery is especially impressive during late July and early August when a showy display of wildflowers carpets the valley floor.

The Handies Peak trail leaves the southeast end of the trailhead parking area and ascends the hillside on the left (east) side of the valley, heading south into the basin through pretty meadows. At 0.7 miles the path crosses a stream and then continues the moderate ascent toward the head of the basin.

At 1.0 mile the trail splits. The path to Handies Peak turns left (southeast), leaving the valley floor and climbs 325-ft. up a moderately steep hillside. At the top of hill the path descends into a shallow basin, crosses the outlet stream for Sloan Lake and then climbs gently across rocky meadows.

Soon the path turns south, climbing steep switchbacks, gaining 200-ft., up to a junction with the trail to Sloan Lake at 1.6 miles. At the junction a short spur trail drops south to the shores of Sloan Lake (12,930-ft.) while the trail to Handies Peak veers left.

The short side trip to Sloan Lake is well worth your time. The aquamarine lake lies cradled in a rugged cirque, anchored to the southeast by American Peak (13,806-ft.). An imposing jagged ridge rises above the lake's south shoreline.

Sloan Lake to Handies Peak

Distance from Trailhead: 5.4 miles (RT)
Elevation at Handies Peak: 14,048-ft.
Elevation Gain: 2,448-ft.

To continue hiking to the summit return to the Sloan Lake junction and follow the trail as it curves to the northeast, traversing the talus slopes beneath an unnamed peak on the ridge extending south from Handies Peak. The traverse leads to the southwest facing flank of Handies Peak where a series of steep switchbacks ascend grassy meadows to the 13,490-ft. saddle on the peak's south ridge, gaining 460-ft. in 0.5 miles.

The way to the summit is now evident. Follow the trail is it steeply ascends the south ridge on scree covered slopes, gaining 560-ft in 0.4 miles.

The panoramic views from the top are some of the best in the area. To the southwest the jagged peaks of the Grenadier Range and the Needles Mountains extend to the horizon. To the north are the distinctive summits of the Uncompahgre Wilderness, including Wetterhorn, Matterhorn and Uncompahgre Peaks. To the northeast is the La Garita Range while to the west/northwest the peaks of the San Juan Mountains near Silverton and Ouray, including the Mt. Sneffels Range, fill the skyline.

After enjoying the views, retrace your steps to the trailhead. Alternatively, combine the Handies Peak trail with the Grizzly Gulch trail to form a long, strenuous loop. The loop can be hiked in either direction. This 10 mile loop gains 3,592-ft. in elevation.

Driving Directions

From Lake City: Take Highway 149 south for 2.5 miles and turn right (south) on County Road 30 toward the Lake San Cristobal. Follow the paved road approximately 4 miles and then continue on the dirt road for about 16.3 miles. The American Basin road begins at a fork where a sign reads "Cinnamon Pass/American Basin." American Basin is to the left and Cinnamon Pass is to the right. Turn left and follow the rough 4WD road, with one stream crossing, for 0.9 miles to the trailhead.

Under good conditions, high clearance passenger cars should be able to make it to the American Basin turnoff. Check with the tourism office in Lake City on current road conditions before starting your journey.

43. Uncompahgre Peak ★★★★★
Distance: 7.8 miles (RT)

Stunning panoramic views are the rewards for hiking to the top Uncompahgre Peak (14,309-ft.), the sixth highest fourteener in Colorado and the highest point in the San Juan Mountains.

Distance: 7.8 miles (RT)
Elevation: 11,430-ft. at Trailhead
Maximum elevation: 14,309-ft.
Elevation Gain: 2,879-ft.
Difficulty: strenuous-difficult

Basecamp: Lake City
Area: Uncompahgre Wilderness, Uncompahgre NF
Best Season: July - September
USGS Map(s): Uncompahgre Peak

Why Hike Uncompahgre Peak

The uniquely shaped summit block of Uncompahgre Peak (14,309-ft.) is a well know landmark in the San Juan Mountains. From a distance the peak looks like a formidable climb but the ascent up the mountain's south ridge is quite doable for hikers that are well acclimated and reasonably fit.

Hiking to the summit is well worth the effort. For most of the way the trail climbs through beautiful meadows with unobstructed views of the peak's south and east faces. Beyond the meadows the trail ascends Uncompahgre's south ridge. As you approach the summit there is one short, steep and slightly exposed scramble before you get back on a good trail for the final stiff climb to the top. The broad summit, which stands apart from the surrounding peaks, offers stunning panoramic views in all directions.

Pick a nice day and get an early start so that you are down from the summit before the onset of afternoon thunder storms, a frequent occurrence in the Rockies. Also, be forewarned that the final 4.0 miles drive to the trailhead is up the rocky and narrow Nellie Creek 4WD road. Do not even think about taking a passenger car up this road.

Walking up Nellie Creek adds 8 miles (RT) and 2,115-ft. to the climb making this a 15.8 mile (RT) hike with an elevation gain just under 5,000-ft.

Trailhead to Uncompahgre Peak

The trail starts at the northeast end of the trailhead parking area (see driving directions below) and ascends northwest on moderate grades through meadows and spruce-fir forest, staying to the right (northeast) of Nellie Creek. At 0.6 miles the trail leaves the last of the trees behind and enters a rocky gully where it climbs switchbacks up the gully's north wall to a trail junction with the Big Blue trail at 0.9 miles.

At the junction the Big Blue trail heads right (north). We turn left (west) on the trail to Uncompahgre Peak. Ahead are stunning, unobstructed views of Uncompahgre's east face and distinctive summit block, which from this angle looks somewhat like a huge lopsided wedding cake.

Follow the trail as it traverses along the top of the gully's north wall. In a short distance you will see Nellie Creek tumbling down a rocky cleft in the wall. At this point the trail starts curving northwest, climbing through the pretty meadows with ever improving views of Uncompahgre Peak. Vistas to the south extend to the peaks rising above the Henson Creek Valley.

At 2.0 miles the trail swings south, heading toward the southern end of the basin. Reach a junction (12,940-ft.) at 2.4 miles. Here the the El Paso Trail branches left (southeast) toward Matterhorn Creek. Bear right at the junction to stay on the Uncompahgre trail. From this point you still have 1.5 miles and a 1,370-ft. climb to the summit.

Beyond the junction the trail makes a wide arc to the northwest, heading toward the Uncompahgre's south ridge and then ascends steeply along the east side of the south ridge.

At 3.1 miles a low point in the ridge provides interesting, albeit restricted views of Matterhorn Peak to the west. Past the viewpoint the trail climbs steep switchbacks up a rocky east facing hillside to the crest of the south ridge (13,860-ft.) at 3.4 miles. At the crest take a breather and enjoy the wonderful views of Matterhorn and Wetterhorn Peaks, Courthouse Mountain and the other summits rising to the west.

The trail now crosses to the west side of the ridge for a short traverse along a narrow, rocky trail with enough exposure to make some people uncomfortable. Next is the most difficult part of the hike, a 125-ft. scramble up a steep eroded slope of loose rock. There are several routes, pick the way that looks best to you and scramble to the top of the ridge.

At the top of the ridge be sure to turn around and note where you ascended the ridge so you can find your way back down on the return. There should be rock cairns marking the best place to descend.

Once atop the ridge the going is much easier. Follow the trail as heads north/northeast, climbing 340-ft. up a steep scree covered slope to the large plateau at the top of the peak.

Uncompahgre Peak stands apart from its surrounding summits, providing breathtaking vistas in all directions. Expansive views to the west encompass Matterhorn and Wetterhorn Peaks and, in the distance, the summits of the Mt. Sneffels Wilderness. To the north/northwest are the peaks and valleys of the Uncompahgre Wilderness. To the south/southwest the peaks and ridges of the San Juan Mountains fill the skyline.

When you are done soaking in the views, reverse course and enjoy the scenic hike back to the trailhead.

At the top remember to keep an eye on the weather. If thunderstorms are building it is best to descend and head back to the trailhead.

Driving Directions

From Lake City: Head west on 2nd Street and then turn left on Henson Creek Rd, part of the Alpine Loop Scenic Byway. Follow Henson Creek Rd for 4.0 miles to the Nellie Creek jeep road. Turn right (north) on the Nellie Creek Road and drive this nasty, rocky and narrow 4WD road for 4 miles to the trailhead. Along the way, the road crosses Nellie Creek twice. High clearance is required. Don't try to take a passenger car on this road.

Walking up Nellie Creek road adds 8 miles (RT) and 2,115-ft. to the climb, making this a 15.8 mile (RT) hike with a 5,000-ft. elevation gain.

44. Cataract Lake (aka Cataract Gulch) ⭐⭐⭐⭐⭐

Distance: 4.2 -10.0 miles (RT)

Beginning in dense woods the trail passes cascades and waterfalls along Cataract Creek, travels through beautiful alpine meadows and visits a scenic alpine lake on its way to the Continental Divide.

Distance: 4.2 – 10.0 miles (RT)   **Basecamp:** Lake City
Elevation: 9,630-ft. at Trailhead   **Area:** Gunnison BLM
Maximum elevation: - 12,200-ft.   **Best Season:** July - September
Elevation Gain: 2,570-ft.   **USGS Map(s):** Red Cloud Peak,
Difficulty: moderately strenuous   Pole Creek Mountain

Why Hike Cataract Lake

This scenic hike ascends steeply up Cataract Gulch to a pretty lake basin and then climbs to the Continental Divide Trail (CDT). Along the way the trail travels through dense woods, passes numerous cascades and waterfalls along Cataract Creek and wanders through lovely alpine meadows. Extend the hike by following a section of the CDT toward Cuba Gulch.

Trailhead to Cataract Lake and the Continental Divide

Just beyond the trailhead parking area (see driving directions below) the trail up Cataract Gulch crosses Cottonwood Creek on a bridge and then begins a steep ascent on switchbacks through dense stands of spruce-fir forest. As you climb the trail crosses Cataract Creek five times without the aid of bridges. Generally these crossing are not a problem although you should be prepared to get your feet wet.

During the first 2.0-miles of the hike the trail gains over 2,000-ft. Waterfalls and cascades along Cataract Creek, spectacular displays of wildflowers and an old miner's cabin will help divert your attention from the steep climb. Be sure to turn around when you get to openings in the trees for nice views of Sunshine Peak (14,001-ft.), located to the north (down canyon) across the Lake Fork Valley.

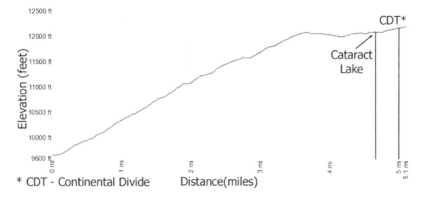

* CDT - Continental Divide

176

At 2.0 miles the grade eases a bit as the trail climbs through meadows with patches of low lying shrubs. Along this section of the trail views open to Half Peak (13,841-ft.) rising to the west of the trail. A short distance beyond the climb resumes and the trail passed a beautiful waterfall at 2.1 miles. This is a good turnaround point for a short hike.

The grade eases briefly at 2.7 miles where views open to a pretty meadow with beaver ponds. Soon the trail turns left (east), climbing steeply up a bluff to the upper basin at 3.5 miles. Here the grade abates as the path ascends on gentle grades through alpine meadows and willow clusters to Cataract Lake (12,100-ft.) at 4.6 miles. The lake lies in a pretty meadow scattered with willows just below the Continental Divide.

To reach the Continental Divide, follow the trail as it curves to the southwest and ascends above the west side of the lake to the Divide (12,200-ft.) at 5.0 miles. A small pond lies cradled atop the divide. From the divide views stretch south down the Pole Creek Valley and beyond. To the north are great views down Cataract Gulch to Sunshine Peak.

The divide is the turnaround point for day hikers. It is possible to connect with the Cuba Gulch Trail by following the CDT west through open tundra for 2.0 miles to the head of Cuba Gulch. You can also walk east along the divide for more great views.

Driving Directions

From Lake City: From Lake City take Highway 149 south for 2.5 miles. Turn right onto CR 30, the road to Lake San Cristobal. Follow the paved road approximately 4 miles then continue on the dirt road for about 8.3 miles. At the fork in the road turn left on CR 35 toward Sherman and drive 1.4 miles. A sign marks the trailhead on the left (south) side of the road.

45. Grizzly Gulch ★★★★
Distance: *8.0 miles (RT)*

The summit of Handies Peak offers breathtaking views of the San Juan Mountains. This alternative route to the top is longer and more strenuous but less traveled than the popular Handies Peak trail via American Basin.

Distance: 8.0 miles (RT)
Elevation: 10,425-ft. at Trailhead
Maximum elevation: 14,048-ft.
Elevation Gain: 3,623-ft.
Difficulty: extremely difficult

Basecamp: Lake City
Area: Gunnison BLM
Best Season: July - September
USGS Map(s): Handies Peak
See Page 170 for Map

Why Hike Grizzly Gulch to Handies Peak

Grizzly Gulch offers an alternative approach to the summit of Handies Peak (14,048-ft.) that is longer and gains more elevation than the more popular hike to the summit via American Basin. The trail ascends the scenic Grizzly Gulch Valley and then climbs the north ridge of Handies Peak to the summit.

The pristine valley provides a degree of solitude not usually found on the route up American Basin. The trail is a good alternative for hikers who do not have a 4WD for negotiating the road up American Basin.

The best time to visit the area is late July and early August when the tundra basin below the peak is carpeted with wildflowers. A small alpine lake in the eastern spur of the basin can be reached on an interesting 0.5-mile side trip.

Trailhead to Handies Peak via Grizzly Gulch

From the trailhead (see driving directions below), follow the path that starts behind the restroom and leads to a bridge crossing of the Lake Fork of the Gunnison River. Beyond the bridge the trail heads straight up the north side of the valley through spruce, fir and aspen for about 0.75 miles. The trail then climbs through a series of avalanche chutes interspersed with small groups of trees.

At 1.7 miles leave the last of the trees behind and continue the ascent through beautiful meadows with wonderful views of Handies Peak. Soon the trail enters a gorgeous alpine basin and for a brief period travels alongside the creek, crossing it twice. Be sure to look over your shoulder on the way up the basin for beautiful views of the Silver Creek Valley to the northeast.

Just beyond the second creek crossing a sign points right (north) to a long switchback that helps ease the climb up the west side of Handies' north ridge. The ascent to the ridge gains over 1,225-ft in just under 1.1 miles. Along the way the trail curves to the west/southwest as it climbs through rocky meadows and crosses a large talus field. A few switchbacks aid the final stiff climb to the ridge crest.

Atop the ridge the trail heads south, climbing rocky slopes for 0.2 miles. The path to the summit is now visible. Continue the ascent for 0.2 miles, now on moderate grades, reaching the summit of Handies Peak at 4.0 miles after gaining 3,592-ft.

The panoramic views from the top are some of the best in the area. To the southwest the jagged peaks of the Grenadier Range and the Needles Mountains extend to the horizon. To the north are the distinctive summits of the Uncompahgre Wilderness, including Wetterhorn, Matterhorn and Uncompahgre Peaks. To the northeast is the La Garita Range while to the west/northwest the peaks of the San Juan Mountains near Silverton and Ouray, including the Mt. Sneffels Range, fill the skyline.

After taking in the views retrace your steps back to your car. Alternatively combine the Grizzly Gulch trail with the Handies Peak/American Basin trail to create a very scenic 10 mile loop. From the top of Handies Peak take the Handies Peak trail down through American Basin to the main road and back to your car. This 10 mile loop can be done in either direction.

Driving Directions

From Lake City: Take Highway 149 south for 2.5 miles and turn right on County Road 30 toward Lake San Cristobal. Follow the paved road about 4.0 miles then continue on dirt road for 12.6 miles. Look for a sign on the left (south) side of the road for Handies Peak. Parking is available in defined areas on both sides of the main road. Under good conditions high clearance vehicles can make it to the trailhead. Check on current road conditions at the Lake City Tourist office before starting your journey.

46. Redcloud and Sunshine Peaks ★★★★☆

Distance: 9.0 - 11.8 miles (RT)

This great hike leads to the top of two of the easiest fourteeners to climb in Colorado, Redcloud (14,034 ft.) and Sunshine (14,001 ft.) peaks. From the summits a sea of peaks and ridges extend in all directions, encompassing large swaths of the San Juan Mountains.

Distance: 9.0 - 11.8 miles (RT)
Elevation: 10,425-ft. at Trailhead
Maximum elevation: 14,034-ft.
Elevation Gain: 3,609-ft.
Difficulty: extremely difficult

Basecamp: Lake City
Area: Gunnison BLM
Best Season: July - September
USGS Map(s): Redcloud Peak

Trailhead to Redcloud and Sunshine Peaks

The trail to Redcloud and Sunshine peaks begins at the Silver Creek trailhead parking area (see driving directions below) and heads northeast, ascending through trees along the west side of the Silver Creek drainage. A little over a mile from the start the trail emerges from the trees and continues up the basin, paralleling the creek. Be sure to turn around during this part of the ascent for ever-improving views of Handies Peak (14,048-ft.) to the southwest.

At 2.7 miles the trail curves to the southeast and climbs to a large basin beneath the north face of Redcloud Peak at 3.1 miles. From the basin the path ascends steeply to a saddle on the ridge between Redcloud Peak and Peak 13561, gaining 650-ft. in just over 0.6 miles. Turn right and follow a very steep trail that climbs up the ridge to Redcloud Peak (14,034-ft.). On the way to the peak you will climb over a false summit. This section of the trail gains over 1,000-ft. in just 0.8 miles.

From Redcloud the path to Sunshine Peak descends from the summit along Redcloud's south ridge on an undulating trail, losing about 515-ft. to a saddle between Redcloud and Sunshine. From the saddle the rugged trail climbs 484-ft. up Sunshine's north ridge to Sunshine Peak (14,001-ft.), reaching the peak in a little over 1.4 miles.

From both summits enjoy panoramic views of a sea of peaks and ridges encompassing large swaths of the San Juan Mountains. To the north Uncompahgre Peak towers above the other summits of the Uncompahgre Wilderness. To the west is a wall of mountains extending from Ouray to Silverton. On a clear day views extend northwest to the Sneffels Range. The Needles and peaks in the Weminuche Wilderness fill the skyline to the south while to the northeast are the 12,000-ft. tundra-clad plateaus of the Powderhorn Wilderness.

Be sure to select a day full of promise and get an early start so you can take your time enjoying the wonderful views from the top and descend before the onset of afternoon thunder storms, a frequent occurrence in the Rockies.

Driving Directions

From Lake City: From Lake City, take Highway 149 south for 2.5 miles and turn right on County Road 30 toward Lake San Cristobal. Follow the paved road approximately 4 miles, then continue on dirt road for 8.3 miles to the fork in the road. Take the right fork (the Alpine Loop Scenic Byway) and drive another 4.2 miles to the trailhead. The trail sign, located on the left, reads "Redcloud

Peak." Under good conditions high clearance 2WD vehicles should be able to reach the trailhead.

47. Devil's Lake (aka Devil's Creek) ★★★★

Distance: 14.0 miles (RT)

Picturesque groves of mature aspen and beautiful views of the Lake Fork Valley and Uncompahgre Peak are a few of the visual delights on this scenic trail following the Devil's Creek drainage to Devil's Lake, lying beneath the western flanks of the Calf Creek Plateau.

Distance: 14.0 miles (RT) to Devil's Lake
Elevation: 8,480-ft. at Trailhead
12,000-ft. at Devil's Lake
Elevation Gain: 3,520-ft. to Devil's Lake
Difficulty: strenuous

Basecamp: Lake City
Area: Powderhorn Wilderness, Gunnison BLM, Gunnison NF
Best Season: July - September
USGS Map(s): Alpine Plateau, Cannibal Plateau, Powderhorn Lakes, Lake City

Why Hike to Devil's Lake

In the northern reaches of the San Juan Mountains lies the Powderhorn Wilderness, a rugged, glacier carved landscape encompassing large expanses of alpine tundra, spruce forests, and several alpine lakes at nearly 12,000-ft. The wilderness harbors two huge plateaus over 12,000-ft., the Cannibal Plateau and the Calf Creek Plateau, that make up the largest relatively flat expanse of alpine tundra in the lower 48 states. The plateaus were created by Tertiary volcanic deposits that are believed to be 5,000-ft. thick in some place.

This trail climbs the Devil's Creek drainage to Devil's Lake, which lies nestled in a tundra-clad saddle between the Cannibal and Calf Creek Plateaus. Beautiful views of the Lake Fork Valley and Uncompahgre Peak are visible from many points along the trail.

Trailhead to Devil's Lake

From the trailhead parking area (see driving directions below) the trail heads east, climbing an old road to the north of the Devil's Creek drainage. Soon the trail leaves the road, climbing switchbacks up the west side of the Lake Fork Gunnison Valley. Along the way the path crosses and/or uses sections of the road. In a little over a mile the trail tops a mesa and then gently ascends across the sage brush clad mesa. At 1.5 miles the path turns northeast through a fence line and into the Powderhorn Wilderness. From the mesa nice views extend west to the peaks of the Uncompahgre Wilderness.

Over the next mile the trail again departs from and returns to the old road several times, traversing through pretty stands of aspen and spruce-fir forest. After walking 2.7 miles and gaining over 1,700-ft. the trail passes an old cow camp containing two wood structures.

At the end of the road the trail curves to the southeast and travels along the base of a ridge through forest and meadows above the north side of Devil's Creek. Near the head of the drainage the path makes a wide arc to the northeast to avoid the talus clad slopes of the Cannibal Plateau.

At 4.5 miles the trail briefly breaks out of the trees as it climbs through an area cleared by avalanche activity. Be sure to turn around and look west where you will see the tip of Uncompahgre Peak peeking above a ridge.

Soon the trail curves right (southeast) and ascends a wide gully between the Calf Creek Plateau (to the east) and Cannibal Plateau (to the west). At 6.0 miles the grade abates. The final mile of the trail to Devil's Lake crosses open meadows dotted with small tarns. The lake lies nestled in a bowl/saddle between the Calf Creek and Cannibal Plateaus, surrounded by a huge meadow. Do not be surprise if you to run into large flocks of sheep grazing around the lake.

The Devil's Creek Trail can be used in conjunction with the Powderhorn Lakes Trail, the Powderhorn Park Trail, the Middle Fork Trail and the East Fork Trail for extended backpacking trips.

Driving Directions

From Lake City: From Lake City take Highway 149 north for 7 miles and turn right (east) on BLM 3021, a dirt road heading northeast. A large brown sign marks the entrance to this road advising that the road is steep and narrow. Follow the road as it crosses a bridge spanning the Lake Fork River and heads up a hill to another dirt road to the left marked with a "TRAILHEADS" sign. Turn left onto this road and continue about 0.5 mile up the road to the Devil's Creek Trailhead. The gate at the bridge does not open to the public until June 15th.

48. Powderhorn Lakes ★★★★★

Distance: 9.6 miles (RT)

An interesting hike through forest and meadows to a scenic lake basin nestled beneath the eastern escarpment of the Calf Creek Plateau (12,644-ft.) in the Powderhorn Wilderness.

Distance: 7.8 - 9.6 miles (RT)
Elevation: 11,140-ft. at Trailhead
Maximum elevation: 11,870-ft.
Elevation Gain: 1,050-ft.
Difficulty: moderate

Basecamp: Lake City
Area: Powderhorn Wilderness, Gunnison BLM
Best Season: July - September
USGS Map(s): Powderhorn

Why Hike to Powderhorn Lakes

In the northern reaches of the San Juan Mountains lies the Powderhorn Wilderness, a rugged, glacier carved landscape consisting of large expanses of alpine tundra, spruce forests, and several alpine lakes at nearly 12,000-ft. The wilderness harbors two huge plateaus over 12,000-ft., the Cannibal Plateau and the Calf Creek Plateau, that make up the largest relatively flat expanse of alpine tundra in the lower 48 states. The plateaus were created by Tertiary volcanic deposits that are believed to be 5,000-ft. thick in some place.

The Powderhorn Lakes lay in a huge glacial-chiseled cirque beneath the eastern side of the Calf Creek Plateau in the heart this incredible wilderness. The cirque's steep rock walls rise 450-ft. to 700-ft. from the lakeshores to the plateau.

An interesting trail travels through a diverse landscape of forests and meadows to the pretty lake basin. The lakes are set amid meadows surrounded by trees. The Powderhorn Lakes trails connects with other trails leading to the high plateaus and the Devil's Creek trail, offering opportunities for extended backpacking trips in the area.

Trailhead to Powderhorn Lakes

The path to the Powderhorn Lakes climbs southwest through a forest of Engelmann spruce along the eastern side of a long valley. At the head of the valley the trail crest a ridge and then drops into a large, scenic, wildflower-filled meadow at 1.5 miles. If you're lucky you may see elk grazing in the meadow in the early morning or late evening. Take a short side trip to the meadow's western rim for nice views to the northwest.

The trail descends gently across the meadow and then skirts its southwestern edge before reentering the trees at 1.9 miles. The trail, now in the West Fork of Powderhorn drainage, follows a rolling traverse, crossing a low ridge before dropping into minor drainage with a small lake set amid meadows filled with willows.

Beyond the lake the trail returns to the trees, climbs a small rise and then loses 130-ft. in 0.2 miles. At the bottom of the drop the path turns southwest, paralleling the unseen West Fork of Powderhorn Creek. Another short, moderately steep climb leads to the top of a small hill at 3.4 miles and the junction with the trail to Hidden Lake, heading west.

From the junction the path descends to and skirts the marshy meadows along the north side of the creek, passing several beaver ponds along the way, and arrives at a trail junction with a sign pointing straight ahead to the Powderhorn Lakes. (The unsigned trail to the left is the Middle Fork Trail that climbs to the Calf Creek Plateau.)

Soon after the junction the trail ascends a small rise and arrives at Lower Powderhorn Lake at 3.9 miles. The lake sits at the eastern end of a large cirque. The cirque's steep rocky walls rise over 440-ft. above the lake to the Calf Creek Plateau.

To reach Upper Powderhorn Lake follow the trail as it skirts marshy meadows around the right (northwest) side of the lake. At the end of the lake the trail climbs a hillside through forest and meadows to the upper lake basin, gaining a little over 200-ft. in 0.6 miles.

Reach Upper Powderhorn Lake at 4.8 miles. The lake lies cradled in a glacier-carved bowl beneath the eastern escarpment of the Calf Creek Plateau. Steep volcanic rock walls rise 500-ft. to 700-ft. from the southern and western shoreline of the lake to the plateau. Good campsites are located on the north and eastern sides of the lake.

The Powderhorn Lakes Trail can be used in conjunction with the East Fork Trail, the Middle Fork Trail and the Powderhorn Park Trail for a nice backpacking trip.

Lower Powderhorn Lake offers fair to good trout fishing as do the streams and beaver ponds of the West Fork of Powderhorn Creek. The Upper Powderhorn Lake sometimes has fish and sometimes suffers from winter kill.

Driving Directions

From Lake City: Drive north on Hwy 149 for just over 24 miles and turn right on Indian Creek Road / County Road 58. Follow the rough 2-wheel drive road for 10 miles. The trailhead sign and parking area are at the end of the road.

From Gunnison: Go 9 miles west on Hwy. 50 to Hwy.149 and turn left. Follow Hwy. 149 south for 20 miles. Turn left on Indian Creek Road (County Rd. 58) and follow the rough 2-wheel drive road for 10 miles. The trailhead sign and parking area are at the end of the road.

49. Cooper Lake ★★★★
Distance: 7.6 miles (RT)

This gorgeous hike travels up a seldom visited valley to a scenic lake tucked in a high basin. Here you will experience a level of solitude not found on hikes to the nearby 14ers. Extend the hike by climbing to a saddle overlooking Lee Smelter Gulch to the north.

Distance: 7.6 miles (RT)
Elevation: 10,650-ft. - Trailhead
12,750-ft. at Bridal Veil Falls
Elevation Gain: 2,100-ft.
Difficulty: moderately strenuous

Basecamp: Lake City
Area: Gunnison BLM
Best Season: July - September
USGS Map(s): Redcloud Peak

Trailhead to Cooper Lake

The trailhead for Cooper Lake is located along CR 30, part of the Alpine Loop Road. (See driving directions below.) On the north side of the road follow the old jeep road (2-track) as it curves around and enters the Cooper Creek Valley, reaching a trail registration box at 0.4 miles. The trail now heads northeast, climbing on moderately-steep grades through forest and intermittent meadows. After walking 1.1 miles the grade levels and then drops gently down to cross the creek at 1.4 miles. Early in the season you will need to wade the creek. Otherwise it is not a problem.

Climb a switchback up the valley's eastern slopes and then enter the trees, passing the ruins of a cabin at 1.7 miles. The trail now ascends up the classic "V-shaped" valley on easy grades, traveling through pretty meadows and scattered trees beneath 13,000-ft. peaks. CT Peak (13,312-ft.) and Gudy Peak (13,566-ft.) rise to the west while Peak 13,484 dominates the view at the head of the valley.

Cross back to the west side of the creek at 2.6 miles. A short distance beyond the creek crossing the trail starts a steep climb up the lowers slopes of Gudy's eastern ridge. You are now ascending toward the lower basin of the West Fork of the Cooper Creek Valley.

As you climb enjoy fine views of Peak 13,484-ft and Every Mountain (13,691-ft.) soaring above the head of the valley. Soon views open up the length of the East Fork of the Cooper Creek Valley. Cooper Peak (13,689-ft.) anchors the cirque of 13,000-ft. peaks ringing the head of the East Fork.

At 3.2 miles the path curves to the left (north/northwest) as the steep ascent to the lower basin continues along the west side of Cooper Lake's outlet stream. The grade abates a bit as the trail reaches the lower basin at 3.4 miles. Here the trail fades as it crosses the lower basin. Watch for cairns marking the route, which stays to the south of a boggy area. Ahead, scree spills down the upper basin's steep headwall.

Soon the steep ascent resumes through tundra and talus-clad slopes up the left (south) side of the headwall. Cross the outlet stream at 3.7 miles and climb on moderate grades to the upper basin and Cooper Lake (12,750-ft.) at 3.8 miles. The stunning lake lies at the foot of a rugged cirque of 13,000-ft. peaks. Gudy Peak towers above the lake to the west. Steep scree-covered slopes ring the north side of the lake.

From the upper basin views extend east to the high peaks rimming the head of the Cooper Creek Valley.

Driving Directions

From Lake City: From the intersection of Highway 149/Gunnison Ave and 4th Street, head south on Highway 149 for 2.5 miles and turn right on CR 30, the Alpine Loop Road, toward Lake San Cristobal. Reset your odometer here. Follow CR 30 for 12.1 miles to a "Y" intersection. Bear right here to stay on CR 30. The road now becomes rougher and soon travels along a shelf below Sunshine Peak for 1.5 miles. Pass the Silver Creek/Grizzly Gulch trailhead at 16.2 miles. The unmarked trailhead for Cooper Lake is located at 17.0 miles. On the left (south) side of the road you will see a small parking area. On the north side of the road is an old 2-track jeep trail. This is the beginning of the trail.

A high clearance vehicle is recommended for reaching the trailhead. 4WD is required if the road is wet. Check road conditions at the Lake City Visitor Center before starting out on this hike.

50. Crystal Lake ★★★★
Distance: 8.2 miles (RT)

A stiff ascent through aspen groves, forest and meadows leads to pretty Crystal Lake set against the eastern slopes of Crystal Peak. Fine views encompass the vast tundra-clad plateaus to the east and the high peaks towering above Henson Creek to the south.

Distance: 8.2 miles (RT)   **Basecamp:** Lake City
Elevation: 8,875-ft. at Trailhead   **Area:** Uncompahgre NF
Maximum elevation: 11,760-ft.   **Best Season:** July - September
Elevation Gain: 2,885-ft.   **USGS Map(s):** Lake City
Difficulty: moderately strenuous

Why Hike to Crystal Lake

Crystal Lake, set beneath the eastern slopes of Crystal Peak (12,933-ft.), is the goal of this hike reached by a steady, moderately-steep climb through forests and intermittent meadows. Views along the way encompass the high tundra-clad plateaus to the east. As you near the lake vistas open to the high peaks rising to the south of Henson Creek.

This hike offers a great workout and is a good option if

weather is threatening the high peaks to the west. It is particularly nice in the fall when the leaves are changing.

Extend the hike by climbing to the summit of Crystal Peak, which adds 2.0 miles and close to 1,200-ft to the elevation gain to the day. From the summit enjoy fine views of Uncompahgre Peak (14,309-ft.), Redcloud Peak (14,034-ft.) and the sea of peaks filling the horizon to the west/southwest.

Trailhead to Crystal Lake

The trailhead for the Crystal and Larson Lake trails is located near the Lake City IOOF Cemetery (see driving directions below). From the parking area ascend through pine and aspen trees along Balsam Drive, now a dirt road, for 0.5 miles to a forest service gate and a signed trail junction. Here we bear left (west) on the Crystal Lake Trail. The trail to the right leads to Thompson and Larson Lakes.

The trail ascends on moderately-steep/steep grades, generally heading west through aspens and pines along an old jeep road. Soon the trees give way to meadows and the trail leaves the road as its climbs switchbacks along the north slopes above Slaughterhouse Gulch. From the meadows enjoy views of Lake City to the south/southeast and Mesa Seco, (12,800-ft.) rising across the valley to the east.

At 1.5 miles the trail enters a beautiful aspen grove. The steady ascent continues through aspens interspersed with small meadows. At 2.5 miles the trail leaves the Slaughterhouse drainage and ascends across a bench, skirting the north side of an old rockslide set amid spruce, fir and aspens trees. Views open east/southeast to the tundra-clad plateaus and peaks rising above Highway 149.

Reach the southern shore of tiny, timber-lined Hay Lake at 2.75 miles. The rocky trail now swings to the southwest and travels through trees, reaching a second rockslide at 3.1 miles. Here the trail swings to the right (west), ascending along the base of the slide before curving to the right (northwest).

After a short climb, the grade abates at 3.3 miles as the trail traverses through scattered trees along an irrigation ditch, high above the east side of

190

Crystal Creek. Openings offer ever improving views of the Redcloud Peak massif and the high peaks towering above Alpine Gulch to the south.

At 3.8 miles the trail curves to the right (north/northwest) as it climbs on moderate grades to a high basin. The grade ease as the trail crests the basin and enters beautiful meadows with stunning views of Red Mountain (12,826-ft.), Grassy Mountain (12,821-ft.), the Redcloud massif (14,034-ft.) and the unnamed peaks soaring above Alpine and Owl Gulches to the south of Henson Creek. Crystal Peak (12,933-ft.) towers above the basin to the west.

Cross the meadow, reenter the trees and then reach the east shore of Crystal Lake (11,700-ft.) at 4.1 miles. The pretty lake, nestled beneath the eastern slopes of Crystal Peak, features a small, wooded island. Nearby are the ruins of an old cabin.

Posts and cairns in the meadows beyond the lake mark the continuation of the trail to Larson Lake, a destination best done as a backpack. The area around Crystal Lake invites exploration. Hikers with the time and energy can climb to the summit of Crystal Peak, which will add 1,170-ft. and 2 miles (round-trip) to the hike.

When you are done enjoying the lake, retrace your steps to the trailhead for an 8.2 miles round-trip hike.

Driving Directions

From Lake City: From Gunnison Ave/ Highway 149 and 4th Street in Lake City, head north on Gunnison Ave/Highway 149 N for 0.9 miles and turn left onto Balsam Drive, signed for the Lake City IOOF Cemetery. Follow Balsam Drive for 0.3 miles to a parking area just past the cemetery, signed for the Crystal Lake/Larson Lakes trailhead.

51. Waterdog Lake ★★★★

Distance: 7.8 miles (RT)

A stiff climb leads to a scenic bench and a pretty lake high above the east side of the Lake City.

Distance: 7.8 miles (RT)
Elevation: 8,730-ft. at Trailhead
Maximum elevation: 11,130-ft.
Elevation Gain: 2,400-ft.
Difficulty: strenuous

Basecamp: Lake City
Area: Uncompahgre NF
Best Season: July - September
USGS Map(s): Lake City
See Page 191 for Map

Why Hike to Waterdog Lake

Waterdog Lake sits in the timberline bowl beneath Mesa Seco (12,800-ft.), high above the east side of Lake City. The first half of the hike is a sustained steep climb up switchbacks, passing through Douglas firs and then lovely aspen groves. The stiff climb leads to scenic Horse Park, a high bench clad in pretty meadows scattered with aspens. Here the grade abates as the trail curves around the north end of the park to meet a jeep road. A moderate climb up the forest lined road leads to the pretty lake.

Meadows and openings in the forest along the trail offer views of Lake City and the peaks towering to the south of the Henson Creek Valley. Station Eleven (10,726-ft.) rises along the west side of Horse Park while Crystal Peak is seen to the west.

The hike offers a great workout and is a good option if weather is threatening the high country to the west. Topping out at 11,130-ft. also makes this a good shoulder season hike or an option for fit hikers trying to get acclimated.

Trailhead to Waterdog Lake

This hike might win the award for the least appealing start with the trailhead parking area located adjacent to the Lake City Water Treatment Plant. (See driving directions below.) From the parking area walk up the road past the water treatment facility to the trailhead located on the right (east) side of the road, just before a house.

The trail immediately starts ascending steep switchback through fir forest on private land. Please stay on the trail. Openings in the trees offer birds-eye-views of

Lake City. The grade abates briefly as the trail passes beneath power lines at 0.6 miles. The respite is short-lived and soon we resume the stiff climb, now on public land. As you gain elevation Peak 13,092-ft. and its neighbors along the south side of Hanson Creek are seen to the southwest.

At 1.1 miles the trail passes through a large, lovely grove of Aspens. Here we lose the views as the trail continues its relentless ascent.

The grade abates at 1.8 miles as the trail turns left (north/northeast) and enters Horse Park, a beautiful expanse of meadows sprinkled with aspen groves atop a bench. Station Eleven (10,726-ft.), rises to the southwest. Horse Park is part of the Vickers Ranch, so you are back on private property. Please be respectful.

The trail now ascends on easy grades through Aspens and meadows along the western edge of the bench. At 2.4 miles the grade levels as the trail curves to the right (east) and crosses the bench. Views from Horse Park extend southwest to Red Mountain (12,826-ft.), the Redcloud Peak (14,034-ft.) massif, Peak 13,092 and beyond. Crystal Peak rises above the valley to the west.

At 3.0 miles the trail crosses Park Creek and soon reaches a dirt road. Turn left (north/northeast) and follow the road as it climbs on moderate grades through aspen and spruce-fir forest to Waterdogs Lake (11,130-ft.) at 3.9 miles.

Mesa Seco (12,800-ft.) forms the backdrop for this pretty lake, surround by forest on three sides. A nice afternoon can be spent lazing around the scenic lake, picnicking and fishing. (Check with the Lake City Visitor Center for current fishing conditions before setting out.)

When you are done enjoying the lake, retrace your steps to the trailhead.

Driving Directions

From Lake City: From the intersection of CO-149/Gunnison Ave and 4th Street, head north on Gunnison Ave for 0.5 miles and turn right on 8 and Half Street. This turn is just past Lake City Auto. Cross the bridge and at the next intersection take a left on Water Street and then right on 9th Street.

Follow 9th Street for 2 blocks and turn left onto Hotchkiss Street. Head up Hotchkiss Street for 0.1 miles to the parking area on the right (east) side of the road, just before the water treatment facility.

From the parking area walk up the road past the water treatment ponds to the trailhead located on the right (east) side of the road, just before a house.

52. Spring Creek Pass East to Snow Mesa

★★★★✦

Distance: 6.4 – 10.0 miles (RT)

Hikers ascending from Spring Creek Pass to the beautiful, tundra-clad plateau of Snow Mesa are rewarded with glorious views of the San Juan Mountains to the west/southwest of the Lake City area. Extend the hike by climbing Baldy Cinco or walking to the ponds at the east end of the mesa.

Distance: 6.4 – 10.0 miles (RT)
Elevation: 10,898-ft. at Trailhead
Maximum elevation: 12,380-ft.
Elevation Gain: 1,482-ft.
Difficulty: moderate-strenuous

Basecamp: Lake City
Area: Rio Grande NF
Best Season: July - September
USGS Map(s): Slumgullion Pass, Baldy Cinco Quad

Why Hike from Spring Creek Pass East to Snow Mesa

Views, views and more views are the hallmarks of this hike climbing to Snow Mesa, the largest expanse of tundra in the lower 48 states. The scenic wonderland is easily visited by driving south from Lake City along Highway 149 to Spring Creek Pass. From the highway the trail climbs steadily through forest and then rocky meadows and sections of talus to the western rim of Snow Mesa in 1.9 miles.

From Snow Mesa views of the San Juan Range extend from the Rio Grande Pyramid in the Weminuche Wilderness to the southwest to Uncompahgre, Wetterhorn and Matterhorn Peaks in the Uncompahgre

Wilderness to the northeast. A near level expanse of tundra stretches as far as the eye can see to the east while Baldy Cinco, Baldy No Es Cinco and three nearby summits rise to the northeast.

On a beautiful day the easy walk across the tundra is a sheer joy, with frequent stops to take in the views. For a shorter hike ascend gently cross the tundra to a high point just to the south of Baldy Cinco. Extend the hike by continuing to the small ponds near the eastern edge of the mesa or climb Badly Cinco and Baldy No Es Cinco.

Keep an eye on the weather atop the mesa. This is not a place to be during a thunder storm. Turn around if you see the weather taking a turn for the worse.

Spring Creek Pass East to Snow Mesa

The combined Continental Divide/Colorado Trails to Snow Mesa begin at Spring Creek Pass on Highway 149. (See driving directions below.) The path immediately starts ascending on moderately-steep grades through forest, marred by trees killed by the beetle infestation. Openings in the trees offer fine views of the San Juan Range rising to the west.

At 1.0 mile the grade abates as the trail breaks from the trees, crosses a meadow and passes a large rock cairn. From the meadow enjoy great views west to the high peaks towering above the Lake Fork of the Gunnison, including Red Mountain, Grassy Mountain, Sunshine Peak and Redcloud Peak. The Rio Grande Pyramid rises to the southwest while Uncompahgre, Wetterhorn and Matterhorn Peaks grace the skyline to the northwest. Ahead views open to the talus-clad slopes beneath Snow Mesa.

Soon the trail reenters the trees and the climb resumes on moderately steep grades. At 1.4 miles the trail emerges from the trees into rocky meadows, ascending along the north side of the East Spring Creek drainage. The meadows soon give way to talus slopes as the trail swings to the northeast, reaching the western rim of Snow Mesa (12,270-ft.) at 1.9 miles.

Upon arriving atop the mesa take time to enjoy the panoramic views of the 13,000-14,000-ft. peaks of the San Juan Range to the west. Snow Mesa, the largest expanse of tundra in the lower 48 states, stretches as far as the eye can see to the east. Baldy No Es Cinco and Baldy Cinco, along with 3 nearby summits, rise above the tundra to the northeast. (Baldy No Es Cinco is the pointy peak to the west of Baldy Cinco.)

The trail now travels east across the tundra on gentle grades. Large rock cairns and brown stakes help keep you on track if snow covers a portion of the trail. Progress will be slow as you stop often to admire the stunning views to the west.

At 3.2 miles reach a high point (12,380-ft.) on the mesa to the south of Baldy Cinco. This point is a short distance beyond one of the large rock cairns. To the east the trail dips into and then climbs out of a broad gully. This is a good turn around point, resulting in a 6.4 mile round-trip hike. On the return leg of the hike the fabulous views are now front and center as you retrace your steps across the tundra and then drop down through the trees to the trailhead.

Parties looking for a longer hike can continue heading east across the mesa, which now descends gently to a group of ponds near the eastern edge of the mesa at 5.0 miles. Along the way the trail crosses two gullies. During the height of the summer the moist tundra around the ponds supports beautiful displays of wildflowers. Totally round-trip distance to the ponds is 10.0 miles with a 1,700-ft. elevation gain.

Alternatively, hikers with time, energy and favorable weather can extend the hike by climbing Baldy Cinco and Baldy No Es Cinco. From the turn-around point return to the last large rock cairn and then start hiking north up the south ridge of Baldy Cinco. As you climb you should see a large rock cairn on the ridge. Aim for this point at approximately 13,080-ft. and then

196

climb to rounded summit of Baldy Cinco (13,383-ft.). Distance from the trail to the summit is approximately 1.5 miles, depending on your route.

Baldy Cinco enjoys jaw-dropping views of the San Juan Mountains. From this vantage point you can now see Lake San Cristobal and the high peaks in the Weminuche Wilderness. San Luis Peak (14,014) and the summit of Stewart Peak (13,983) rise to the east.

From Baldy Cinco it is relatively easy to bag Baldy No Es Cinco. Start by descending the talus slope along Baldy Cinco's western slopes to a saddle at 12,900-ft and then climb to the rocky summit of Baldy No Es Cinco (13,313-ft.). Total distance is about 0.9 miles. Near the top of the ascent you are treated to dramatic views of the peak's sheer north wall. Atop the summit is a very tall rock cairn and more fabulous views.

After you are done taking in the views descend Baldy No Es Cinco's southern slopes, initially through a talus field and then tundra clad meadows, to the CDT/CT. Turn right and return to the Spring Creek Pass trailhead in 4.2 miles. Total distance for hiking Baldy Cinco and No Es Cinco is about 9.8 miles with 2,900-ft. of elevation gain.

Driving Directions

From Lake City: From the Lake City Tourist Information Center, at the junction of Gunnison Avenue (Main Street) and Gunnison Street, follow Colorado 149 South for 17.7 miles to Spring Creek Pass. Turn right into the Spring Creek Pass Campground. The day use parking area is located on the right side of the spur road before you reach the loop for the camping area. Carefully cross to the east side of Highway 149 to the Continental Divide/Colorado trailhead to Snow Mesa and San Luis Pass.

53. Spring Creek Pass West to Jarosa Mesa

★★★★
Distance: 8.8 miles (RT)

Hike a section of the Continental Divide/Colorado Trail from Spring Creek Pass to Jarosa Mesa for great views of the San Juan Range, including Uncompahgre Peak, Matterhorn Peak, Red Mountain, Redcloud Peak and Sunshine Peak.

Distance: 8.8.0 miles (RT)
Elevation: 10,898-ft. at Trailhead
Maximum elevation: 12,025-ft.
Elevation Gain: 1,267-ft.
Difficulty: moderate

Basecamp: Lake City
Area: Rio Grande NF
Best Season: July - September
USGS Map(s): Slumgullion Pass Quad

Why Hike from Spring Creek Pass West to Jarosa Mesa

A contiguous section of the Continental Divide and Colorado Trails (CDT/CT) crosses Highway 149 to the south of Lake City at Spring Creek

Pass. The pass offers easy access to sections of the trails heading east to Snow Mesa and this trail, which heads west to Jarosa Mesa.

The CDT/CT to Jarosa Mesa initially travels along an undulating dirt road on easy to moderate grades. As you head west views open to the high peaks in the Weminuche Wilderness to the south/southwest along with Baldy Cinco and Baldy No Es Cinco atop Snow Mesa to the east.

Half way through the hike the CDT/CT leaves the road and follows a path that ascends on moderate grades to the top of Jarosa Mesa where stunning, panoramic views open to the high peaks of the San Juan Range. Prominent peaks visible from atop the mesa include Red Mountain, Uncompahgre Peak, the Matterhorn, Redcloud Peak, Sunshine Peak, Half Peak and the Rio Grande Pyramid, to name a few.

When you are done taking in the views retrace your steps to the trailhead. Views of Baldy Cinco and Baldy No Es Cinco keep your company for the return journey to Spring Creek Pass.

Spring Creek Pass West to Jarosa Mesa

The Continental Divide/Colorado Trails (CDT/CT) to Jarosa Mesa begin at Spring Creek Pass on Highway 149. (See driving directions below.) From the day use parking area, walk along the west side of the campground's loop road to a dirt road, signed for the Continental Divide/Colorado Trail, heading west. This road is open to vehicles but is seldom used. You are more likely to see a few mountain bikes.

The road ascends on moderately-easy grades through trees to a high point at 0.7 miles. Here the trees give way to meadows and the road now descends on easy grades. Views soon open west to Jarosa Mesa, our destination. To the south/southwest are far-reaching views of the high peaks in the Weminuche Wilderness towering above rounded hills and beautiful valleys. Behind you (east) are ever improving views of Baldy Cinco and Baldy No Es Cinco rising above Snow Mesa.

Reach the low point along the road at 1.6 miles. From here the road now ascends on easy to moderate grades, passing through some trees before coming to a junction at 2.6 miles. To the left is the continuation of the road. We bear right on a signed trail for the CDT/CT.

The trail now ascends on moderate to easy grades across a grassy meadow. To the west are the willow clad slopes beneath Jarosa Mesa. At 3.0 miles the trail swings to the left (west) and climbs on moderate grades up meadows-clad slopes edged by willows. Along the way turn around for more great views of Baldy Cinco and Baldy No Es Cinco to the east.

At 3.9 miles the grade abates as the trail reaching the top of Jarosa Mesa. Here stunning views open to the peaks of the San Juan Range. To the west Red Mountain, Redcloud Peak and Sunshine peak towering above the Lake Fork of the Gunnison. Uncompahgre Peak and the Matterhorn grace the horizon to the northwest. Half Peak and a sea of unnamed summits are seen in the distance to the west while the distinctive Rio Grande Pyramid rises above its neighboring peaks in the Weminuche Wilderness to the southwest.

It is now an easy stroll across Jarosa Mesa, accompanied by nonstop views. A good turn around point is located at 4.4 miles, the high point (12025-ft.) on the trail along mesa. Beyond this point the trail starts to descend to a saddle beneath the west side of the mesa.

When you are done enjoying the views, turn around and retrace your steps to Spring Creek Pass for an 8.8 miles round-trip hike.

Driving Directions

From Lake City: From the Lake City Tourist Information Center, at the junction of Gunnison Avenue (Main Street) and Gunnison Street, follow Colorado 149 South for 17.7 miles to Spring Creek Pass. Turn right into the Spring Creek Pass Campground. The day use parking area is located on the right side of the spur road, before you reach the loop for the camping area. The campground includes an outhouse. The Continental Divide trailhead is located at the beginning of a dirt road on the west side of the campground's loop road.

Viewpoint

Jarosa Mesa

Spring
Creek
Pass

Hwy
149

54. Cannibal Plateau ☆☆☆☆
Distance: 5.0 miles (RT)

This great half day hike ascending Mesa Seco features splendid views of the San Juan Range rising to the west of the Lake City area along with the Slumgullion Earthflow, a huge, slow-moving landside that broke off the west side of mesa.

Distance: 5.0 miles (RT)
Elevation: 11,050-ft. at Trailhead
Maximum elevation: 12,360-ft.
Elevation Gain: 1,900-ft.
Difficulty: moderate-strenuous

Basecamp: Lake City
Area: Rio Grande NF
Best Season: July - September
USGS Map(s): Slumgullion Pass Quad

Why Hike to the Cannibal Plateau

Mesa Seco rises above the Alfred Packer Massacre Site, located to the south of Lake City. In the winter of 1874 Packer is believed to have murdered and ate his four travel companions in the vicinity. This half day hike, which climbs the southeast slopes of Mesa Seco to an overlook on the western edge of the mesa, is named after the incident.

The climb to the mesa is accompanied by fine views of the peaks rimming the south side of the Lake Fork of the Gunnison and the summits rising to the southeast of the mesa, including Baldy Cinco and Baldy No Es Cinco. A short detour atop the mesa leads to an overlook with dramatic, birds-eye-views of the Slumgullion Earthflow, where a part of the Mesa broke off and slid down the hillside. The large, slow-moving landslide extends for 4 miles and covers over 1,000-acres.

Beyond the overlook the trail continues ascending to a point where hikers leave the path and blaze a route through the tundra to viewpoints along the Mesa's western ridge. Here terrific vistas open to the high peaks in the San Juan Range including Uncompahgre Peak, Matterhorn Peak,

Wetterhorn Peak, Redcloud Peak, Sunshine Peak, Red Mountain and the summits along the Lake Fork.

Hikers can extend the hike by continuing up the ridge crest toward one of the high points on the mesa, accompanied by nonstop views, or turn around and return to the trailhead for a 5.0 mile round-trip hike. No matter the destination this is a great hike.

The trail is open to ATVs (excluding jeeps), bikes and motorcycles. Vehicle use is typically light. Keep an eye on the weather. The mesa is above the timberline and not the place to be during a thunderstorm.

Note: The trailhead is a short distance down County Road 50, a good, 2WD dirt road. The road can be slippery when wet.

Cannibal Plateau Trail

The Cannibal Plateau trail begins on a dirt road off of County Road 50 (see driving directions below). Note this road is open to ATVs, motorcycles and bikes but not jeeps. It is lightly used so you will probably not run into many, if any, vehicles on the trail.

The road ascends on moderate to moderately steep grades through meadows and trees up the southern slopes of Mesa Seco (12,800-ft.). At 0.7 miles the road curves to the right and starts up a switchback. Here a brown post marks a faint path, closed to wheeled vehicles, heading straight up the meadows. This is an old, steep trail that shortcuts the switchbacks. I recommend staying on the road, which climbs on more reasonable grades.

The road now climbs the switchbacks on moderate grades. At 1.1 miles the trail emerges from the trees and views open southwest to the ridge rimming the east side of the Lake Fork of the Gunnison. Bent and Carson Peaks rise above the ridge. Red Mountain dominates the views to the west. As you gain elevation the summits to the north of Henson Creek join the scene.

Nearer-at-hand are views of the multi-hued cliffs of Mesa Seco rising above the Slumgullion Earthflow, a mass wasting that started 700-years ago when a large section of mesa broke away and started sliding down the hill. The slow-moving landslide, which is 4-miles long and covers over 1,000-acres, blocked the Lake Fork of the Gunnison. The resulting natural dam formed Lake San Cristobal. A second earthflow that started 300 years ago is still active and moving at a rate of about 20-ft. per year.

Views continue to expand as you climb. On a clear day Redcloud, Sunshine and Half Peaks soon appear to the distance to the west/southwest.

At 1.5 miles the road, now a two-track, crests the mesa as it continues ascending on moderately-easy grades through meadows and clusters of willows. At 1.7 miles the track reaches an intersection with a faint trail branching left. This 0.3 miles round-trip detour leads to an overlook at the edge of the Mesa where the Slumgullion Earthflow broke away from the plateau and slowly slid down the hillside. The gaping maw and the massive tongue of yellow and orange earth extending toward the Lake Fork of the Gunnison is an incredible site. Use caution near the unstable edge.

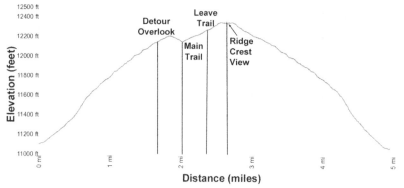

Beyond the intersection the path travels through meadows with views north to the mesa's rounded summits. To the southeast Baldy Cinco, Baldy No Es Cinco and several unnamed 13,000-ft. peaks grace the skyline.

At 2.1 miles (2.4 miles including the detour to the overlook) the trail curves to the right and continues ascending the mesa for 3 more miles, well below the ridge marking the western edge of the plateau. You will probably wonder how you are going to see more views if you continue ascending well below the ridge crest.

The answer is to look up and spot three tall rock cairns rising atop the ridge. Leave the trail and start angling up toward the cairns. Stay on the grass as you ascend, skirting patches of rocks and scree.

After walking about 0.2 miles the route crests the ridge and an amazing panorama springs into view. To the northwest a sea of high peaks, including Uncompahgre Peak, Matterhorn Peak and Wetterhorn Peak, fill the skyline. To the west Redcloud, Sunshine and a host of 13,000-ft. peaks rise beyond the aptly named Red Mountain. Lake San Cristobal is seen bellow the mesa at the foot of the Lake Fork of the Gunnison.

On a nice day ascend along the ridge crest enjoying ever evolving views as long as time and energy permit. Alternatively, when you are done enjoying the views, retrace your steps to the road and the trailhead. If you didn't take the detour to the Slumgullion Overlook on the way up, certain do so on the way down.

Total distance for the shortest up and back hike that includes a trip to the Slumgullion Overlook and a trip to the ridge crest is 5.0 miles (round-trip) with a 1,900-ft. elevation gain.

Note: On the drive back to Lake City stop at Windy Point for views of the Slumgullion Earthflow from a different angle along with more great views of the high peaks rising to the west/northwest. Also, watch for the historic sign pointing to the turn for the Alfred Packer Massacre site, situated beneath Mesa Seco, to learn more about the history of the infamous Lake City cannibal, Alfred Packer.

Driving Directions

From Lake City: From the Lake City Tourist Information Center at the junction of Gunnison Avenue (Main Street) and Gunnison Street, follow Colorado 149 South for 10 miles and then turn left onto County Road 50. Drive 0.1 miles on CR 50 to the signed Cannibal Plateau trailhead on the left side of the road. There are several spots to pull off the road and park near the trailhead.

Appendix A: Hiking Tips

Staying healthy and safe in the backcountry.

Hiking in the backcountry is a wonderful experience but can also be hazardous if you are not properly prepared. Here are some tips to help you to stay healthy and safe. For more backcountry hiking safety information check out the Hiking Safety tips from the American Hiking Society.

Trip Preparation

Your trip will be more enjoyable and safer if you take the time to plan it at home. Use forest recreation maps, topographic maps and trail guides to create an itinerary, calculate mileage and elevation gains, understand the terrain and learn about any potential hazards.

Take someone with you. Traveling with at least one hiking companion adds to your safety margin.

Before leaving home always leave your itinerary with a relative or friend. Write a full account of who is going, where you are going and when you will be back. For overnight trips include where you plan to stay each night.

Check current conditions posted on the forest service website to find out if there are any know hazards such as slippery roads, high fire danger and flash flood warnings. If possible, stop by the nearest Ranger Station before your trip to get the latest information.

Get in shape before the trip. Do not attempt a trip that is beyond your physical capabilities. Fatigue often leads to injuries.

What to Pack

Sudden shifts in weather are one of the backcountry's greatest dangers. Dress in layers and take the gear needed to keep you warm and dry if the weather turns for the worse. It may seem silly to carry a hat, gloves, rain gear (including pants) and a Polartec when starting your hike on a beautiful sunny day. But you will be glad you have carried all this gear if you get caught in high country during a ferocious afternoon thunderstorm with gale force wind, plummeting temperatures, hail and heavy rains.

I recommend that you bring a warm fleece or wool pullover, a waterproof jacket and pants, a hat, sunglasses, sunscreen, lip balm, insect repellant, first-aid kit, pocket knife, flashlight or headlamp, waterproof matches, maps, compass, a mirror and whistle for signaling if you are lost. Wear sturdy boots that are broken in and are comfortable and know how they respond to wet slippery surfaces. A trekking pole or walking stick can be very helpful in maintaining your balance in hazardous conditions Take plenty of water and food. It's very important to drink water! See the section on dehydration under hazards.

Weather

Before you leave check the current weather forecast and change your plans if necessary.

Weather in the mountains is unpredictable. A beautiful sunny day can turn nasty in a blink of an eye. Keep an eye on the weather. High passes, exposed ridges, areas above the timberline, open meadows and isolated trees are dangerous places to be during a lightning storm. Respect Mother Nature and head downhill when you see storms approaching.

During July and August thunderstorms are most common in the afternoons. Your best bet is to get your butt out of bed early and plan your day so you are down from the high passes and ridges by early afternoon to avoid any potential bad weather.

Heavy rains can cause rivers and streams to rise rapidly. The stream you rock-hopped across on the way up the trail can become a raging torrent that becomes hazardous to cross. When in doubt, wait out the storm and let the rivers go down before trying to cross. Move to higher ground and avoid gullies and drainages.

Hazards

Giardia: Don't Drink the Water!!! Giardia, a microscopic organism that can cause severe diarrhea for up to two weeks, is widespread. You should assume all waterways are infected. The most effective treatment to make water safe to drink is to boil it. A good filter can also remove most harmful organisms present in mountain water. Choose a filter with a pore size less than 0.5 microns or a Steripen. These filters will effectively remove most harmful bacteria and protozoa (including Giardia) or, in the case of a Steripen, sterilize the water. Another option is to use iodine tablets to disinfect water collected on the hike. For short trips take a supply of water from home or other domestic sources.

Dehydration and Heat: Heat exhaustion and heat stroke can result from continued exposure to high temperatures and inadequate or unbalanced replacement of fluids. Adults require two quarts of water per day and four quarts or more for strenuous activity at high elevations. To maintain a high energy level and avoid dehydration by:

- Drink 8 to 16 ounces of water before hiking.
- Drink frequently when on the trail.
- Drink as much water as possible during lunch and throughout the evening.
- Limit caffeine drinks such as coffee or cola.
- Avoid alcoholic drinks.
- Plan ahead for drinking water. Don't allow water to run out before resupplying.
- Take breaks in the shade.

Prevent sunburn by wearing lightweight, light colored, and loose fitting clothing that allows air to circulate and sweat to evaporate while offering protection from direct sun. Bare skin absorbs the sun's radiant heat and raises body temperature. Understand the signs and symptoms of heat disorders including heat cramps, heat exhaustion and heat stroke.

Hypothermia: Hypothermia, caused by rapid loss of body heat, is the most dangerous illness of backcountry travel. Hypothermia can occur even in the warm summer months. Symptoms of hypothermia include: apathy, confusion, drowsiness, loss of coordination, pale or cold skin, uncontrollable shivering, shock, slurred speech and weakness.

To prevent hypothermia, wear non-cotton clothing in layers, including a waterproof outer layer, that allow you to adjust to changing weather and temperatures. To treat hypothermia get the victim out of the wind and any wet clothing they may be wearing. Because skin-to-skin contact can quickly warm somebody back up again, place the victim in a dry sleeping bag then have one or two heat donors surround the victim. When fit for travel, carry or help the victim walk out and get medical attention as soon as possible.

Lightning: During a lightning storm avoid mountaintops, ridges, trees, rocks, and boulder fields. Go to a low-lying area and move away from others in your group. Turn off your electronic devices and remove any metal objects you are carrying including jewelry, watches, keys, knife, etc. Make your body a single point ground by putting your ankles and knees together and then crouching down. This posture lessens your chances of being a lightning rod or of a charge entering one foot from the ground, traveling through your vital organs and exiting through your other foot. Do not lie flat on the ground because electrical current from a strike can easily travel through your vital organs this way too. If your hair stands on end, immediately take the above safety precautions. A lightning strike could be eminent.

Altitude Sickness: Altitude sickness may occur if you overexert at high elevations (above 5,000 feet) where oxygen supply is reduced. Symptoms of high altitude sickness include nausea, dizziness, confusion, and fatigue. Before hiking at high altitudes it is best to acclimatize yourself by sleeping at these elevations a night or two. If you or someone in your party experiences altitude sickness symptoms on a hike, do not go any higher! Descend as quickly as possible and, if symptoms get worse, get medical attention.

Fatigue: Exhaustion and fatigue occur because the person may be pushing too hard and is embarrassed to ask the group to slow down. A good principle of backcountry travel is take it slow, rest often, drink and eat snacks frequently to restore body energy and stay warm.

Fatigue slows your awareness and preparedness to hike safely. Watch out for other members of your party getting fatigued and take appropriate action and care.

Leave No Trace

Always practice Leave No Trace technique with hiking and backpacking. Please visit the Leave No Trace website to learn about the 7 Leave No Trace Principles.

Other Useful Tips

Hiking on Variable Terrain: Identify safe routes and local conditions. Test and use secure footing and never run down slopes. Step over logs, not on them. Know how to fall; protect your head and back and roll with the fall. Take extra precautions when encountering steep, loose, or wet trails.

Horses and Pack Stock: When you encounter travelers who have horses or pack stock, move off the trail on the downhill side and let them pass. Horses are easily frightened and have the right-of-way on trails.

Fall Hunting Season: We recommend that you don't hike alone during hunting season and that you stay on established trails. All hikers, as well their dogs, should wear at least one piece of florescent orange clothing during hunting season.

Bears: Bears are generally shy and will avoid people. If you should encounter a bear on the trail, back away slowly while facing the bear. Before you hike in Bear Country be sure to read Be Bear Aware, published by the Sierra National Forest.

Appendix B: Ouray – Food, Services, Resources and Links

Food, Lodging and Services

Ouray Mountain Sports - ouraymountainsports.com - 732 Main St.

Buckskin Booksellers - www.facebook.com/pages/category/Bookstore/Buckskin-Booksellers-212152978801758/ - 505 Main Street

Ouray Grocery - facebook.com/ouraygrocery - 621 Main Street

Ridgway Mountain Market - ridgwaycolorado.com/businesses/amenities-services/ridgway-mountain-market/, 490 Sherman St, Ridgway, CO, (11 miles north of Ouray.

Mouse's Chocolate and Coffee - mouseschocolates.com, 520 Main Street

Accommodations - Condos, cabins and home vacations rentals, B&B's, hotels/motels and campground/RV parks listings from Ouray Tourism - visitouray.com/lodging

Restaurants, Bars and Breweries - visitouray.com/dining-drinks

Resources and Links

Ouray Visitor Center - visitouray.com – 1230 Main Street

Uncompahgre National Forest - Ouray District Office, 2505 S. Townsend, Montrose, CO 81401, 970-240-5300 - www.fs.usda.gov/gmug

Ouray Trails Group - Short descriptions of area trails - www.ouraytrails.org

Short trail descriptions are also available from the Ouray Information Center - visitouray.com/hiking

The San Juan Skyway, a stunning 233-mile loop that crosses four high passes and connects Ouray to Silverton, Durango, Cortez, and Telluride (going clockwise around the loop). https://www.codot.gov/travel/scenic-byways/southwest/san-juan-skyway

Campgrounds and RV Parks

U.S. Forest Service: Amphitheater Campground - is located on the side of a mountain above the east side of Ouray, Colorado at an elevation of about 8,400 ft. It is tightly designed with loops and camping spurs among Gamble oaks and mixed conifers. There is a scenic overlook in the campground with views of Ouray and the "Amphitheater," which was formed by a volcanic explosion. Firewood is available for a fee. The campground is best suited for tents, but RVers can utilize sites 3 through 15. Total RV length should not exceed 35 feet. (www.fs.usda.gov/recarea/gmug/recarea/?recid=32522)

Ridgway State Park Campground - This is a full-service facility with 258 RV/tent sites, 25 walk in tent sites and 3 Yurts. The campground is located in 15 miles north of Ouray in Ridgway State Park, a facility that includes a beautiful reservoir, picnic and playground areas and trail system. Fees apply. cpw.state.co.us/placestogo/parks/Ridgway

Private Campground – 4J+1+1 RV Campground - 790 Oak Street, Ouray

Tours and Attractions

Ouray's Hot Springs- A great place for kids of all ages! visitouray.com/hot-springs

Box Canyon Waterfalls and Park, located on CR 361 off Highway 550 just south of Ouray, is an interesting geological formation featuring a 285-ft. waterfall plummeting through a narrow box canyon. www.ci.ouray.co.us/city_offices/city_resources/box_canon_waterfalls_vs2.php

The San Juan Skyway between Ouray and **Silverton**. The route traverses jaw dropping scenery littered with mining relics and climbs over 11,018-ft

Red Mountain Pass. https://www.codot.gov/travel/scenic-byways/southwest/san-juan-skyway

Yankee Boy Basin, to the southwest of town, provides opportunities to visit several ghost towns, view beautiful Twin Falls and, during late July/early August, see spectacular displays of wildflowers. http://www.narrowgauge.org/4x4/html/yankee.html

The **Alpine Loop** is another popular route leading over 12,000-ft passes to the **Lake City** and back. Route requires a high clearance/4WD vehicle. Check on current road conditions and the skill level required to drive the route at the Ouray Visitor Center. https://www.colorado.com/articles/colorado-scenic-byway-alpine-loop

Bachelors Syracuse Mine Tour - http://www.bachelorsyracusemine.com/ - 1222 County Road 14, Ouray, CO

Appendix C: Silverton Food, Services, Resources and Links

Food, Lodging and Services

Silverton Grocery - Groceries, snacks, beer, video rentals. 717 Greene St.

Outdoor World – Hiking, backpacking, fishing gear along with maps and guidebooks, 1234 Greene Street

The Coffee Bear - Coffee and tea, fresh-baked breads and pastries, homemade light fare, 1309 Greene St. https://www.coffeebearsilverton.com/

Lodging Info - from the Silverton Chamber of Commerce - www.silvertoncolorado.com/index.php?biz=yes&bizstatus=viewcat&cat_id=8

Dining Info - from the Silverton Chamber of Commerce - www.silvertoncolorado.com/index.php?biz=yes&bizstatus=viewcat&cat_id=7

Shopping Info - from the Silverton Chamber of Commerce - www.silvertoncolorado.com/index.php?biz=yes&bizstatus=viewcat&cat_id=12

Resources and Links

Silverton Visitor Information - //www.silvertoncolorado.com

Uncompahgre National Forest - //www.fs.usda.gov/gmug

San Juan National Forest - //www.fs.usda.gov/sanjuan

Campgrounds and RV Parks

A & B RV Park - Full hookups; 30 & 50 amp; large spaces; TV; showers; laundry. 1445 Mineral St.

Red Mountain Motel, Cabins & RV Park - 38 full hookup sites. Camp, jeep, ATV, OHV, fish, hunt; tent, snowmobile. Motel (summer only), cabins (year round); laundry. 664 Greene St. - www.redmtmotelrvpk.com

Silver Summit RV Park - 640 Mineral St., www.silversummitrvpark.com

Molas Lake Park - Camping, cabins, fishing, hiking, horseback rides & canoeing. 6 miles south of Silverton on Highway 550, Molas Lake.

South Mineral Campground – Take Highway 550 2 miles west of Silverton and turn left onto Forest Rd. 585. Follow 585 for 4.4 miles to the campground which has 26 sites. Dispersed camping sites are located along much of FR 585 between the highway and the South Mineral Campground.

Tours

Old Hundred Gold Mine Tour - 4 miles northeast of Silverton - 1-800-872-3009 or www.minetour.com

Mayflower Gold Mill Tour - 4 miles northeast of Silverton - www.sanjuancountyhistoricalsociety.org/mayflower-mill.html

Appendix D: Telluride Resources and Links

Food, Lodging and Retail

Clark's Market - Supermarket - 700 W. Colorado Avenue - www.clarksmarket.com

Village Market, 157 S. Fir St.

Baked in Telluride - 127 S. Fir Street - www.bakedintelluride.com

Maggie's Bakery & Cafe, 300 West Colorado Avenue

Between the Covers Bookstore and Espresso Bar - 224 W. Colorado Avenue - www.between-the-covers.com

Jagged Edge - Sporting Goods, Maps and Books - 223 E. Colorado Avenue - www.jagged-edge-telluride.com

Telluride Sports - Sporting Goods, Maps and Books - 150 W. Colorado Avenue - www.telluridesports.com

Telluride Accommodations Directory - www.telluride.com/lodging/

Resources and Links

Telluride Tourism -700 W Colorado Avenue - www.visittelluride.com

Uncompahgre National Forest - www.fs.usda.gov/gmug

San Juan National Forest - www.fs.usda.gov/sanjuan

Camping and RV Parks

Alta Lakes Campground - Take Highway 145 south for about 10 miles to the Boomerang Road, Alta Lakes. Drive 5-miles on the rough road to the campsite located a 11,200-ft. Dispersed camping, pit toilet, free. (www.fs.usda.gov/recarea/gmug/recreation/camping-cabins/recarea/?recid=34056&actid=29)

Matterhorn Campground – Located 7 miles south of Telluride on Highway 145. This campground has showers, dumping station/sewer hookups, electric hookups. (www.fs.usda.gov/recarea/gmug/recreation/camping-cabins/recarea/?recid=32376&actid=29)

Sunshine Campground – 12 miles south of Telluride on Highway 145 on the right side of the highway. There are 18 sites, 2 wheelchair accessible compost restrooms, metal tables and fire grates at each site. (www.fs.usda.gov/recarea/gmug/recreation/camping-cabins/recarea/?recid=32454&actid=29)

Telluride Town Park Campground – Located along the river at the east end of town. (www.visittelluride.com/accommodation/telluride-town-park-campground)

Woods Lake Campground – Travel west on Highway 145 toward Placerville for 9 miles and turn left on Fall Creek Road. Follow the road to Woods Lake. The campground offers 41 designated sites, hand pumped water and vault toilets.
(www.fs.usda.gov/recarea/gmug/recreation/camping-cabins/recarea/?recid=32380&actid=29)

List of Other Area Campgrounds - Includes both public and private campgrounds. (www.visittelluride.com/places-to-stay/rv-camping)

Appendix E: Lake City Resources and Links

Food, Lodging and Retail

Lake City Accommodations and Campgrounds - businessdirectory.lakecity.com/directory/Search/lodging-travel-category-159470

Country Grocery Store - located at 916 N State Highway 149 in Lake City, https://www.facebook.com/The-Country-Store-623737871029777

Lake City Bakery - 922 N Highway 149, recommended for pastries, breads and other goodies. Good place to stop for coffee, breakfast and lunch items. https://www.facebook.com/Lake-City-Bakery-1087821594642917

Chillin Internet Coffee Shope and Cafe – 205 Gunnison Ave., Great place to satisfy your caffeine addiction. Also severs breakfast and lunch. https://www.chillininc.com/

The General Store - located at 252 S Gunnison Ave in Lake City stocks housewares, hardware, camping and fishing supplies, books and more.

Resources and Links

Lake City Visitor Center - 800 Gunnison Avenue, Lake City, CO, http://www.lakecity.com

Grand Mesa, Uncompahgre and Gunnison National Forest - Near district office: Gunnison District Office at 216 N. Colorado, Gunnison, CO, 970-641-0471, www.fs.usda.gov/main/gmug/home

Short Trail Descriptions from the Lake City Visitor Center, https://www.lakecity.com/mountain-town-activities/walking-hiking-horseback-riding

Trail and Road Conditions - provided by the Lake City Visitor Center, www.lakecity.com/plan-your-colorado-trip/trail-road-conditions

Tours and Attractions

Hardtack Mine Tour - This underground mine tour describes the tools and techniques used by hard rock miners and includes exhibits explaining local mining history and equipment along with a rock gallery showcasing the mine's huge collection of rocks and minerals. http://hardtackmine.com/

Hinsdale County Museum -Nice local museum with displays chronicling the area history. www.lakecitymuseum.com/

Silverthread Scenic Byway - Head south on Highway 149 to see the Slumgullion Earth Slide and take in the views from Slumgullion Pass. Take a side trip to Lake San Cristobal, the Rio Grand Reservoir and the historic town of Creede. www.codot.gov/travel/colorado-byways/south-central/silver-thread

Last Chance Mine - See the ruins of the old mine and collect rock specimens. https://www.coloradodirectory.com/creede-mine/

Creede Underground Mining Museum - Retired miners lead tours of a closed mine, explaining the equipment and methods used to extract minerals. www.undergroundminingmuseum.com/mining-museum.html

Wheeler Geologic Area - An amazing area of eroded outcroppings of volcanic ash in the La Garita Mountains, northeast of Creede. Arrange to see this geologic wonder with a local jeep tour operator or backpack into the area on one of several trails in the Rio Grande National Forest. https://en.wikipedia.org/wiki/Wheeler_Geologic_Area and http://www.fs.usda.gov/recarea/riogrande/recarea/?recid=29264